THE DIARIES OF
WILLARD MOTLEY

THE DIARIES OF
WILLARD MOTLEY

EDITED AND WITH AN INTRODUCTION BY **JEROME KLINKOWITZ**

FOREWORD BY **CLARENCE MAJOR**

THE IOWA STATE UNIVERSITY PRESS, AMES   **1 9 7 9**

JEROME KLINKOWITZ is Professor of English at the University of Northern Iowa. His booklength studies include *Literary Disruptions* (1975), *The Life of Fiction* (1977), *Vonnegut in America* (1977), *The Vonnegut Statement* (1973), descriptive bibliographies of Kurt Vonnegut (1974) and Donald Barthelme (1977), and the anthologies *Innovative Fiction* (1972) and *Writing Under Fire* (1978). He has contributed chapters to *Black American Writers: Essays in Bibliography, Surfiction: Fiction Now and Tomorrow, The New Fiction, American Literary Manuscripts,* and *Seeing Castaneda* and has published essays in *The New Republic, The Village Voice, Partisan Review, Black American Literature Forum, Yardbird Reader,* and many other journals in the United States, Europe, and Australia.

FRONTISPIECE: Photo by Carl Van Vechten. Permission granted through the courtesy of Saul Mauriber, photographic executor of the Carl Van Vechten estate.

FOREWORD © 1975 Clarence Major

Composed and printed by
The Iowa State University Press
Ames, Iowa   50010

First edition, 1979

PS
3563
0888
Z463
1979

Library of Congress Cataloging in Publication Data

Motley, Willard, 1909–1965.
      ⸱ The diaries of Willard Motley.

      Bibliography: p.
      Includes index.
      1. Motley, Willard, 1909–1965—Diaries. 2. Novelists, American—20th century—Biography. I. Klinkowitz, Jerome.
PS3563.0888Z463   1978   813′.5′4 [B]   78-16782
ISBN 0-8138-0140-0 cloth
ISBN 0-8138-0705-0 paper

CONTENTS

CONTENTS

FOREWORD

WILLARD MOTLEY, along with a minority of other black American authors, from the beginnings of American literature to the present, wrote fiction in which the question of race was not a central theme.

Most of Motley's characters were white. There is a black American tradition of fiction by black authors dealing solely with white characters. Examples are Zora Neal Hurston's *Seraph on the Suwanne,* Richard Wright's *Savage Holiday,* James Baldwin's *Giovanni's Room,* Ann Petry's *Country Place,* Frank Yerby's *Foxes of Harrow,* Samuel R. Delany's *Dhalgren,* and Charles Perry's *Portrait of a Young Man Drowning.*

Many black writers, on the other hand, have made fiction about black characters but with no overwhelming special commitment to racial problems. Examples among them are Charles Wright, Ishmael Reed, Jean Toomer, William Demby, John Wideman, LeRoi Jones, and Robert Boles.

There is also a long tradition of white writers writing about black people. One of the most successful is Gertrude Stein's "Melanctha," in *Three Lives.* Gertrude Stein's Melanctha emerges as a "real person." Most white writers, however, have invented black characters who represent "problems" of society or who are idiots or savages. Exceptions in varying degrees would be Herman Melville's *Benito Cereno,* William Faulkner's *Light in August,* Harriet Beecher Stowe's *Uncle Tom's Cabin,* Carl Van Vechten's *Nigger Heaven,* William Styron's *The Confessions of Nat Turner,* Bernard Malamud's novel *The Tenants* and his story "Angel Levine," and Shane Stevens's *Way Up Town in Another World.* These authors, in these books, are concerned with race as well as with other aspects of the question of identity.

Willard Motley always saw his characters as real people, never solely as sociological puzzles or ethnic beings. Motley's Italians have social habits that are characteristic of the Chicago Italian-American community, but the reader is also allowed to see and to feel them, to know them, on other levels.

When Robert Bone, in *The Negro Novel in America,* accuses Motley of nearly plagiarizing Richard Wright's *Native Son,* Bone must not have thought much further than what the book reviewers of the day were saying. Fact is, *Knock on Any Door* (the Motley book Bone refers to) came along in a tradition well worn. Motley simply wrote a type of novel that had been popular since Stendhal's *The Red and the Black*. *Native Son* was hardly the best example of a prototype for *Knock on Any Door*. Motley was certainly no innovator. But neither was Theodore Dreiser or Sinclair Lewis. Whose shoulders were they standing on? The answer is too obvious.

Generally, Willard Motley did not and has not received serious critical attention until recently, in such periodicals as *Proof: The Yearbook of American Bibliographical and Textual Studies, The Negro American Literature Forum,* and *Resources for American Literary Study.* The serious Motley scholars are Jerome Klinkowitz, who uncovered Motley's literary archives, Jill Weyant, Ann Rayson, Charles and Karen Wood, Bob Fleming, James Giles, and John O'Brien. A few popular literary studies of Motley in relation to modern and contemporary Negro fiction have appeared, but they have, almost without exception, dealt with everything written by blacks as though the racial reference constituted a fixed form, a genre.

Like many other writers of both quality and commercial fiction, Motley left, after his death, many unpublished manuscripts. Constance Webb and Michel Fabre indicate that Richard Wright left a long detailed diary, at least one unpublished novel, and many shorter works. There is an unpublished autobiography of Jean Toomer. Claude McKay left several unpublished novels and a number of miscellaneous manuscripts. Well known is the fact that Ernest Hemingway left unfinished *Islands in the Stream* and several other manuscripts. John Berryman's *Recovery* was not finished. The natural question that arises is: If the work is inferior or unfinished, should it be published? I can say without reservations that the publication of Willard Motley's diaries will not damage his reputation. The quality of thinking and feeling expressed in them, even the writing, can only enhance his image. They are, so far, his best published work.

It is not unusual for an author's unpublished manuscripts to reveal a side of the person not previously known. Richard Wright's "Island of Hallucination," Claude McKay's "Romance in Marseilles" and "Harlem Glory," and Jean Toomer's unpublished fiction and autobiography serve respectively as indexes to the fact that these writers have been dealt with in critical terms based solely on the range of their published works, which, obviously, does not tell the full story. Willard Motley's unpublished works indicate a writer who tried many techniques and themes, sometimes with real success, as with the book "Adventure," a sensitive account of bumming across country in the spirit of Jack London and before Jack Kerouac's *On the Road* appeared.

Motley's "Adventure" indicates a whole new aspect of the writer the public has not been aware of. In an essay on Motley by Charles Wood, Karen Wood is quoted. She says Motley's "view of Los Angeles and its citizens shows such an affirmative love for humanity that one can never again view Motley simply as a traditional naturalist. . . ." ("The *Adventure* Manuscript: New Light on Willard Motley's Naturalism," *Negro*

American Literature Forum.) Charles Woods's point is that Motley was not limited to "a sordid and deterministic view of man."

Willard Motley was a conventional writer and a conservative person. In an essay by Jerome Klinkowitz and James R. Giles called "The Emergence of Willard Motley in Black American Literature" (NALF), the reader witnesses an exchange of letters between Motley, Chester Himes, and Carl Van Vechten—subject: Himes's controversial novel, *Lonely Crusade,* which deals with a young Negro struggling to maintain his own sense of integrity while being used by American communist and labor groups. Motley apparently assumed Himes's book represented an attack on whites. Motley wrote and published a negative review of the book, then wrote Himes an apology for his inability to like the book.

Carl Van Vechten, meanwhile, saw something tragic and something sympathetic in Motley. Motley was no doubt a tragic figure. He was also certainly a very sympathetic person. But he was also sensitively intelligent and a totally committed writer. Writing was almost his whole life.

The extent of Motley's sincerity is dramatically demonstrated in the diaries. He was a thoughtful and shy person; even during the single time I talked with him, one day in the summer of 1960 in Chicago, this was obvious. These diaries reflect a passionate young man with an optimistic outlook. Motley was more interested in expression and impression than in meaning and reason. His published novels, the manuscript "Adventure," and the diaries support this judgment. He had a democratic spirit. It is given expression throughout the diaries in Englewood High School episodes and later in the traveling episodes. When Motley was abused, he did not strike back; he tried to find in himself the strength to withstand the abuse. He was instinctively nonviolent—hence the irony of the "tough little iron man" and the "tough"-looking expressions on his face in photographs that appeared on the covers and jackets of his novels. Fighting back, as the diaries indicate, was an activity Motley managed in a more subtle manner. His sense of himself was hardly racial, though he never denied his racial heritage. Most important to Willard Motley's vision of "unadorned" life was his lower middle-class outlook.

Motley was devoted to beauty and especially to the idea of male beauty. Nick Romano, hero of *Knock on Any Door,* was based in part on a handsome Mexican named Tino N——, whom Motley met while traveling through Denver, where N—— served time in a detention home. For a writer as realistically, as graphically, as naturalistically oriented as Willard Motley, the whole idea of internalizing certain aspects of real persons for the purposes of fiction was a natural process. In trying to help Joe, Motley assumes the role he later assigns to one of his characters, a writer, Grant Holloway. Holloway is white.

In the diaries Motley invents a reality based on his own life. When he describes the process of inventing and living with his characters, especially with Nick, it is with the same compassion and care he gives to real people in real life, before, during, and after the writing of *Knock on Any Door.*

There is an innocent sort of intelligence in the diaries. Motley relates his many conversations with friends and he finds, almost always, a lot of joy in the "deep" discoveries about "life" during these talks.

While in high school he refers to his existence as an "ugly desert." He sees himself as very plain. He finds himself seeking handsome friends, seeking "the beautiful in life." Even this early he describes schoolmates who resemble Nick.

This, a condensed version of the diaries, begins January 1, 1926, and ends June 1, 1943, when Willard Motley was thirty-three, four years before the publication of *Knock on Any Door,* his most celebrated previously published work.

Clarence Major

PREFACE

WILLARD MOTLEY (1909–1965) was a dedicated and self-conscious literary naturalist, saving every detail from his own life and the larger life about him. In their original form, his diaries can exhaust the patience of even the most interested reader. Motley began them as a teenager in 1926 and continued them with an almost religious perseverance, making daily entries through August 1943, the year his first novel was accepted for publication; from then on the massive revisions of his first book and eager work on a second monopolized his attention. But his twenty-eight volumes of diaries, written longhand in pencil and supplemented by newspaper clippings and letters, served him as the journal of a writer's apprenticeship, totaling nearly one million words.

Motley's use of his diaries matured with his growth as a writer. As a youth, he exhorted himself in the conduct of his life as well as his writing; in his late teens, when he began submitting stories to national magazines, the diaries served as a logbook of submissions and rejections. In the 1930s, however, Motley undertook three transcontinental trips—one by bicycle—in deliberate search for story material, and at this point the diaries became virtual first drafts for published material. His travelogue piece "Assault on Catalina," published in *Outdoors* magazine for April 1939, is a virtual transcription of diary material. Again, as a literary naturalist, Motley hesitated to falsify experience by too much rewriting. For his novels, though, he worked differently. Here Motley saw himself as the sociological researcher, leaving his own middle-class circumstances to seek out the deeper truths of life. And, like a researcher, taking and assembling field notes were part of his task. Motley would first record an experience in his diaries, following it through several days of research. Then he would copy fragments on loose sheets of paper. These in turn would be written up as paragraphs and in the final process of composition would be arranged into chapters. As each piece of material was incorporated into the novel, the original notation would be crossed out—but retained as part of Motley's growing record.

A specific example of Motley's method may be traced from diary to first-draft story to novel. On August 11, 1937, Motley's diary records his meeting with a young inmate at the Denver, Colorado, reformatory. The scene itself is visualized at once in literary terms, and Motley uses fictional techniques to record it: development by dialogue, framing, developing characterization, conflict, and so forth. This experience was then written up as a story for *Ohio Motorist,* where it was published as "The Boy" in August 1938 (the sketch has been republished by Robert E. Fleming in "The First Nick Romano," as cited in the bibliography). "The Boy" was in turn rewritten as the first encounter between Grant Holloway and Nick Romano in *Knock on Any Door.*

As Motley's first novel drew to its conclusion, the author wrote diary and fiction side by side, as the closing sections of this edition show. From Skid Row to the Court House to his room in the slums, Motley would roam back and forth, finding original material only to shape it into fiction sometimes just hours later. Each became a living process, accounting for the great vitality of Motley's writing. No matter how negative superior reviewers might be, faulting Willard Motley for his sentimentality and ignorance of literary tradition, all had to admit the driving energy of his fiction—a quality directly attributable to his methods of working from the diaries of his life.

THE WILLARD MOTLEY PAPERS

In 1969, as an Assistant Professor of English at Northern Illinois University, I was selected as a Regional Associate Editor for the volume *American Literary Manuscripts,* edited for the American Literature Section/MLA by J. Albert Robbins. My assignments were libraries, historical societies, and museums in my home state of Wisconsin.

By June 1971 my work had proceeded to the Rare Book Room of the University of Wisconsin Library; there I found eight large file cartons containing Motley's papers from 1957 through 1963, which the author had donated with the hope of stimulating a purchase of his larger collection of papers. Sensing the value of this latter material, I traced its location to the attorney for Motley's heirs, Mr. Walter Roth of D'Ancona, Pflaum, Wyatt & Riskind, who directed me to a basement on 87th Street off Dr. Martin Luther King Drive on Chicago's South Side, where Motley's papers filled an entire room. Notes and manuscripts for his published novels, several unpublished manuscripts, letters, clippings, memorabilia, and the twenty-eight volumes of diaries accounted for the bulk.

Through the generosity of Motley's niece, Mrs. Frederica Westbrooke, the papers were loaned to Northern Illinois University, where they were photocopied and catalogued; several graduate students eventually based their dissertations on the Motley Papers. Meanwhile, I completed a descriptive catalogue of the Wisconsin collection, which was published in *Resources for American Literary Study* for Autumn 1972. The full range of the Motley Papers revealed the frustrations of his career as a commercial writer; this story is told in "The Making and Unmaking of *Knock on Any Door,* " published in *Proof* for 1973.

EDITORIAL PRACTICES

In editing the diaries, the major principle has been one of selection. Redundant or simply boring material has been completely excised; on the other hand, careful attention has been given to presenting an honest picture of Motley's life as he perceived it. Therefore certain instances of adolescent excess have been allowed to stand as examples of Motley's early romanticism and self-image. Few deletions were made for the years 1941, 1942, and 1943, where Motley's working methods are most dramatically detailed. None of Motley's writing has been changed; though not a superior student, he was always a proper and correct writer, as evidenced by his ability to write professional copy for the *Chicago Defender* when barely out of his childhood. Occasionally the surnames of Motley's friends and associates have been deleted at his family's request.

ACKNOWLEDGMENTS

Northern Illinois University and the University of Northern Iowa supported my work on the Motley Papers with research grants for basic expenses. Especially helpful were the services of Kathleen Hinton Colonnese (who prepared outline-summaries of each full diary), Karen Gold of Englewood High School, and Julie Huffman-Klinkowitz. Many other colleagues and students contributed time and effort to Motley's cause and can be thanked best, I hope, just by seeing this book appear—the honest record of a young black author who prized friendship more than anything else.

Jerome Klinkowitz

INTRODUCTION

"**WILLARD MOTLEY**," Langston Hughes wrote in 1967, ranks among the "ten most noted names in American Negro writing." W. E. B. Dubois, Paul Laurence Dunbar, Richard Wright, and the others, plus Hughes himself, have all been the subjects of historical study and literary acclaim; but years after his death Motley's story remained untold and his name hardly mentioned, despite the fact that two million copies of his novels were in print and that the literary modes he exploited still prevailed in American popular fiction. His story, though not foreboding, is problematic, and resists the designs of criticism—which may be the reason he merits silence or disdain in the literary histories of the period. Motley was a black author who wrote almost exclusively of white characters, and whose artistic style and political ideology seemed a decade behind the vogue of such authors as Richard Wright and James T. Farrell. He deviated from the path of conventional artistic development, and such departures are hard things for literary historians to handle.

Looking closer, one finds the story of a young man from a reasonably comfortable, middle-class background turning to the lower depths of life in an endless search for stronger currents and deeper truths. Raised and educated in an almost entirely white neighborhood, where a mixture of several racial and national groups discouraged any special identity, Willard Motley had to school himself in ethnic realities no less than the social ones he so ardently studied in his adopted neighborhoods of Chicago's Maxwell Street and Skid Row. His father was a Pullman porter on the "Wolverine," a train on the New York City to Chicago route. His brother Archibald grew up to become a famous artist, while his sister Florence (called "Flossie") has stayed close to the old neighborhood most of her life. But Willard chose a more complicated way of life. Economically he fought the Great Depression, bumming his way from coast to coast and working every imaginable part-time and para-professional job. Intellectually he suffered embarrassments for his slim experience in the literary forms of the past. But personally he was most distinguished by a remarkable dedication, from his earliest ambitions of childhood, to become a major writer. Motley wrote at least ten times the amount of fiction that eventually saw publication in his four novels, and his personal records are of similar expanse. A literary naturalist, he saved everything, and because of that we can know all the more about him.

Race, a subject of little concern to the early Motley, became by the end of his life a major personal issue. In 1963 he wrote *Time* magazine about James Baldwin's militancy, and a heavily edited version of his letter appeared in the June 7 issue. Willard Motley, born July 14, 1909, on West 60th Street in Chicago, remembered half a century later the conditions of his youth, as reflected in the carbon typescript of his letter filed at the University of Wisconsin.

Sir: James Baldwin, the "professional Negro," needs an answer for his attack on liberals, Chicago (and other northern cities) and white people in general: [marginal note: We were the only Negro family in the neighborhood] During Chicago's race riot I was a boy and didn't understand why my father had me piling rocks up in the hall by the front door. The curtain was down and he stood behind the door with a rifle. If memory serves correctly, next to him, also with a rifle stood his white neighbor and friend.

The mob came. Perhaps fifty or more. A woman neighbor a block and a half down the street from our house stopped it and wagged her finger under the leader's nose and said "Don't you dare bother that colored family down the street or you are going to have trouble with all of us." The answer: "No we're going to the West Side to get some niggers." As they approached our house the woman across the street ran out and stopped them, telling them the same thing. They walked past our house without looking at it. In high school I coached a girls' (white) basketball team and the pastor of the church wanted me to join but being a good Catholic (at the time) I refused. After high school I coached a neighborhood football team and in Washington Park on Sundays (James T. Farrell's park) most of the crowd (white) rooted for us—I believe because the team was white and had a colored coach.

My experiences are a little different from those of most Negroes in that I have never lived in a Negro neighborhood, instead: Near Maxwell and Halsted, that wonderful place where all nationalities live within a couple blocks of each other, in an Italian neighborhood and finally east of Michigan Boulevard on the near North Side where I was perhaps the first Negro (aside from living-in servants) to live. Not bad for Chicago, eh?

If I understand correctly, Mr. Baldwin does not like liberals (does TIME?). Well, I have news for him. There are thousands of radicals, liberals and just plain, ordinary people of good heart and have none of these prejudices he has taken his stake of land out in.

Finally the next time I go to Chicago I must go by way of Birmingham or where ever else there is trouble for I feel it is time for every man, woman and child of good will to stand up and be counted.

Except for the 1919 riots, Motley's youth was innocent of racial concern. His interest was in writing, as early as when editor Lucius C. Harper persuaded Robert S. Abbott, publisher of the black community newspaper, the

Chicago Defender, to begin a children's column, "Bud Billiken," written by the youngster Willard Motley. Although the paper featured news of racial pertinence, Motley's column even at this date bespoke the author's personal belief in universality of concern; reflected, Motley might assume, by the Chinese "billiken," god of things "as they ought to be."

Idealism is the key to Motley's childhood and adolescence. Chicago is a city of neighborhoods; whether designated by parish, ward, or natural boundaries, each demographic center has its name, reputation, and strong local spirit. Willard Motley's neighborhood was Englewood, surrounding a shopping district at 63rd Street and Halsted on Chicago's South Side; and Motley's youth, especially his high school years, is distinguished by a lusty chauvinism for this part of town. Lest the spirit of his early diaries be misunderstood, the reader must be aware that enthusiasm for the Englewood high school teams reveals not only student spirit but also implies a life-style natural to any Chicago youth, all the more so in the earlier part of this century when the neighborhoods were at their strongest.

In 1926, at age sixteen, Motley began a set of diaries that were to be faithfully continued until 1943, the year he completed his first and best-selling novel, *Knock on Any Door.* "Awful lonesome; need a chum," wrote Motley on his diary's first page, and he proceeded for seventeen years to create and sustain a personal, sometimes imaginary world. Facts are duly recorded: team sports, his adolescent newspaper work, school friendships, transcontinental trips, and an interminable series of projects. All, he is led to admit, are his own substitute for simple, natural companionship, and so as the years and the volumes of his diary draw on he becomes the self-conscious artist, weaving impossible ambitions (great romantic loves, a spectacular college career) not as a record of fact but as his life might be, as it "ought" to be. Always counterposed are the events—depression economics, growing racial complications to love—which make of Motley a hard-nosed realist at the same time he strikes his lofty ideals.

Willard Motley graduated from Englewood High School in Chicago on January 31, 1929, and after a year and a half of fruitless attempts to find a steady job, he set about collecting experiences and adventures for his stories. In June and July of 1930 he bicycled to New York, with no money and only the generosity of strangers, themselves experiencing the first summer of the Great Depression, to see him through. In the fall of 1933 he made an abortive, almost explicitly fantastical attempt to attend the University of Wisconsin as a spontaneous football hero. Through high school Motley had submitted scores of stories to *Boy's Life* and similar periodicals, although very few were ever accepted and published. Nevertheless he lived his life as material for fiction, and when he dreamed of himself as a great writer it was not simply as a goal, but as a way of creating the very substance he wished to write about. His experiences in New York, in Madison, and ultimately on a nine-month hobo trip (repeated a year later) to California, Colorado, and the Pacific Northwest yielded much material for stories, often transcribed directly from his diaries.

By 1938 Motley was living in the Maxwell Street and Skid Row neighborhoods of Chicago, mining his travel journals and collecting material for his novel of "real" life in the city. In Denver he had met a young reformatory inmate who was to be the genesis of Nick Romano in *Knock on Any Door,* and every day in his new neighborhood Motley, now used to living on hardly any means at all, was seeing countless Nick Romanos growing up from altar boys into candidates for Death Row. His stories were being published, but usually for little or no payment, and in one case, as the editor of *Outdoors* magazine suggested, in barter for some fishing tackle or a hunting jacket. In 1940 a letter of rejection from a small literary magazine, *The Anvil,* included an invitation to meet the editors, Jack Conroy and Nelson Algren. With this introduction to literary (albeit proletarian) society, Motley found his way toward WPA Writers' work, Newberry and Julius Rosenwald Fellowships, and the stimulus to complete his novel "Leave Without Illusions," later retitled *Knock on Any Door.*

Motley's diaries end in 1943, with his novel written and soon to begin the rounds of publishers. That the book became a best-seller (300,000 copies in hardbound during its first year of publication, over 1.5 million in paperback through 1975) does not imply that Motley found success as a writer. Thirteen major houses rejected the book, Motley later claimed, because of thematic references to miscegenation (eventually tempered by the book's final publisher). When it was accepted, the firm's editor-in-chief demanded massive revisions, for matters of length, language, and sexual reference—and for fear that because of its brutal portrayal of Chicago, the city's police would censor the book and the school board would cancel orders for the company's texts. Motley traveled to New York, and after searching for a midtown hotel that would accept blacks, spent several months with Ted Purdy, a specially hired editor, reducing his manuscript from 1 million to 250,000 words and altering its unique material to fit the style suitable for a more readable novel. A preface Motley had written in 1943 was the first to go, for reasons of space and aesthetics, and also because it described a novel and a novelist's method that were no longer there.

An apprentice author can expect to have his work so altered, but fifteen years later, working on his third (and highly anticipated) novel, *Let No Man Write My Epitaph,* Motley had to repeat the same arguments for his editor. "I feel," he wrote Hiram Haydn in 1958, "that the writer is the lay figure in the hands of his characters and material rather than the other way around and that they—the characters and materials—dictate his style. I want to be a writer speaking not for but 'with' my characters; that chameleon who can wear the coloration of the environment he deals with." "Don't make me too respectable and polished," he pleaded in his P.S.; but publishers had their own ideas of how a black best-selling novelist should write, and to the end of his career Motley would fight such pressures. His novels were rewritten, and even when made into movies were diluted a second time. What would have otherwise been the noteworthy fact of a black novelist leading the best-seller lists, and having his work transposed to the film by Humphrey Bogart, became instead an entirely different story, as Motley wrote a friend in 1961:

KNOCK ON ANY DOOR was sold for $50,000. However I lost $100,000 on this sale. M-G-M was running a contest for "Best-novel-of-the-year" for which they were to pay $150,000 and KNOCK was chosen, a script written and presented to Breen office for approval. The book-script was turned down by that great body on the grounds that it encouraged juvenile delinquency, was immoral, indecent, etc. Mark Hellinger later bought the rights for the book and on his death Bogart bought them from his estate. His company (Santana, I believe, after his boat) produced it and Columbia released it.

With no creative control, Motley could only write the actors with advice, as he did John Derek, in 1948, who was starring in his first role:

I have written to [director] Nick Ray today too and pleaded with him to come to Chicago if only just to see West Madison Street and the actual localities of the book. There's nothing like it on Main Street I assure you and hope that he will come to Chicago, that you can come along with him. We could wear old clothes and tramp West Madison day and night until both of you got the feel and tempo of the street, the people down there.

Again, fifteen years later, Motley made the same proposal to James Darren, who played Nick Romano, Jr., in the film of *Let No Man Write My Eiptaph*. Darren actually accompanied Motley, but with no visible effect on the film.

The writing career of Willard Motley became one of frustration. The high promise, reflected in Arna Bontemps' letter of 1946, sending word of Motley's Rosenwald Fellowship, was not fulfilled. Despite his strong sales, critics expressed dissatisfaction with Motley's work—dissatisfaction shared by Motley himself. On the eve of *Knock*'s publication, Motley wrote his editor of his plans as a writer, plans no less ambitious than the many projects outlined day to day in his adolescent diary. Included were books not only with white characters but, an innovation for Motley, with black characters in racially pertinent themes. But such material remained—and finally died—in manuscript.

The two subsequent novels Motley did produce—*We Fished All Night* (1951) and *Let No Man Write My Epitaph* (1958)—were formed in the mold of *Knock on Any Door,* yet never enjoyed similar success. For the last decade of his life (1955–1965) Motley lived in Mexico, where now, painfully conscious of the prejudices against his race, he found a more hospitable culture (in 1963 he wrote Roy Wilkins of the NAACP about the feasibility of organizing Latin-American–oriented protest against racial prejudice). His fiction, now often set in Mexico and reflecting the racial universality he saw there, met great resistance from New York publishers and literary agents, and little of it was published. Motley's *Time* letter, however, did attract attention, and the *Chicago Sun-Times* asked him to amplify his comments for a feature article. Titled by Motley "Some Thoughts on Color," the *Sun-Times* ran it on Sunday, August 11, 1963, as "Let No Man Write Epitaph of Hate for His Chicago," omitting these important paragraphs:

Inter-marriage? And why not? Some sense should be talked into a senseless situation. Again, to use an old observation, an old cliché, there has been much inter-marriage, of course, as any man with eyes can see, dating from the first slave girl to the present—one needs only to look at the brownness, lightness and whiteness of so many Negroes. Perhaps not marriage, but a mating, a mixing of bodies. There has been an awful lot of desegragation for over a century.

Every time there is a crossing of lines, an international or inter-racial marriage (of whatever races) a small hurrah arises in the guts of me. Why not an international, interracial man, looking much like a man? He would probably be tan of color with wavy hair, slant eyes and high cheek bones and no one would have to go to the beach to get sun-tanned, some women to the beauty parlor to get their hair curled, others to have it straightened—and we could go on from there to solve our psychological problems—god knows we have a few.

At the time of his death in 1965 (from intestinal gangrene, the final ravages of a poor diet and too much beer), Motley was working on a novel, *Tourist Town,* which displayed the corruptions worked upon a small Mexican fishing village. Never marrying, Motley nevertheless adopted a Mexican street urchin as his son. Perhaps despairing of publication, Motley had spent his last years exploring the themes he wanted to: interracial affairs, homosexuality, and other issues considered too sensitive for respectable commercial publishing. By the mid-1960s, however, American life and its literary market were opening up to the frank and honest treatment of such themes, and Motley's unfinished manuscript was quickly trimmed to manageable length, retitled *Let Noon Be Fair,* and published in the style of another best-seller. Without the author at hand to protest, the book met even colder reception than the two previous novels, and the career of Willard Motley closed on a very minor note.

The discovery of the Willard Motley Papers, and the work being done on them, suggests that his career was indeed important. For the best-selling black novelist of his day, Motley's manuscripts and letters reveal even more literary substance behind his work. His diaries are the closest record we can have for the genesis and development of the artist, and in Motley's case all the more so because of his carefully noted, self-conscious ambition as a writer. June 1, 1943, the morning after he wrote the last page of *Knock on Any Door,* Motley confided to his diary that "I hadn't realized how long three and a half years [of writing] are nor how dear Nick had grown to me. I feel as if one of my arms had been cut off. Three and a half years of my life—ten years of Nick's life." Close enough to his characters in his writing to actually be them, Willard Motley through his diaries offers the reader a similar chance to see inside the life of a young black man and complex literary artist.

A Willard Motley Bibliography

NOVELS BY WILLARD MOTLEY

Knock on Any Door. New York: D. Appleton-Century, 1947.
We Fished All Night. New York: Appleton-Century-Crofts, 1951.
Let No Man Write My Epitaph. New York: Random House, 1958.
Let Noon Be Fair. New York: G. P. Putnam's Sons, 1966.

SELECTED STUDIES ABOUT WILLARD MOTLEY

Bayliss, John F. "Nick Romano: Father and Son," *Negro American Literature Forum* 3 (March 1969): 18–21, 32.

Bone, Robert A. *The Negro Novel in America,* revised edition. New Haven: Yale University Press, 1965, pp. 178–79.

Bontemps, Arna. "Famous WPA Authors," *Negro Digest* 8 (June 1950): 43–47.

Breit, Harvey. "James Baldwin and Two Footnotes," *The Creative Present,* edited by Nona Balakian and Charles Simmons. New York: Doubleday, 1963, pp. 1–3.

Eisinger, Chester E. *Fiction of the Forties.* Chicago: University of Chicago Press, 1973, p. 70.

Ellison, Bob. "Willard Motley" [interview], *Rogue* 8 (December 1963): 20–24, 75.

Fleming, Robert E. "Willard Motley's Urban Novels," *Umoja: Southwestern Afro-American Journal* 7 (Summer 1973): 15–19.

———. "Willard Motley's Date of Birth: A Corrected Error," *American Notes & Queries* 13 (September 1974): 8–9.

———. "The First Nick Romano: The Origins of *Knock on Any Door,*" *Mid America II,* edited by David D. Anderson. East Lansing: Midwestern Press, 1975, pp. 80–87.

———. *Willard Motley.* Boston: Twayne, 1978.

Ford, Nick Aaron. "Four Popular Negro American Novelists," *Phylon* 15 (1954): 29–39.

Gelfant, Blanche. *The American City Novel.* Norman: University of Oklahoma Press, 1954, pp. 12, 185, 232, 236, 248–52.

Giles, James. "Willard Motley's Concept of 'Style' and 'Material,' " *Studies in Black Literature* 4 (Spring 1973): 4–6.

Giles, James, and Jill Weyant. "The Short Fiction of Willard Motley," *Negro American Literature Forum* 9 (Spring 1975): 3–10.

Giles, James, and Karen McGee Myers. "Naturalism as Principle and Trap: Theory and Execution in Willard Motley's *We Fished All Night,*" *Studies in Black Literature* 7 (Winter 1976): 19–22.

Grenander, M. E. "Criminal Responsibility in *Native Son* and *Knock on Any Door,*" *American Literature* 49 (May 1977): 221–33.

Hazard, Eloise Perry. "First Novelists of 1947," *Saturday Review* 31 (February 14, 1948): 8.

Hoffman, Frederick J. *The Modern Novel in America.* Chicago: Henry Regnery, 1954, pp. xiv, 149, 205.

Hughes, Carl M. *The Negro Novelist.* New York: Citadel Press, 1953, pp. 148, 178–93, 197, 243–47, 251, 253, 261–63, 273–74, 277.

Jarrett, Thomas D. "Sociology and Imagery in a Great American Novel," *English Journal* 38 (November 1949): 518–20.

Klinkowitz, Jerome, and James Giles. "The Emergence of Willard Motley in Black American Literature," *Negro American Literature Forum* 6 (June 1972): 31–34.

Klinkowitz, Jerome, and Karen Wood. "The Making and Unmaking of *Knock On Any Door,*" *Proof* 3 (1973): 121–37.

Klinkowitz, Jerome, James Giles, and John O'Brien. "The Willard Motley Papers at the University of Wisconsin," *Resources for American Literary Study* 2 (Autumn 1972): 218–73.

Major, Clarence. "Willard Motley: Vague Ghost After the Father," *The Dark and Feeling.* New York: The Third Press, 1974, pp. 95–98.

Rayson, Ann L. "Prototypes for Nick Romano of *Knock On Any Door,*" *Negro American Literature Forum* 8 (Fall 1974): 248–51.

Rideout, Walter B. *The Radical Novel in the United States.* Cambridge: Harvard University Press, 1956, p. 263.

Schraufnagel, Noel. *From Apology to Protest.* Deland, Florida: Everett Edwards, 1973, pp. 44–47, 100–101.

Weissgarber, Alfred. "Willard Motley and the Sociological Novel," *Studi Americani* (Rome) 7 (1961): 299–309.

Weyant, N. Jill. *The Craft of Willard Motley's Fiction.* Doctoral dissertation, Northern Illinois University, 1976. *Dissertation Abstracts International* 36 (1976): 7429A.

――――. "Lyrical Experimentation in Willard Motley's Mexican Novel: *Let Noon Be Fair,*" *Negro American Literature Forum* 10 (September 1976): 95–99.

Wood, Charles. "The 'Adventure' Manuscript: New Light on Willard Motley's Naturalism," *Negro American Literature Forum* 6 (June 1972): 35–38.

Unsigned. "America's Top Negro Authors," *Color* 5 (June 1949): 28–31.
_____. "The Return of Willard Motley," *Ebony* 13 (December 1958): 84–88, 90.

THE DIARIES OF
WILLARD MOTLEY

1 9 2 6

Fri. Jan. 1st: Awful lonesome; need a chum. Picked on you friend diary. We'll be in close company while I am trying to strike up a true pal and a lot of real chums and buddies. Spent a rather dreary and uneventful New Year at home. Dreamed.

Resolved: That I make that old varsity squad this year and become a crack half-back!

Be a regular fellow.

Sat. Jan. 2nd: Sat around thinking about friendship, football, and Lillian. Retired about 10:30.

Sun. Jan. 3rd: Blue Sunday. Church. Movies. To-day is end of holiday, vacation. Oh boy! Englewood and the basketball season tomorrow!

Tues. Jan. 5th: Wonders will never cease! Made a successful Latin recitation this morning. Must make note of it, pal diary, as it is not an every day occurrence. Saw Charlie Chaplin in "The Gold Rush" to-night. Two whole days of school and I haven't seen her yet, pal.

Wed. Jan. 6th: School. Played basketball over at Weldon's.

Thur. Jan. 7th: Gazed upon her beautiful face today! Gee the thrill that rushes through me when I look at her! She's the prettiest girl I've ever seen.

Fri. Jan. 8th: Weldon wanted me to go skating with Matt and he and the rest of the old gang. Haven't any ice skates. My chances to pal around with the regular fellows seem slim. Well I've got one true sympathetic pal, diary.

Had a fine time in E. C. (easy) Smith's class dodging heavy questions which she was flashing left and right. The old gal kept me in hot water all period.

Fri. Jan. 22nd: The "E" Weakly, my queer creation, made a big hit on its first appearance at school to-day. Even Miss Hedeen smiled a little. Some of the fellows who represent school teams were awarded their "E's" at the assembly to-day.

Tues. Jan. 26th: Wow! Passed in four majors. G in Latin from Miss Knutzen. E from Miss Cross in English. G from Mr. Patch, algebra teacher and an E from "Easy" Smith.

Mon. Feb. 1st: Got registered in most of my classes. Made my first day at the coal yards. Boy but my muscles ache. Helped one of the men fill a wagon of coal and shoveled coal all afternoon.

Wed. Feb. 3rd: I saw her! Went to coal yards. Nothing to do. Climbed up on top of the coal bin and watched my friend "the foreigner" shoveling coal to the mouth of one of the bins. Imagined I was an American Spy. Went to gym where I watched Leon and Red practicing for the track team. The "Reds" play tomorrow evening.

Thur. Feb. 4th: Cowboy Allen started the day with a short lecture on citizenship. Citizenship seems to be her weak point. She accuses Alex van Telligan of being a non-American, dirty, low-down, turkey trodden foreigner because he spells the van in his name with a small v. This is uncitizen-like and is not an American name spelled thus claims the offended. Spent the noon recess tossing a baseball around with Louie and John. Johnnie has something on the ball besides the cover. Nothing doing at the coal-yards. Home. Supper and to gym. Bed at 10:30.

Mon. Feb. 8th: School. Played catch after classes with John. The announcement that the scandal-shouting, truth speaking outroaring sheet "Motley's" *E Weakly* may really be has brought many rumors and much gossip in 215. Things are humming. Played Hockey with Minton and Jucy this eve.

Tues. Feb. 9th: "E Weakly" subscriptions coming in.

Thur. Feb. 11th: School. "E Weakly" announcements caused quite a sensation. Had to talk about it in class. You know how I felt as I am a rotten speaker. Schwartz talked about the money end of it and Price as our baseball manager spoke about our baseball team. Was nominated Room Reporter and also as Englebooster Delegate. Rejected both.

Mon. Feb. 22nd: Art Staff and Mickey Schwartz were over. We worked on the paper. Got copies out on the Hektograph. It took all night.

Tues. Feb. 23rd: The whole school laughed! Especially the sophs. A few freshies are nursing hurts. Who cares about the freshies though. Big sensational, uproaring success.

Then the bolt into the blue—The faculty won't allow us to publish the paper any more! Mr. Lucas and Davidson, our new principal, are greatly opposed to it. Is there no way to publish it? We are holding a meeting tomorrow.

Wed. Feb. 24th: S'all off. Mr. Davidson won't give his permission. Talk of a sophomore protest, other rooms have had room papers. Several English teachers who saw paper liked it. Louie's English teacher, Miss Hardy, wanted to keep his copy. Miss Hedeen was given a copy. She liked it.

Thur. Feb. 25th: Englewood won the first two games in the semi-finals.
The lights won 17–10.
The heavyweight basketeers led on by Capt. Hinkley won a "thriller" 11–10. Fisher, light headed, rangy, center dropped in a free throw that won the game in the last 50 seconds of play.

Fri. Feb. 26th: Watched a couple basketball games tonight at the gym with Joe. Later his brother, Willard, dropped in and showed me some wrestling grips as he tossed me around on the mat.

Sat. March 6th: Our lights play the Lane lights for the city championship to-night. There is only one thing between me and that game—the price. I'm flat.
Go it, lights!

Fri. March 19th: Today was roughneck day at Englewood! All the fellows wore sweat-shirts and came to school without ties on, in shirt sleeves, etc. Had my neck nearly yanked off once because I didn't belong to the royal-rowdy revolters gang. Their motto is—Semper sic gentlemen (and teachers)—or something like that. Decided to take my tie off. Cowboy was on the war path for us rough-neck indians. And boy did she ride us! She started in by telling us that the President, big bankers, and famous rich men weren't roughneck. (Personally I'd rather be a Red Grange than any aforesaid.) Ended up with a lecture on citizenship. We had to go out of the room and put on our ties. When she wanted us to recite she called us roughnecks. She kept referring to our class work and you know, pal diary, I'm no geom shark.

Thur. April 22nd: School. Had not only a sub in English but also a good time. Zika gave Howard a slip for 7 days of study hall for disorder in division. That would keep him away from basketball practice. I took the slip and sat the period out for him while he practiced. Henri (the Mysterious Female) sat two seats in front of me and I couldn't resist the temptation of having a little fun with him. He talked to Mr. McGee about it and Mr. McGee talked to me. He asked me my name and as he was looking right at the slip I answered Winston Howard. I could imagine how Henri's face looked. You should have seen him. He edged around until he could see the name written on the slip. I held my breath and waited for the explosion. Catching his eye I shook my head and flashed a meaning look at him. But I expected him to give me away any minute. I had to pick up scraps of paper on the floor for Mr. McGee, as many of the other poor helpless victims who have come under the sword of his queer justice have had to do.

Tues. May 18th: Spent the second and third periods writing an English theme. In Journalism today Miss Zander said "I see Willard Motley that you had time to play ball." She had seen me from the "E" Weakly office yesterday evening playing ball with the fellows. I am on the very verge of failing and have a lot of back-work to make up. Teachers will peep! We have to interview some of the teachers for practice.

Thur. May 27th: Frank Dalrymple was back to school today! He hurt his ankle in a motorcycle accident. (This confidentially for he is supposed to have hurt it on the diving board.) Frank is a nice fellow and one nobody could help from liking. He's done some great things for Englewood and is the kind of modest, honest, clean cut athlete, and friend that I would like to be and am striving to be. I hope to be an intimate friend of his some day.

Tues. June 1st: Went to see about a place to rent for the proposed Englewood Athlete Club.

Fri. June 25th: Bid farewell to my classmates and embark on my summer vacation. Must get to work and raise some muscles.

Dave, a young fellow on the next street (he's about 13) has a little bird house in a tree in his back yard. This evening when I was passing by he was tacking on a sign.

F O R   R E N T
D O N ' T   A P P L Y —
J U S T   M O V E   I N

I wonder if birds believe in signs?

Big, good-natured Mr. Ryan was on his porch today when I passed by. He was singing and humming. I said he must be happy. He claimed, "Yes— my wife's gone out."

To bed at 11 o'clock.

Wed. June 30th: Went to the downtown library. Got some books on football. Met Earl Howard at our house. He is Winston Howard's cousin. He plays football on a southern college team and he weighs 210 pounds.

Mon. July 12th: Went to see about job at coal yards on Wallace and 59th Street. It's a Consumer Branch Coal Yard. Went over there at 7 o'clock this morning. Saw the yard foreman at about 12 o'clock and he assigned me to a job emptying a huge boxcar of coal containing about 40 tons. Had very little done by 6 o'clock when I quit. Awfully tired.

Tues. July 13th: Started to work at 5:30 and was finished at 12:30 and got my 4 dollars for the job. Talk about getting hardened up. That coal yard surely will harden one up.

Wed. July 14th: My birthday. I am 17 to-day. My year of hope: football—friendship—love—
   Celebrated by tackling my second coal yard job. Put in a hard day. Me and my partner hauled in 12 tons of coal. Delivered it to a cottage on 85 and Bishop. The fireman who lives there tipped us a dollar. Got awfully tired at times but imagined I was playing with Englewood and battering a Hyde Park or Lindblom team. It helped some. Made $3.30. Took a hot and then a cold bath. Made me feel fine and fit as a fiddle. Walked up by school. Treated myself to a pint of ice-cream to celebrate the great day. To bed.

Sat. July 17th: Earned $2.
   Gus, the foreman at the yard, is the typical big, broad, coarse, genial foreman. I can see him now in his slouch felt hat, steely blue eyes peering from under the slouch brim quizzingly (some word! sounds great!), his coal smeared shirt of a coarse blue material and his darker blue overalls. Was rather surprised to find that he's partly bald. Expected to find that he had long stringy white hair, faded worn and yellow at the ends or bushy rebellious black hair. Have never seen him without his companionable blue shirt and bluer overalls and slouch hat. It's his daily costume. He cuts a picturesque figure stradled on the high line. He told my partner that he was surprised that "the kid" had lasted. I'm not surprised. There's a backfield position open on Englewood's varsity this fall for a good player. I'm working on it.

Tues. Aug. 3rd: Work. Went up by school. A lot of the younger fellows were climbing the roof of the Englewood gym and were climbing into an open window to the swimming tank. Told them to come out. They wouldn't and loudly claimed they held no such ideas.
   I feel it's my duty to report it. One of the young kids are liable to get drowned in there. They have no business there anyway. That tank belongs to Englewood exclusively. Then again it might seem like tattling to tell. Any fellow ought to be able to stand a prank. I'm up in the air diary old pal. The diary is the place to come to unburden one's self, is it not? Boy, I wish you could advise me. Should I go to Cliff the janitor? Should I let it go? But if one of them was to get drowned I'd feel partly to blame.

Mon. Sept. 6th: Was over to park with Jordan. Drop-kicked back into form. Can do between 35–40 I believe. Pack up for school, football and friends tomorrow. Oh Boy!

1 9 2 7

A FORWARD

A forward isn't supposed to look backwards but in looking back over the old year, the year of 1926, I find that in a way my ambitions were partially fulfilled. I only hope that this new year which I am now living will be *really* a *happy* one. My greatest day of 1926 was on Thursday, September 30th, when I scored a touchdown against Saint Aquinas and my ambitions seemed to be becoming a reality.

Looking ahead I cannot see what is in store for me but can only hope that I will make the football team and play all season and be an outstanding star. It is not impossible and I feel confident that I *can* make the team and fulfill myself to my own idea of the way I would like to be. Friendship and Football!—

Mon. Jan. 3rd: School opened for the spring term today. Willard, Bob, Howie, and I with handshakes and greetings and friendly gossip fell again into that friendly spirit we had enjoyed last year. Read a ''swell'' Barbour story in a magazine at the library this afternoon.

Met Roy and Chuck tonight at the Englewood gym. Walked home with Chuck. We stood on the corner for a while talking. I saw Lillian today. She seemed to look right past me. God how I love her! I wonder how it will all end—

Thur. Jan. 6th: Turned in my football suit today. Quaint asked me how my foot was. Went over to the Community House gym this morning and shot baskets with a fellow I didn't know. There was an athletic assembly; Willard and I went down together. Johnny Weissmuller, world champion swimmer was at our assembly. He came up upon the platform with Coach Quaint. Johnny's the sort of fellow you like right away—at first sight. I was sold on him. He is very tall—about 6 ft., 6 in., broad shouldered and sandy headed. He was dressed in a light tweed suit and is rather nice looking. He leaned on Quaint's shoulder right up there on the stage. That was my first likeable impression of him. Quaint who is very short looked even smaller under Weissmuller's long arm. Johnny ran a finger down the side of Quaint's face and smiled. Grinning he held a foot out on the footlight protector and looked at it as at something he hadn't seen before. He winked at someone in the balcony. Everybody was laughing and applauding. Everybody liked him immensely. Quaint told us about Johnny and about a meet tonight at which Quaint claimed he was going to lower his previous world's record. Johnny whistled under his breath, rolled his eyes and nodded his head towards Quaint as if to say "Listen at him." Then Mr. Quaint left him to talk to us. He walked around, put his hands in back of him and appeared a bashful school boy. Quaint came back and made his speech for him.

Quaint's speech—

"Boys AND—girls of Englewood HIgh school—I am—glad to BE—HEre—and I THank—you." I can't write it as funny as it sounded the way Quaint said it punctuating it with all the markings of a bashful school boy making his first speech. Weissmuller was applauded and applauded and then applauded some more. He was cheered—he was clapped. Finally he came back upon the stage and opened his mouth for the first time. "Want to hear another speech?" he challenged in a boylike tone. Grinning he beaconed for Quaint!

—Then he was gone . . . leaving a pleasant memory of the great athlete he is. I really liked him. He seemed to be the way a champion or an athlete should be . . . boyish, modest, natural—the way I'd like to be.

Thur. Feb. 24th: School. Miss Beatty wanted to see me at her desk about the football theme I wrote, "Why I Like Football." She didn't think it was wholly original but took my word for it, saying that if I wrote it I was to be complimented on it. She gave me an E+ on it there at her desk. It started off much as a little article about our LaSalle Midgets team did that appeared in the Post two years ago and I will take this article as well as the first two writings of the theme to school tomorrow and show her as I wouldn't want her to think that I copied.

Wed. March 23rd: We won the city championship tonight—and how!

Got an "L" about 6:30 for Loyola gym. Met Micky, Horn, Harry, and another fellow. We had a swell time on the ride out there.

The gym was packed with about 5,000 students and our band had arrived and took possession of the balcony in the huge Loyola gym from where they played Englewood songs. The crowd was noisy and wild with enthusiasm. Lane took to the floor first and after a delay our quintet trotted in. Boy! The outburst of pent-up enthusiasm. We were cheering madly. The cheerleaders trotted out on the floor and led us through a series of cheers as the balls bounced against the backboard.

Saw Louie when he came in and yelled at him but the cheering from the stand was so noisy that he didn't hear me.

Mr. Apkin's little son, about 4 or 5 years old, was there dressed in a

tiny purple and white basketball suit just like the regulars. He went out and
shot with them.

He shot from nearly under the basket pushing the ball upward with his
tiny arms. Three or four times he tried then the ball went through. The
crowd cheered and clapped their hands.

And then the tip-off!

Boy, it was a game and a half. Jim Snyder starred for Englewood
although he sunk but one basket. He was the mainstay on both offense and
defense. Ossie played a wonderful game too. Darrow Smith went out on
personals, which were called very strictly on the team, in the first quarter.
Poor fellow. He was crying as he left the game. However he contributed one
basket for Englewood. Englewood jumped into a 7-1 lead and led 12 to 7 at
the half. The final score was 20-17.

Gosh! It was a real championship game! We got out of the gym early
and although promising ourselves that we would not pay our fair if we won
didn't have enough followers. Howie Smith with his wife and little boy were
at the game and rode home on our "L." We pulled down all the windows
and proceeded in having a grand and glorious celebration. There were a
couple Lane fellows on the "L" and we had a good time with them. They
were a decent sort though.

Gee if I had only waited and come home with the bunch. Half of them
crashed the "L" there at the Loyola station, while many followed the band
which paraded just behind a big Pierce-Arrow in which our champs were
being carried home.

Playing loudly, singing, and shouting they paraded all the way to the
loop where a couple of fellows proceeded to stand in the middle of the street
at State and Madison and broadcast to the world at large that Englewood
had just won the City championship.

Pupils rushed through the loop streets stopping everything and yelling
"Who won—Englewood! Yea!"

They paraded to the Tribune Tower where the basketball fellows were
to have their picture taken and demanded instant attention. Photographers
took snaps of the team, band, and wildly yelling followers of our South Side
stronghold.

Many rushed into the Oriental Theatre and booed Paul Ash, not allowing him to proceed with his act until he had yelled "Yah Englewood!"

Finally he obligingly lead the band through a—

"Yah Englewood!"

Then the band and many of the students, both boys and girls, rushed
the loop "L's" brushing aside all opposition. (In the "L" I came home on
which was an early one we had all the windows down and raced with
another "L" bearing south side rooters back to their stronghold. We shook
hands with fellows on the other "L.")

The band played "Hail! Hail! The gang's all here, we're from
Englewood High School! We're from Englewood High School! Rah!" and
enthusiastic drunk Purple rooters paraded through the cars cheering and
pushing aside the guards.

The rooters were singing and having a fine time. Several others decided that the light was bad for their eyes and decided to put them out. They succeeded and also ripped away advertisements and broke out the windows.

Police who attempted to board the car at loop stations were held at bay although one detective succeeded in entering with a long lead pipe in one hand. One of the fellows stuck a trombone between his legs and he went down with a crash. The bell cord was snatched down and he was bound and set on the back platform to cool off.

The train of wild rooters sped on. At the 58th Street Station a reception was held for the Jackson Park express and, as the police leaped on the car, they were apparently having as much fun as the students.

Fifteen of our number were locked up in jail until three o'clock when they were released.

The rest broke up and the same crowd who had rushed out upon the Loyola floor to carry the victors to their dressing and wrought a sensation in the loop went home happy and smiling.

Boy! One great game!

A great time!

A grand and glorious night as a climax to a wonderful season.

Thur. Oct. 20th: Talked to Muriel in Spanish. Ed was telling me the other night about Lillian's dad owning three bakerys, a cafe, and three cars. I can't see what a girl like her could possibly see in me. She doesn't!

Mon. Nov. 7th: Auggie, Art, and I were standing on the corner at 61st and Princeton when we got into a conversation with a boy hobo. He was only 17. Was hard though. Told us some of his experiences. He came into Chicago on a milk dairy truck. Was supposed to meet the driver again. Missed him, however. Was flat broke. Hadn't eaten since yesterday morning.

Most bums have their "line" but our bum seemed to be sincere and I'm quite sure that he told the truth.

He was going to "steal a flop" (as he put it) in the dairy until morning. Walked him to the dairy where the out-of-town truck picks up milk cans. The dairy is about half a block from our house. I told him to wait for me and that I'd go home and get him some soup. I did. Brought him some in a quart bottle of milk. Brought some bread too—stole them out of the house. Got caught. Bawled out. Misunderstood. Didn't explain.

Watched our tramp gobble it all down. Auggie came back with a sandwich and a half and two buns. These he put in his pocket. I gave him 15 cents. All that I could rake together. He didn't want to take it but I forced it upon him. He promised to write me and tell me some of his experiences.

Tues. Nov. 22nd: The football team left for Pine Bluff today. Louie went! Bully for him! Wish I could have gone with him.

Went to the Literary Club meeting today. Read my story—"That Roommate of Mine!"—an excuse for a football story.

Sat up until 11:30 writing on my latest story—"Leo Clayton, Water-boy, Substitutes."

Miss X (Cross) is going to look it over for me and I am to hand it to her tomorrow.

Sun. Dec. 25th: Christmas finally drew to its dreary end. Awfully lonesome day. Wonder how Lillian spent today! and Muriel?

Wonder what Louie did all day?

1 9 2 8

Sun. Jan. 1st: Another new year.
New Dreams—
New Hopes—
New air-castles built over the charred ashes of '27.
Here's to love, friendship, fun—sports—and yes, luck.
Maybe 1928, a huge rapped mysterious package holds for me what I hold so dear in life.
Who knows?
All that I ask of this infant year has been sealed in an envelope (to be read on New Year 1929) written as the bells, sirens, whistles and guns ushered out the old year and acclaimed the new.
Well dear little diary and true faithful friend you are two years old to-day. Congratulations!
And may this year be your and may I say *our* biggest and best year.
That's all today, little pal.

Wed. Feb. 8th: School. Printed the Cheerleader this morning—big headlines!
Shot baskets with Mush in the gym 7th and 9th hours. We went over to the Community House. Talked about a banquet at the end of our season and about the team next year and college. Lou and I are doubtlessly going to Illinois or Wisconsin and Mush may decide to come. Gee if about 4 or 5 of us could all go together.

Wed. Feb. 29th: This the extra day of the year was dull and commonplace and I could very well have done without it.
To gym first hour where our indoor baseball team beat the other team 33 to 3 and we only batted one inning before the bell rang.
Joe and I went over to the Community House and played dominoes 7th hour Spanish where we're still having that dumb German substitute.
Watch the team practice. Home. Shot some baskets down at the gym this eve. I had my eye working great. Scrimmaged with North Church. Home. Dead tired. Wrote brother a letter. He's in New York having a one-man show and has sold two pictures for $900 in two days.

Thur. March 1st: Late to school.

There was a "pep" assembly 4th hour today. Gee! It was great.

Mr. Davidson spoke first and said that if we win tomorrow Monday we'll be excused at 2:30 and that there will be a snake dance through Englewood lead by our band and our champs on a finely decorated truck.

You see they're having the game at day time and there is only 1,000 tickets allowed each school and as Quaint said ours are almost gone. There's to be no tickets sold at the gate either and the game is at day so that there will be no repetition of last year's performance. It was novel last year but if it reoccurred again there would be nothing nice about it.

Fri. March 9th: Went in to see Miss Cross. She met me in the hall and told me to come in. There's a contest going on in a school magazine, a magazine published for the schools and subscribed for by her for her classes. It's a national contest of creative work and the prizes are $100, $50, and $25 and there are many different branches to get into.

She liked my article "The Fightin' Purple" and suggested that we submit it. She thinks it's great and said that it would be wonderful for them to accept what my own school turned down and said that with a little revision there would be none better in the contest and that I should take a prize and if I didn't she wasn't going to subscribe for the *Scholastic* anymore. She said that the article would go over easily unless there were a couple dough heads on the "jury" who struck at that use of the dash that I have used in describing football. She liked that part though and thinks it was almost genius in me to use the dash that way. She surely encourages one!

She said that she is going to work on this and feels almost as if it were her own. You see the contest closes Monday at midnight and all mail to the contest must have been stamped before this time. On the 28 of April the *Scholastic* prints its student-written number in which appears the work of all the prize winners and many others.

Miss Cross gave me the article making suggestions on corrections after going over it closely for nearly an hour in class and told me to type it and meet her in the library tomorrow morning as she wants it off Saturday night.

She said that she would look over my story "Clayton, Water Boy, Substitutes" and bring it with her tomorrow.

Wrote the article over this eve and retyped the story "After He Was Dead" to give her too.

Sat. March 10th: Met Miss Cross downtown in the library at a quarter of ten and for nearly two and a half hours sat there reading, cutting, revising and writing.

She liked "The Fightin' Purple" the way I've written it over and after putting in a pile of punctuation marks that I left out and correcting the spelling she gave it to me with the other, "After He was Dead," and told me to type them at home and be sure to get them out tonight. I did.

She took the track story home to cut it as it is 6,000 words long and the word limit in the contest is 3,000.

"The Fightin' Purple" was submitted as an essay while the others go in the short story division.

Fri. March 16th: Saw that girl who was in Miss Cross' room last week when I went there. Learned that her name is Anne. When I first saw her it was that eve when she had to come in after school for being late. Miss Cross wasn't in the room at the time and she asked what I was "in for" and said "Now don't forget. I got here just after Miss Cross left!" (Miss Cross had been gone about 15 minutes!) Anne began writing on the board. She was drawing something and would step back and squint at her work. She was the very breath of blossoming youth—defiant—healthy—rare.

She had the prettiest and the most frank eyes I'd ever seen. I asked her what she was drawing. It was a design and she told me so.

Sat. April 14th: Continued my writing tonight on the Fightin' Purple Series. Bought a two pound box of graham crackers and munching on them while seated at my writing table in a cast-off but beautiful smoking jacket (I don't smoke so we'll call it a lounging robe for convenience) I felt really great. I should get a lot of ideas, all dressed up like this.

Secreted crackers under the dresser, laid aside the er—lounging robe and went to bed.

Sun. April 15th: Wrote all day. Took a walk this eve. Was in a wonderful mood—a very imaginative mood. Came back and donning "lounging robe" dashed off two pages of "Wilbur Marther's Diary."[1]

Tues. May 15th: At this writing I have earned the title of "The Red Grange of Englewood." We played touch and our gang won 18-6. Dick and Lou did most of our passing. Lou hurled one to me early in the game that gave us a big gain. In all, I got away for two of our touchdowns, both times snaring passes from Weisberg. Once, after catching the ball I did some good dodging, getting past three men in good fashion to score, Lou, blocking one man, great.

Once I pretended, on defense, to "suck in" but saw, out of the corner of my eye, Benny, hurling a pass to his end.

I ran towards the play and with my back to the ball, nabbed it over my shoulder and started out, circling around the opposite end. I faked it toward the middle, eluding a couple men in this manner, and then streaked to the opposite sideline, going about 25 yards in all. Boy, I really travelled on that play!

Well—I'm no slouch!

I can go!

The linemen worked in the pit today. We had catching passes, falling

---

1. A fictitious biography of his alter ego.

on the ball and taking out men on interference. Dick Weisberg had charge
of the backs and called on me to show them how to fall on the ball, take out
a man and etc. I was an example. He called on me for all of this and soon I
found the fellows watching me and asking me questions. I seem to be pretty
popular and they all seem to like me. I don't know why. I don't seem to
have a great personality, and although I am greatly attracted by many
fellows it seems hard to make staunch friends with them.

Tues. Sept. 4th: Well dear diary the towers of dear old Englewood were
once again sighted above the tree tops and school once again opened as I
made my way to the campus once again.
     My last fall—my last semester—
     A babble of voices—faces, old and new—laughter—and hand shaking.
     Englewood had been painted and cleaned from top to bottom and I im-
mediately ambled up to Senior Hall meeting, on the way, innumerable old
friends.

Sat. Sept. 15th: This morning was hard to live through. Finally it became
time to go out to Grand Crossing where the team dresses and in due time the
whole squad rumbled up to Normal Park in various moods. I climbed out,
trembling somewhat, and entered the stadium. I was to start! I practiced
catching punts with June Baldwin and Asconio while later Palmer had
Asconio and I drop-kicking to the west goal.
     Finally the kick-off and with it some of my tension wore off.
     It would be the most wonderful thing of my life if I could describe how
in my debut I ran wild against our opponents, but truth is not stranger or
more fanciful than fiction. I was rotten!
     I was supposed to, above all, on our formation, be sure that my in-
terference got ahead of me before cutting off tackle. The trouble is,
although I didn't know it I was running too slow and my Charlie-horse
bothered me some. However I played all of the first half but three minutes
when Lee Washer was sent in for me with instructions to *run!*
     As I left the game I heard my name on the lips of the crowd for the first
time and although I left the game in shame I shall not ever forget that
supreme thrill!
     The score was 0-0 at the half but Lee was going great all the time, and
picking his holes nice, and late in the 3rd quarter broke off left tackle for a
25 yard run to the two yard line from where Asconio, our captain, plunged
it over. The final was 6-0, and my substitute had won the game! Most likely
I'd be his substitute from hence forth!

Mon. Dec. 24th: Up to gym. Orville gave me a pleasant surprise by drop-
ping over to the E. C. H. today and I had his annual to give him. He shot
baskets with me and it seemed like old times again! Or's a deadeye now.
You should have seen him pop 'em in from all over the floor. He seldom
fails on a long and as for set-ups that he used to sometimes miss, he never

fails on now. We shot baskets for several hours. I'm getting to be a regular dead-eye now too—me and my old one-handed shot! I feel as if I'm going better now and have a better eye than at any time previous in my basketball career.

Or is rooming with the President of the Freshman Class at Illinois. He's also playing on a frat. team—jumps center, of course—a team that has won seven games and lost none and are on the way toward the intramural championship on a league of 34 teams! Regardless of all this Or turned to me once while we were shooting and said—"Say, Mot, do you know I really wish I was back playing with the Purple A. C. again—I'd give anything!"

Isn't that funny now—Life is awfully unproportional and once we make friends and live in one sphere of happenings it is hard to adjust to another—In fact we don't care to.

Tues. Dec. 25th: Dull—dull—endless day was Christmas—Much as many of my other Christmas's. Life is really miserable when you have no inseparable pal nor a girl or sweetheart to be with, to talk with, to laugh with on such days of wholesome joy and when dreams seem empty.

Thought of Lou and reviewed our friendship again.

1 9 2 9

Thur. Jan. 24th: Lunch at Baldwin's. Henry treated me to a soda on a part of a quarter he won on our championship game. My "Man Friday" is old loyalty itself!

Boy how I hate to leave. I moan it every day. Practically all of the grads feel as I do. Englewood's a great old place and we're going to miss it plenty!

Gave Fred an invitation to the surprise party. He and Johnny are the only non-Purple A. C. fellows invited. February Fifth has everybody wondering.

After lunch Mush and I went back to Englewood. Of course I met fellows and girls galore I knew and yelled hello to. Mush laughed. He's always kidding me about my popularity and always stopping to speak to every "four out of five." He said he wishes he was as popular as I.

I told Mush how I hated graduating and starting all over at college— when I get there!

He said, "Gee, Mot, you don't need to worry. You make friends easily—you're friends with everybody."

Now that's a royal compliment! If only I had as much confidence in my personality!

I'm really a lonely old duffer after all. What I really, really wish is that Louie was my inseparable pal—that we were always together.

And then there's girls I like and yet I've never had five minutes with one alone under the moon!

At that I feel that Louie and I have one of those death-defying friendships that are made overnight in youth. I'd go a long way for him.

Sat. Jan. 26th: Well I'll graduate. I got my final marks—
U.S. HISTORY—G
3B SPANISH—F
3A SPANISH—F
PRINTING—E
Civics—G

Mon. Jan. 28th: Commencement night!!!—Three nights into the future!!!

No classes any longer. To school at 9 to practice our graduation exercises.

They seat us on the stage according to our rank. The girls are seated on one side and the boys on the other. The class officers, members of the Honor Society and T. D. I. are seated in the first row. And so on—down to us low brows!

All lettermen are seated on the stage.

You know our stage is too small to seat the entire class and only those prominent in school life get seats on the stage where proud parents can see and gurgle. For mine, although seated on the stage, I'd rather sit before— have everyone sit below than have some of our classmates seated in the audience, a thing they'll remember all their lives. There's fellows down below, regular fellows, who are far above some of the scrawny rats they've got on the stage because they belong to the T. D. I. or got 5 in Physics and Chem and History!

Stop!—you'll talk yourself right into a job as an orator or off the stage!

I'm seated next to good old Micky Schwartz. He's a clown!

We practiced the march on and off the stage but no one was in step. It's plenty hard to keep time to the fool thing and we take the stage as slowly as the old folks home would—so that we look dignified!

While the line was waiting outside to start the march back in Micky and I ducked into the rear of the lunchroom and bought cup cakes and sandwiches!

After the exercises Will, Micky, Howie, Mush, Lou, and I wandered around the building and recalled memories of our four years here. We finally wound up at the E. C. H.

Downtown this afternoon to buy a pair of shoes and some things for our surprise party.

Sick. Stomach ache!

Thur. Jan. 31st: Willard Motley—former Englewood High School pupil— that's how it'll read from now on!

I went up to school at about 7:30 this evening and went down to the lunch room where we grads met and donned our caps and gowns with joking comments and laughter. We looked like a school of monks!

Gus and I sat on one of the lunchroom tables and talked, our gowned legs dangling. Will Starke arrived shortly. Howie shouted that he had discovered ice cream in the freezer and we all stood around him, shielding him with our gowns from the waitresses who were serving the night school pupils, as he grabbed several plates from a neighboring tray and dished them up!!! We had to eat the ice cream with our fingers but it was mighty good!

Then the inseparables once again, Mickey and Mush, arrived and Mickey stuck his hand in the freezer and pulled out a fist-full of ice cream! Just like Mickey!

Then motherly teachers ordered us out into the hall to line-up outside of the auditorium. We raised hell in the hall and Lee Washer, coming from his place in line, blew his breath in my face and asked me if I could smell anything. Lee had to get braced up.

Mickey was feeling awfully bad because of the sudden death of his grandfather and wasn't as comical as he would otherwise have been.

We marched in all well and good, but once on the stage we raised hell! We talked and joked and told jokes the entire two hours and a half. Mickey was a clown, hiding his grief. Mickey offered me some candy but I was afraid to eat it, afraid that they'd see us in the balcony at least. The girl across the aisle, wearing her cap collegiate and with her legs crossed asked for gum and we threw her over a piece. Then, nothing would do but that Minnie Lubershane have a stick. I made faces at Will Starlee down the aisle and watched Johnny Baldwin chew gum noisily throughout the entire show.

Mickey and I then resorted to pointing out friends in the audience.

Later I was called out in front with the other grads who have won major letters to receive an athletic diploma. We were—Mickey, Asconio, Johnnie, Lee, Jack, Leon, Eddie, Louie, Jim, and Joie (also myself).

Then the diploma march and a freedom I'm not at all crazy about.

Good-bye dear, dear old Englewood—I'll never, never forget you or all the great times I've had under your green tiled roofs.

Mon. Feb. 4th: The date has been changed for the surprise party until tomorrow, but today found me busy making plans.

I made the two cakes for the party which took all morning and most of the afternoon.

The big cake is a monstrous thing—I call it "the Leaning Tower of Pisa." It is snow white and dotted and sprinkled with beautiful tiny candies that glow like stars. It has 18 candles on it, four pink, and fourteen lavendar, artistically arranged and placed in tiny holders. It has five large layers and three small top layers that constitute the "tower."

The other cake is a three layer gold and silver cake and has iced on it—
BIRTHDAY GREETINGS
LOU AND WILL

After making the cakes and icing them I went out and made the final purchases.

Fri. March 1st: School. Fred's a "Hi-Y" pledge and was telling me some of the things they are made to do.

Today at noon one of the members made him get down on his knees and propose to a girl in the hall. At first the girl said no but when she saw through the plot she said yes and the fellows told Fred to go with her then.

Wouldn't that be a great little start for a love story of college life with the fellow taking the girl by the arm and telling her, whispering to her to please walk just around to the end of the corridor with him. The beginning of an acquaintance. Maybe I will write it some day. You know my diary is going to be a real gathering source for all kinds of stories.

Fred continued that on the street car the members of the "Hi-Y" made one pledge look for the "lost cord" under the seats. They took another fellow's money and all filed into the car telling the conductor that the fellow on the end had the fares!

Another fellow pledge of Shewell's was made to "wrestle with temptation."

Jim Custer had to wear a huge dog collar to school today and had to sit in Cowboy Allen's class in the front seat with it on while a member watched from the door. Cowboy Allen!—poor Jim!

Fred's ducking them!

Thur. May 9th: Asked Mr. Quaint if I could help him with the coaching and he has turned the entire backfield over to me.

He announced before the entire squad after practice this eve that I would be the backfield's regular spring-practice coach and have full charge. I instructed in pivoting and handling the ball this afternoon.

After practice I caught some 50 yard passes off the able arm of Hoppy Thompson.

Thur. May 16th: Over to the E. B. Church gym this eve and started home about 10:30 with Bud Peterson. We met Eloise and stood talking and joking and holding her hands in front of her house. Her little sister, Alice, came to the door and said that her dad did want her to come in the house but when he found out that it was "Motley" he said it was alright!

Fri. June 21st: I will remember this day as long as I live. Today I truly fell in love for the first and last time—

Today walking north in the third floor corridor, having just come from my salesmanship class, I saw beautiful E—— at her locker and stopped to ask her to write in my annual. My request must surely have sounded like a plea as she answered, "Why of course I will!"

I had no pen but she offered me her own along with her annual that I might write in her book too. I politely asked her to write in my book first. She stood against her locker, my annual held in one hand, her pen moving gracefully over the page. And then the most surprising, the most wonderful revelation of my life made known its light. E——'s eye lids, like soft petals of a flower, were lowered on my book and her lashes were as long, dark, curly crescents. As I stood looking mutely at her my soul cried out and my heart burned in my eyes and made caressing tears well up. Over and over the words came soundlessly to my lips, words that I should not have cared to stop had I the power—"I love you!—I love you!—I love you!—I love you!" They seemed the essence of my life and my soul stood revealed to itself.

But poor, speechless mute that I am, the words will never be coined that could justly express my feelings. It's like a dream come true. I can remember the one most impressive dream of my life, a dream I had when I could have been no more than three years old. I dreamed of the most beautiful blue sky that ever was. This sky, it seemed, was so near that it could have been touched. And it was sprinkled with gleaming silver stars—A dream I'll never forget.

Today was like the dream reviewed—the dream come true. This old world will never be that old cheerless, beaten place again. No matter how life treats me, no matter though I never, never see E—— again (and the tears fill my eyes here and I beg God to be merciful) I will always be happy—happy for having met love and known love. Now I shall die happy.

E—— is the most wonderful, the most beautiful, the sweetest girl on God's gold and green earth and I love her, love her—have loved her always though I never knew it until 2:30 this afternoon.

When I came home this evening after the happiest day of my life which rivals sweetly all the happiest days of the world's greatest loves, I sat in the parlor, my annual opened at her picture, my eyes misty. I was possessed with a queer trembling. The streets outside the window were golden paths and the leaves that rustled on the trees were love songs.

Now—as I write—her picture with her dear signature sits before me on my desk! That paper could be so honorably treated and that every student who bought an annual could be so richly rewarded as to be able to look on the likeness of her!

This is honestly, truly the first time I was ever really, really, in love and I who have never kissed a girl am saving all my love, all my happy thoughts and moods for this one girl, this fairy girl of girls with the eyes of a saint. I love her. I'd marry her today if she would have me. Were she bad, nay the worst girl on earth, which is as impossible as evil in God, I'd love her—love her.

But then, and inward tears brand my soul, it all seems so impossible that she could care, she—an angel like her—me—a cad—a devil—human clay!

And then there are other reasons, the one reason, which I care not to inscribe here as it is a thing that the world could not understand, would think me going out of my class. Only those who have really loved will understand. This reason has always stood in my way and is my one regret in life, feeling and being as I am. And for all that I claim no race but that of humanity!

But even friendship at this late date seems almost impossible.

And after Tuesday, just two scant days, I may never see her again. Never! Never! What a nasty old word—and on the other side I'll always love her! I have watched her in the halls, since I first saw her, and we exchanged greetings but today something burst in me and I learned that I love her. I always thought her beautiful, and adorable but now I know she is no less than an angel in human disguise.

In my book she wrote—

"To Willard—I'm awfully glad that I got acquainted with you and I sincerely hope you'll make good in whatever you undertake.

E——."

She is glad—glad—glad to know me! It's a song that makes my heart beat and my hand is none too steady nor my eyes any too dry! Beautiful, wonderful, loveable E——!

I'd give up anything, everything for her love. I mean it. Even writing which I had always considered my great love, until today, would be a sacrifice meagre. That's how I feel about her.

In her book I wrote, and feared I wrote too much—"To a wonderful girl and may we always be friends." And I dared not write more—though wonderful should have been preceded by *the most.*

Outside, as I sat in front of school having a picture drawn in my annual I caught a glimpse of her purple and white blazer as she sat talking to Tony Skupas and another swimmer. Tony waved, smilingly, at me and in that minute I was insanely jealous of him.

E—— turned!—and smiled!—And said that she was mad at me because I didn't write more in her annual!
Joy!—Unlimited!

Tues. June 25th: Her birthday!

I no longer live in a world of reality. I wander all day dreaming daydreams of E——. I can no longer bear the thoughts of any other girl. Haven't been up to the library to sit next to Ruby. Don't care to. Anne wanted my gold basketball but she didn't get it.

I love E—— more than anything in this world! Life—fame—fortune is nothing—love is real—love is all. Were that I were but a mole on her arm, her pet dog, or the necklace that caresses her neck! Then I would ever be with her. I love her—I love her.

When I got to the assembly hall this morning she was in a front seat, but turning, she saw her girl friend in a back seat and waved. She then caught sight of me where I stood in the rear aisle and waved! Glory of glory!!

E—— —E—— —E—— —I love you!—love you!

I watched the grads march that I might see her gracefully appear from under the balcony wing and take her place on the stage.

After the practice marching I have no idea how I spent the time until I saw her in front of school at noon time. The senior banquet was over and she stood with the seniors in their purple blazers before Mr. Armstrong's window, cheering him. She approached me on her way to the main entrance and I said hello to her. "Birthday greetings!" I added and she said smiling, "Why who told you it was my birthday."

I told her that I am good at riddles and thought she should have a birthday about this time of the year!

From noon until five o'clock was a period of anxious, agonizing waiting and watching. I walked through the halls that were now empty and past her locker, my eyes filling with tears. I knew she was at the senior dance and often walked past the gym that I might be as near as possible to her. I could imagine her floating fairy-like across the gym as that day when I stood in the balcony and saw her in Lee Washer's arms dancing.

I waited happily—I had to see her again.

At about ten after five I happened to be sitting in front of school with some fool of a little under-classman girl when E——, coming from the dance, crossed to Baldwin's.

"Hello Willard!" she called and my name was spoken in the sweetest and friendliest way I've ever heard or hoped to have it pronounced! God I love her so. I'd give up home, life, honour—anything for her—to serve her!

I said goodbye to her and asked her if she had had a good time at the dance. She said the music had been terrible.

At the class prophecy, given on a senior program at the assembly hall this afternoon, before the dance, the scene at the gate of heaven, with this year's seniors trying to enter, was acted out.

After school this eve I played handball—it's the only way I can stop thinking, thinking!—Tex and I winning six games before losing one in the dark.

Tomorrow Englewood plays for the championship in baseball against Lane Tech. There was a huge assembly hall pep meeting today and I'm going to the game, more for the chance to see E—— than anything else although I'll be rooting for Englewood to win her first championship in baseball since 1889!

Wed. June 16th: Englewood won the baseball championship of Chicago 3-2 this afternoon at Cub's park.

Sun. June 30th: It still seems wonderful to me that dear God ordained it that I should go home Friday evening at such a time as E——'s footsteps would be matched with mine. I can no longer go past the spot under that slim, young cottonwood tree where a dream came true without a heavenly thrill of joy.

If God, if fate, if destiny—call it what you may, but if that which rules petty man's affairs will give E—— to me there is nothing else I would ever ask of life. To have her would be to receive more than a king, a saint, could ask for.

Tonight while sitting in the parlor in pensive mood, thinking, dreaming of her, I chanced to look down at my hands and then my eyes filled with tears—

Sun. July 7th: These few days since my last entry have been spent on the crest of hopeful dreams and in the black depths of gnawing despair. I haven't seen her or heard about her but all I know is that I love her and will go on loving her eternally.

Friday, the anniversary of my second week of loving her, I spent in watching clouds chase over the evening sky. And I got as much comfort as possible out of the fact that the same stars I enjoyed from my window twinkled down on her, that I love the same stars she loves.

Today was almost unbearable. You know, dear diary, how dreary Sundays pass for me. To forget I sat for several hours at my typewriter writing up "Second Team Stevens" which I am going to send away to some magazine.

I also got an inkling of a plot for a football story. It is to deal with a boy who fails to make the team at school because of some difficulties, goes to the rival factor and beats his old school, only to feel no joy in it. The story is to end on the eve of another of these crucial battles with the hero against his "mother" school, anxiously awaiting the whistle that he may battle away for his "first love" and redeem himself. Of course this is only the raw material and I don't know what the finished product will read like.

Thur. July 18th: Worked for Miss Rathjie all day and then went shopping at the 5 and 10 cents store for more paper to write more stories on.

"Second Team Stevens," a robust, healthy, ambitious youth went out in the world today with the "Boys' Life Magazines" as his goal with a smaller, weaker, pinch-cheeked brother—"Clayton, Waterboy, Substitutes," who I expect to see come limping home again shortly.

Thoughts of E——, which sometimes gnaw into my very soul, send me flying to my table to write—to work—

Tonight there was a beautiful full moon that I would have loved to show to E—— and a breeze that tugged encouragingly that would have made exploring the world together ecstasty! Enthralling world!—wasting at my feet!

Tues. July 23rd: Up until 2:30 last night writing on "For the Love of Lakewood."

"Clayton, Waterboy—" came back today as I expected.

Wed. July 24th: Down to school and up by E——'s locker or what I believe was her locker where I found a size tag which I am sure came off her purple and white blazer. I will keep that little piece of purple and white paper as long as I live—that little scrap of paper which her dear fingers touched.

Down to the gym where I played basketball at which I went great. I fed the ball well, played the floor in great style and shot accurately.

Typewrote on that new story this afternoon and then went down to school where Jucy and I won 6 games of handball, losing none.

I'm turning in rather early tonight.

Thur. July 25th: Received a card today from the Boys' Life Magazine which read:

"Your communication of recent date has reached us and will receive early consideration."

I priced orchids and they cost $2.50 apiece!

Nothing's too expensive for E—— though—she's wonderful and I'd give up my life for her. Maybe, if I get a job soon I can send her a dozen at Christmas time.

Mon. Aug. 12th: "For the Love of Lakewood" came back from The Boys' Life which was indeed a great disappointment. I surely thought it would be accepted. But steer clear of disappointment. Disappointment causes more failures than anything else and is more dangerous because it is thought harmless. A team fights hardest, has more spirit and gameness when behind, but still in the running. Surely I would be ashamed of any man, any friend of mine, who would lay down and invite life and fate to kick him just because he happened to be down at the moment. Then surely any such mood is foreign to my make-up. Battle fate with both fists. There is no failure—only success in its different stages.

Decided to send the story to the Open Road Magazine but have been twice rejected by that magazine in a month. They might not even trouble to read it!

Tues. Sept. 3rd: School opened again today and all roads hereabout lead to Englewood. But it's a blue and gold road that I'll never take again. It seems so funny, so sorrowful, that only a year ago I hurried back to the campus and to the gridiron to make the team and to meet E—— and love her and now as today's sun rises it finds me without either. But such is life— just a puff of wind across the sky of time.

Me—my class-mates—my team-mates, my friends of last fall have been cut down as green grass under the blade of a lawn-mower. And campus life no longer gives any account of us. Englewood moulded us and has turned us out, forgetting us as the mother hen her grown chick.

I sat by the front window in the same chair I did when I came from school that June day with the song of love in my heart, and watched perfect droves of students back to Englewood. And I knew a home-sickness I've never known the like of while when Fredericks brought the "E" Weakly home that had a familiar, intimate atmosphere about it I could have wept all over it. But I didn't—I laughed with joy at seeing it. Today at school they're getting their football suits and happy students are gathering at Baldwin's and in front of school to link arms and tell summer adventures.

Wed. Sept. 4th: Downtown to look for a job today. Found nothing. Went to five employment agencies. Years ago a high school graduate was a novelty but this is no longer true. High school grads can starve too!

Down to school tonight and Ben Kaplan and I sat in the misty stargleaming and shadow-blanketed Englewood back campus, sitting on a window ledge of the old Lewis building and staring out upon the running track as we talked softly, whispering beliefs and puzzlements to each other— debating with our own doubting and reasoning faculties.

We talked about everything.

We discussed war and the silly, school-boy helplessness of it where whole nations act as puppets in the hands of money and other prime reasons. We talked about prejudices and religions—the Christian and Jewish beliefs, beliefs of the Catholics. We discussed winning and losing in games and in life, and I broached the mental attitude. We talked about childbirth, and life again—what it is, what it means and talking about it only left us more puzzled.

Then we talked about happiness, and happiness was a subject we could and did discuss with both bliss and pessimism, and I stated that I believe life is much better than it would have been in the Garden of Eden, that living and lying (no, not dying!)—loving, striving, doing, knowing happiness, sweating—ever striving is altogether a lot more fun than sitting all day long in the Garden of Eden playing with a tiger! I think Benny would have traded this life for the garden. I would, sometimes, too. But having known and loved E—— and Englewood and having had for friends and school-mates such fellows as Lou, Jack Davidson, Gus, Bob Henle, Lon Levin, Will Starke, Ben—and oh countless others and having known the urge to write. I believe my answer final would always be in favor of this dear old painful globe as is!

Then the talk turned to athletics. Benny said that he always thought he'd have been happy if he could have made a team. I said that I thought that I'd be happy if I made my major "E" and now that I have it I have found that happiness laid in playing. While now I think that my real happiness would have been in scoring just one touchdown—just one! Or winning a game for Englewood.

Then we discussed the other side of athletics. We talked of athletics being a show—being a way of showing off. And it is too! I have felt the selfishness of it all. Of myself. Of the team and my team-mates. This was only at times though but players are selfish and almost mean at times. I've sometimes hated myself for it. Sometimes I've hated the other fellows of the team for it and for showing off. Grand-standing.

But I love athletics. It's so like the old medieval days, the days of knights. And one can use one's imagination. And there's such a glamour and in actual play an entire forgetting of one's self in the spirit of it all. It's really wonderful to have a fine body and to play! All this Ben and I talked of; I'm just giving it to you second hand dear diary.

Then we became cynical to the point of stating that all life is a showoff—Sham (a good name for a story) (Gathering material now). People are so artificial in public and forever try to make others think they are what they are not. While when with friends when it seems that we are "putting on" it is then that we are really being ourselves—being ourselves as we would best like to be rather than that person of our making that we are in public, a thing that has become more than conventional.

Yes, Ben and I hit on some deep stuff tonight and we both really enjoyed ourselves in thus "letting down."

Tues. Sept. 15th: Practiced tonight. Light shadow scrimmage. There's several "Prima Donnas" in the Liberty line who come out all dressed up every night to watch practice and to be admired. But backfield is always intact but the line can't be relied upon.

However I've thought of a way to interest the line. Where there's competition there's always strenuous action. I'm going to send for a bronze football medal, similar to the Cheerleader awards and offer it as a weekly reward to be won and worn for a week by the linesman who shows up best in the weekend game and who has shown the best team spirit all week. The fellow winning this award the most times at the end of the year will keep the medal. The backfield each week will decide the winner.

Wed. Oct. 2nd: Went up to school this aft to see Tom. We're becoming the best of friends. Isn't it funny how one can be drawn toward a person from the first and become really fond of the person. No not funny, but wonderful. For is there anything in this world though it be searched from its vaulted ceiling to the depths of its earthly cellars as beautiful, as inspiring, as joyous as true friendship?

When God allowed man friendship he on the spot forgave man his earthly sins and fairly balanced all life's foes and discords. Thank God that I have known Louie!

I have always sought and admired the beautiful in life.

In friends, in girls, even in football and in daily reality I look for the beautiful. Probably this is to dispel so much of the ugly desert of my existence and of my own catalogued plainness. But don't go away, dear diary, with the idea that I am cry-babying. I am not. My life has had its sweet and refreshing oasis too.

In friends I have always looked for the handsome ones, though I don't mean this word in the physical alone. This may be just to study their delightful personalities and moods and again it may be to dispel that overburdened market of the ordinary, of the plain, of which life is crowded. It seems that friendship in beauty can be beautiful, that the mind and imagination and love faculties can be given complete and happy liberty. It would be hard, would it not, imagining an extremely plain, a dull personality possessed person, having the beautiful qualities of love, and courage, and forgetfulness of self? It would be hard to associate them with the daring, with great conquests. And so much of our life depends upon these dreams, these illusions with which we garb ourselves, our friends.

Tom is the handsome, slim, bouyant type with just a touch of the whimsical and melancholy. He is boyish almost to the extreme and his face is one that doubtlessly makes girls thrill to its handsomeness and fellows think of true and mischievous friendship. While to an old fool like me with the desire to write he brings pictures of Galahad, of Lancelot, of dreamy eyed poets, of devilish boarding school boys. His personality seconds all these hues.

And though I don't expect a deep or lasting friendship here it will be fun to be around Tom for a while at least, to study him, to phantom him, if only to picture him as the hero of a book at some later date.

Louie, my friend, is of the handsome type too. Then too he is the kind of fellow who folks find it hard to make friends with—but who, once a friend, no man nor God-made law can put aside!

Everybody doesn't like Lou: He's sort of cold, sort of blunt, rather ruthless, though ruthless is far too strong a word. He has a touch of the born fighter, the upright young man.

It was these things, linked with his cold, handsome eyes, long drooping eye lashes, his square fighting chin, and finely chiseled nose (as perfect a nose I have failed to find) and that about him that seemed to speak of a soul that wanted to be understood but that unseeing people passed up for hardness that won in me a death defying friendship.

Louie's a great chap—a real fellow—the best pal a fellow ever had!

In friendship, as in love, I have always imagined the perfect kind. The kind that sent pals, arms linked, swinging down the avenue. The kind that sees friends stick through thick and thin. The kind that has its sunshine, its devil-may-care, all-consuming rapture in a world that weeps!

In love, in looking for perfection I have found it in E—— —my E—— in a far more beautiful world than this, a heaven, a paradise of my own imagination in which love, and friendship, and laughter alone count.

*   *   *

I have entirely forgotten myself tonight and let my emotions and feelings that I intended to carry as traditions, as ideals, in the most secret closets of my heart, escape. Nothing restrained and now I have said my say. But tonight I feel that old haunting, familiar mood. That mood that overwhelms me, allowing me the peaks and the depths interchangeably and combined.— One moment serene as if on the verge of a happy realization while the next that old glow of longing that chases tears to the back of my eyes, and restlessness to my heels, a restlessness that sends me for an aimless, pursued turn around several blocks.—Written while possessed by a mood that mixes longing, hope, love, and some unexplainable something hopelessly.

Thur. Oct. 3rd: Did nothing much all day but wait for the time when I was to see Tom and play handball with him. He didn't appear on the courts and I was perfectly miserable. I know I am never perfectly happy unless I am in the company of E—— or Louie and now it seems that Tom is about to join this group, too.

I'm trying not to let our friendship grow too deeply, trying hard. For fate separated first Louie and I and then E—— and I. I am trying to maintain the impersonal sort of friendship that accepts any congenial companion but fastens loyalty to none. The nice to everyone attitude. This asks for nothing in return but pleasant agreeableness at the time.

If you expect nothing you are never disappointed.

But I find that I am becoming attached to the slim, handsome Tom and his quaint, beautiful personality.

Probably our friendship will amount to nothing more than comradeship on meeting at the handball courts but I know that he is one of those rare persons whom I shall always feel a real thrill of well being on meeting. Jack is another. Good old Jack!

Then too when thinking of fellows like Louie and Jack there is comfort in the thought that somewhere there is someone who cares and understands you. That somewhere there is someone with whom you can be perfectly natural; someone who is to you as the sun to the flowers.

Mon. Nov. 4th: Downtown looking for work all day. One employment agency wanted to give me a job for $12 a week and wanted the first weeks salary! Can you beat it! And me a high school grad—but of course that means nothing nowadays.

Thur. Nov. 28th: Thanksgiving.

A family battle featured the day. I have hypocritically tried to keep everything of a disagreeable nature out of these writings as far as possible as these are my sunshine books. However I never miss these fights.

It's at times like these when humans are shown to be so soft, so hysterical, so foolish. It seemed all so unnecessary.

Sat. Dec. 21st: This eve, after supper, I took my typewriter to a "loan bank"—not a pretty announcement but fringed with loyal love when it is realized that I had no money and pawned it to get flowers—money for E——'s Christmas flowers and for her powder jar. Went to several places before they'd take it. One man acted as if he thought I'd stolen the typewriter. The fellow I did business with was a nice sort. I borrowed $12.50 on the machine—enough for the flowers. I intend going down to get my typewriter the evening after I get paid. Downtown and bought that beautiful musical powder jar which I only hope E—— will like and will keep. It is exquisite—plays Rio Rita and Rose Marie—is orchid in color, oval in shape and has a pretty little light green puff.

When I was down the street a ways with the typewriter Joe called me and said someone wanted me on the phone. I told him to take the number. It was Louie! Good old Louie! I would have come back had I known it was he. Called him at 10 this eve but no one answered the phone.

Sun. Dec. 22nd: An argument here this eve about my pawning my typewriter and the presents I am using the money for. Anyone who understands the situation can imagine the stand taken. But love needs no defending; love has no shame; love is all consuming. Sometimes I think that the garden of paradise would have been better after all. But would E—— have been there?

Love always was painted a fool by persons unfeeling and un-understanding.

Wed. Dec. 25th: Worked until 3:15. Home. Sat thinking of E—— all afternoon and evening. Louise was over. Louise is 31, an interesting woman.
She, brother's wife, Fanny, and I played cards but they could see that
something was wrong with me. Fanny kidded me about E—— and Louise
won my confidence. I told her the whole pitiful story. Brother's wife
discouraged me and said it should be broken up.

Later in the dining room Louise made me dance with her, something I
do very poorly, and she talked to me. We discussed life. She told me that I
was making a mistake by letting people know my feelings, that they
wouldn't understand me. (But I had to tell someone—confide in some!) She
told me that she too loved someone as I too love. A cigarette burned in a
saucer and I watched its smoke curl up from the plate. Again we danced.
She said—"Don't let people know your feelings—this life is a pretense."
"Sham!" I almost hissed. "Yes, a sham!" She asserted. Louise is very interesting. She has been operated on seven times, married young, is
separated from her husband who loves her but she doesn't love (loving that
fellow—as I love) and is now making a home for her mother of which she is
very happy and proud. Her dream is a career. She thinks that when disappointed in love one shouldn't give up but fight for a career. She says that
she hopes to be the finest designer ever someday and I could see that she
believed in herself and believed what she said.

But I can't draw my thoughts from E—— nor even form my words
straight. How I love her!—love her! How I wish that she might care or
befriend me.

I wonder how she liked the flowers, what she said, if she is angry with
me for sending them. I almost am doubtful that I should have sent them. I
am most unhappy.

1 9 3 0

Thur. Jan. 2nd: Tonight Tex, Jim, Frank, and I coming from the E.C.H. saw lights in the Englewood High gym and went over there. I want to explain what a coward I am—explain what happened tonight but hardly know how. We were coming out of the gym, where a team was having solitary practice, and Frank stopped at the door holding it open, to light a cigarette. Tex and I were walking together behind him, mounting the steps to the door. A heavy set, fierce looking, elderly man yelled at Frank to close the door but Frank merely stood there and the man made a break for Frank but when he got to the door Frank stood down the street, 40 paces, in the niche of the building, peering out, and looking very funny. Tex and I giggled and this man ordered us to move on. Naturally Tex and I took our time and this man, then addressing me, said "Come on, beat it—" and called me a name, a name that hurt. I stood there and he catching up to me on the sidewalk outside ordered me on again. I told him that he wouldn't call me that if I were a man like him. A crowd, out of the gym, was gathering. Frank, hurrying up from the rear . . . said, "He's a nice fellow and you haven't any right calling him that! It wasn't a nice thing to call anybody!"

And then that man hauled off and smacked Frank full on the cheeks—slaps that belonged on my cheeks if anyone's—before the crowd came between, cutting us off. And I stood here inert, so shocked at the speed of the attack—stood there like a coward, arms at my side instead of in this beast's face. Coward! Coward! My conscience screams at me now—and it is true. A coward after all my ideas of glorious battle and spunk like the knights of old when hard pressed. After all the fight that I thought football had taught me. I would give five years of my life to have it to do over and a broken nose if I could but have landed two blows at that man, if I could have jumped on him like a wild man possessed, jump on him like he did Frank.

A kind faced, elderly man and the old detective asked us to go on and not start anything.

—And Frank who is only 15 or 16 years old and a slim, frail kid stood wiping the tears from his cheeks and smiling and saying that he wasn't hurt though his cheeks showed red. And he had fought to free himself from several men after that beast had hit him, crying, "Let me fight him, let me go!'' God this is something I'll never live down. I never had anyone defend me before nor did I ever dream that I would act so horribly yellow.

E—— is a wise girl, not to come to me, if she does care—and because of that horrible name that man called me. I would ruin her life. She would be unhappy. People may look down on her. That could never be. If she cared and came to me would I send her back or again act the coward? I am sure that I would send her away. I will always love her but I couldn't see her destroy herself, her charm, her lovely Self.

And if in sending her, I could have previously fought tooth and nail for Frank, fought for him until the blood shown on my face, and in the presence of Tex, I could feel that the sending of her was less painful.

And Frank wasn't even an intimate friend, merely an acquaintance whom I haven't always treated with the best of graces. And he stood by me and my muscles were paper, my blood water, my spunk not at all. Hide a face that burns with shame but knows not how to express braveness.

—Oh God! It hurts, this world of yours and we must be bigger than ourselves every time. I must be nice to everyone—nice as I was in a crisis today—nice and soft!—

Thur. Jan. 16th: Over to Stan's store. (Bought a maroon silk scarf and three pair of imported English hose for Louie's birthday the 2nd of next month while downtown yesterday.) Art and Jack bent over a chess game in the back booths while all the young bloods and the present sweethearts crowded the store, laughing and shouting—shaming the Tower of Babble to insignificance. At a store like Baldwin's (Stan's now) where the ritzy gather, the "big shots" on the teams, the popular girls, the "higher ups" and "mightier than thou" gather one often feels the pretenses, the sham these young folk put on, the snobbishness. The fellows act as the possessors of any immediate girl that happens to appeal to them at the time. To them life whirls dizzily and they "gag" their way through. It seems a pity the money and strife and heartache many of the parents of these "children" go to in order that theirs may look alluring and infatuating to the particular boy friend at the time, and all male observers, over a hot dog sandwich or a malted milk; that she might have the background and atmosphere to cultivate a "line" and a baby lisp!

Mashed!—all of them.

On parade.

Happy? No. Just playing a game. Education a sugar coated pill. A toy to play with.

The fellows, friends without, hating in their hearts, jealous. Each fellow in opposition with the other.

The gym was a relief after this mood for at the gym the fellows are frank and above board, earnest and enthusiastic. Here life is real. One is a gladiator or a knight, fighting and playing. No pretenses here. Only a healthy imagination. If one is selfish and all for himself he reveals it. Conceit expresses itself. One knows really where he stands with his fellow mate.

And then I thought that mayhaps those youths of that select circle that prominade at Stan's are only trying to escape the reality—the heartbreak of honest life—life as it really is—life unadorned.

Perhaps they are trying to build of the ruins, the havoc that all the ages before have wrought and dying, left. Perhaps youth, headstrong and impulsive, wants to live its life and make it a better one than that that our apparent unsuccessful, unhappy parents have had.

But when an aim as worthy as this borders on snobbery then the aim is lost and we are not improving but just keeping the turmoil bubbling.

Sun. Feb. 2nd: Back home I tuned in "Art Castle and His Castles in the Air" at the Club Metropole. I phoned in a request for "Love Me" and not ten minutes later, at a little after twelve, they announced that "Love Me" was to be played for Mr. Willard Motley—and my name was pronounced right.

Sat. Feb. 8th: This eve I met little Rich and we each held up a hand with two fingers pressed close together—our insignia on meeting. He's a beautiful kid—about 11 or 12 years old, big, round eyes, oh so brown, that can widen with wonderment or twinkle with mischief. His hair, the color of his eyes is fascinating in its tumbled misbehavior—gosh I hope that some day I will have a little boy, a son just like him. He's beautiful, he's full of life and youthfulness. He makes me think of a beautiful woman in a garden with her children tumbling on the lawn, her arm in mine, her hair brushing against my cheek.

Wed. June 4th: Well, old man, here I am again. Several things have happened since we last had a few minutes together. Monday Miss Arney left on her vacation for California to be gone a month. I seem to have gotten over my infatuation for Ray's friendship rather successfully. I saw that our friendship would, if any, be rather hopeless and that he and Kelly more or less belong together.

Again it seems that I must give up hoping for, seeking that perfect friendship and place ambition as my goal. Ambition!

However I am somewhat like "Peter Westcott" a character in one of Hugh Walpole's books—"Fortitude." He, when young, was forever worshipping, loving or idolizing someone. I have now turned to Rob in who I see a lot of sterling qualities. He's young. If I could be his friend, help him, be a factor in the moulding of his character I'd be glad. Tonight we walked home together and talked. There's just a something about me that requires me to be highly interested in some human being all the time and there's no use fighting it down for it is quite impossible and these "overnight" friendships shall probably all inspire stories for all who I have been interested in I have known quite thoroughly. This made the breaking and the delusions all the harder. But as for a divine friendship I have put that out of my mind. I am just, I suppose, one of those unfortunates who will never know its sweetness. Had things been a wee bit different probably Lou and I would have been the death-defying friends. But this is all past—

Two of my stories came bounding back like boomerangs today and were sent out this afternoon. I've just got to take these rejections like a man. Typed on the latest—"Lovely Muriel Cohen" today and will probably finish it and start on another I've been thinking of tomorrow if the mood hits me. I've made up my mind to hang on to Chicago until I sell a couple of stories and get enough money to get to New York where I will write or more than likely get a job on a ship and sail!—sail!

Wed. June 25th: I'm getting ready to go. Yes my dream of going to New Jersey and visiting the Englewood High School there, of New York, of a job in ship-board, of Europe, is about to materialize. I have finally worked up courage enough to go. I'm making my plans now. It is to be by bicycle to New York City! Getting camera film—buying a series of books for my diary—expect to be gone about two years.

That Bob, 14 year old youngster of the neighborhood here who has bummed to Colorado wants to go with me—has wanted to go all along. I hate the idea of a young fellow like him along. I'd have to be over-careful that nothing happened to him. But, should he go, I'd be the child most likely, for he's done this before and I would probably need him more than he'd need me. Then too it would be terribly lonely alone.

This eve I saw his mother on her front porch and asked her if she really didn't care if Bob went as he has tried to make me believe. She said that she wants him to go with me; she long ago, it proved, gave her permission for him to go, and seems to think he'd be safe with me.

Thur. June 26th: This has been a most interesting day. This morning I went down to school and I snapped a couple pictures of Englewood High School to take to New Jersey with me. Also got a snap of Rob and one of Richie.

Sat. June 29th: My bike is nearly ready for the road. Am making final plans for trip. To leave Wednesday or Thursday morning. Stored my things away at home, locking my diary up. Sat on Louie's porch this eve while he played his mouth organ and little eight year old Susie, his sister, snuggled as close to me as she could get.

Wed. July 2nd: The time for parting has nearly arrived! At last I am to have adventures, to feel life beat and caress, to live!

Spent the entire day fixing up my things. Made sandwiches, bought canned goods, packed my clothes.

Joe, who has been away for several days on a drunk but who called me up last night as he thought I was going Wednesday, was home this morning. He bought me some camera film. I don't know how much money I'll have to take with me as I'm flat broke and too damn proud to accept anything from my friends although all of them want to give me most anything I want or need.

Dear Richie was over about ten with his little puppy "Buddy" and I took their picture together. Dear, dear Rich—the dearest kid who ever lived! We sat on the lawn, or rather lay on our backs looking up at the leaves of the trees in my back yard and at patches of blue and white of sky. "Buddy" danced over the lawn. I'll never forget that little scene—Rich with his head on my chest joking, "Buddy" on the lawn, Spot's grave at the side on the little crooked path to the back gate, and memories—memories of all my youth and life here in Englewood crowding down from the blue patch above the tree-tops and stinging my eyes with their beauty. (I am reading this July 13, 1934, on the eve of my 25th birthday. This was the perfect moment of my life. Would to God I could have died exactly then or that my whole life would be just this over and over—it would be could I arrest time.)

Bill "Red" was by and he's almost broken hearted because he can't get a bicycle to go to Gary—that is as far as Gary with me. These youngsters surely think a lot of me and tonight I am honestly so proud of their friendship for me—undeserving as I am—that I wouldn't change places with any other human being in the world.

Isn't it funny, when you go away like this, that you then realize that people really think a lot of you and that all people are good. Everyone.

These youngsters' friendship dwarfs all other things to me. Even success—writing—fame—fortune—E—— friendship—the one great friendship seems inferior. My life would perhaps be perfect now if I could just step out of it like a shiny new garment and lay it away to be admired.

Thur. July 3rd: Well here I am sitting on the stump of an old tree off the highway and just at the door of Michigan City, Indiana, with a broken pedal on "the Englewood Knight Errant," without a partner, and at a place where some would be ready to go back. The "Knight Errant of Englewood" is chained to a tree down the road a little. I have just been across the street to a small filling station where I got a drink, a young fellow of about 17 being very nice in showing me how to work the pump. I have always had an aversion to well water but water never tasted better and I will pay this particular well another visit shortly. I am at the time eating Toasterettes but they don't taste as they did when Richie and I ate them in the kitchen at my house!

A series of unfortunate occurrences led me to be seated on this old tree stump which is probably full of snakes. First, Bob, who started out with me, had to be a sap and tell me to go ahead to Michigan City where he would meet me and then my pedal had to break. I haven't seen Bob since before 2:30 and it's close to 6 now. It looks as if he, my knap-sack and canned goods and all are gone. He's a pain. I have to be after him all the time to keep him away from the cars that fly by, he gets things in his eyes, he has to stop and lie down, the knapsack gets heavy!—Right Richie was when he named me "Mopie Lard" and said I shouldn't take him. Wish I hadn't. I wish I could get my knap-sack and leave him in Michigan City where he claims he has people.

Well just thought I'd write to explain conditions. More later, including all the events leading to this tree-stump.

I *do* wish Bob would come if ever! The highway is empty of anything that looks like a bicycle. Well all I can do is wait until dark and then push on. (And I had a delicious can of peaches, not counting pork and beans and spaghetti in that knap-sack!)

*   *   *

Well! And the adventures I started out for have started and with a vengeance! Of course!

At 6 this eve I was sitting on an old tree stump waiting for Bob and that knap-sack and at 10 here I am in jail for the first time of my life! But it is O.K. for I intended going to that gorgeous state prison there at the entrance to the town and asking to sleep there for the novelty of it.

Well sitting on the road there by the bike grew monotonous and the water-pump across at the filling-station and a possible acquaintance with the youth over there most tempting. The water was good and so was his conversation. We talked about school—his Michigan City H.S. where he wrestles. We talked about my trip and soon he was acquainted with this silly occurrence 13 miles out of Michigan City. We watched the highway and I drank plenty of my host's cooling water. Funny but I haven't been hungry, only thirsty and have wet my lips at every possible fountain. That funny fountain—or rather pump, where my host invited me to drink, is a joke and includes a mild shower bath.

At nearly eight o'clock this eve when I had given Bob up and was waiting until it grew rather late that I might go and apply for a berth for the night at that new state prison of theirs—then couldn't I brag about having slept in Indiana's state prison—by my own request!

A police squad drew up for gas and one of the police asked me where I was going and if that was my bicycle across the street. It developed when I later asked him to drive me back along the road that I might possibly find Bob, that he had been in town and was at the Salvation Army! And how did he get in town without me seeing him!

Well there was nothing to do but haul my bike all the way through this horrible, ugly town with its uglier mannered police (see later developments) uptown to find that fool. Shook hands with my host at the water-pump who gave me his name as Arnold and we parted. (He had previously given me a map of Indiana and pointed out the route to me.)

This town makes a wonderful impression at its front gates and promises great things but falls down in the middle after its beautiful prison and nice brick houses are passed. Ragged little stuccoed shacks drag along to the tail of the town. They must be rather proud of that State Prison and ashamed of their Salvation Army and miserable Police Station where I am.

My pedal broken and night all about in the streets I was unable to ride and there being no sidewalks along the route I had to trace I pushed "The Knight-Errant of Englewood" about two miles and was about to turn left to the Salvation Army that I never saw when I heard Bob yell and saw him perched on the steps of the Police Station. He had been here since five o'clock he said!

The desk-sergeant questioned me. Wrote my name down. Held my keys, told me to pack my things in a corner of the hallway upstairs and I was sent down to a cell. It was only by allowing my grip to be searched did they let me take my diary down.

This compartment is divided into five filthy iron-barred cells with upper and lower berths and ill-smelling toilets in the cells. The "beds" are iron nettings and those who wish may take a wooden sort of mattress from a pile in the corner. I haven't tried their "beds" yet but know that they will remind me of the Chinese "beds" Mr. Nichols told me about. The cells are not locked and there are about five fellows here. They're all young. One a Jewish fellow with a good education, I believe, gave himself up that he might sleep for the night. He has a pal and they are talking about "the road" in the first cell to the left, occupying upper and lower berths. They are headed for Pittsburgh. Amos 'n Andy are coming on the air now, which means it is 10:30 and we can barely hear the strains of their theme song. The Jewish lad was out of his berth to hear it but couldn't as it was too faint. The other inmates are all asleep. One lad's mother, a poor old wrinkled, white headed lady came and peered in at her boy through the bars and said, "What are you in here for son?" She was all pathos. Another lad had been beaten by the police because of some affair with girls.

—I can hear Amos 'n Andy now—a novel experience—through a cell floor!

The cell doors are not locked and we are allowed the freedom of a narrow sort of a corridor. I am seated on the floor in it with my back to a cement post where I can best get the advantage of a single cell light. At first my companions were interested in my writings and I had an audience but they doubtlessly wearied of watching my pen slide over the paper and have gone asleep.

Oh most magnificent Michigan City Prison and dear police force with a special word for the officer who searched me for a knife. I will have a lot of fun at your expense should I write an article about this experience for a magazine or newspaper.

A tiny cell window at the rear of our "abode," which I recently tried by standing on the "mattresses" gives out to a rather sad courtyard over which an eerie half moon keeps sentinel and upon which the pale lights of a few houses look.

But enough of this! I have yet to tell how I got into the Michigan City Jail. (And by the way Bob is spending the night at the Salvation Army. However I wouldn't change places with him for the world as this is all very interesting. And why worry the circumstances when one has pen and paper if even a weak light?)

Prison on the first night out!

*   *   *

I arose at five o'clock this morning after getting to bed late and being unable to sleep for thinking of my adventure. At six-thirty I was ready to go, Fanny giving me 20 cents, all she had, for stamps, and Joe a quarter. Chester, Jerry, my mechanic, Frank and dear Richie were on hand to see us off.

—Youth—a young sun—and young adventures!—
At last romance and adventure!—At last to live!—
A horizon chaser!—

*   *   *

On the street Bob wanted me to ditch my bike and hitch-hike the rest of the way. Never! I'll pedal into New York City—and every bit of the way! I told him he could if he liked. He would like to but said "You won't be mad will you?" I must be a very clever actor the way I concealed my elation! In the alley behind the Salvation Army he gave me his bicycle tires which was indeed a great break. I tried to get one of his pedals off to exchange for one of mine but this was impossible.

Starting out with 51¢ in my pocket I now had one cent. I found another penny in my back pocket which doubled my purse.

On the city's main street Bob and I parted. I am supposed to meet him in Baltimore. My bicycle with two small grips on the rear loaded with 3 shirts, 3 towels, socks, a suit of underwear, a camera, writing paper, envelopes, address book, a few snaps, bike tools, two books for my diary, a dictionary and synonym (I intend if I get a job on a steamer to study these two books until I have a mastery of their words), two song sheets, razor, face and yellow soap, shaving brush and a few other odds and ends and two spare tires and a knap-sack loaded with cans of pork and beans, peaches and spaghetti, small frying pan, knife, spoon, fork, can opener and a blanket was well loaded down. In fact it looked much like a small pack horse. And, yes, it was hard pumping.

I rode to the gateway of the city and there got a map for I had lost mine in chasing after Bob last evening. Then I went across the road to where I had parked my bike yesterday and climbing a tree-stump and facing Chicago I fired a salute to Richie in birthday greeting. You may recall that I purchased the fire-crackers, "three inchers," on the road yesterday for 10¢ when ice cold pop was selling at the next stand for 5¢. The fire-crackers were 6 in number so each represented two years of Richie's life. After they had cracked their salutation I climbed my bike and pedaled back through Michigan City and out on the highway, following route U.S. 20 now. At about 11 I stopped at a little grove, drank a lot of water that was pumped from a well and tasted of tin òr some metal. I hated it but it was cool and what I required. Here I rested for perhaps half an hour, ate a can of sardines and some toasterettes and wrote to Mrs. Fitzgibbon and Red. This grove, where I sat under a tiny pear tree, is reached just before one enters Springville Orchard.

On the way to South Bend one encounters Rolling Prairie. Nothing was ever named more perfectly. There is nothing but rolling hills and huge prairies of golden and yellow grains or prairies of dense trees. This long stretch was the most difficult of my entire trip so far. One particular hill must have rolled upward 500 yards in three huge laps. Often I had to push up hills and the land seems to go on up and up. At places where the hills slope downward I made about 40 to 45 miles coasting which was great fun.

On one heaven-provided downward sweep I coasted fully two miles without exaggeration. After this things took a turn for the better.

I reached South Bend's outskirts at three o'clock. South Bend is beautiful and its streets are the widest I've ever seen which made it very easy for me. I rode to the "Y.M.C.A." hoping to be able to get a bath there but it being the 4th of July their gym dept. was closed.

I decided to find the South Bend High School football field and sleep there for the night. You know that in 1928 I played there for Englewood and played one of my very best games, helping Englewood's belated rally a great deal. I thought it would be fun sleeping on the field—the battle-field on which I had once played. I rode all over town looking for it, was directed several times and lost my way as many times. Once I missed it by a street and rode two miles out of the way.

In looking for the field I stumbled on perfection, on a paradise, a something that I cannot put to paper without doubting its real existence.

I once approached what appeared to be a very high-hilled park. The grounds ran upward for perhaps 300 yards on a gentle slope and a perfectly laid red brick driveway led up. Trees, hundreds of them, perfectly arranged, hid the top of the hill and its possibilities.

Trembling with an unknown thrill I entered the huge stone gateway and pushed my bike up the hill. Immediately I felt as if I had stepped from the world of reality and into the pages of a fairy book. Never have I seen such shade as those trees gave other than in my day-dreaming and in rare etchings.

An intruder, a wanderer, I stood about the grounds admiring it all. To me it seemed that I had come from Chicago only to enjoy this.

The top of that hill held nothing but six to eight mansions. But never have I seen such perfection, such placement in architecture and in nature! Stone dogs stood at door-stoops, bay windows allowed the air to enter those wonderful homes, a private swimming pool lay in the rear and a mermaid, I won't call her a girl, for nothing is real here, dripped in the water. Unfortunately there was too much shade for a picture to be taken, if camera could, indeed, have caught this bewitchment!

I forgot everything! I sat there, buried my face in that perfect carpet of turf—time went, eons passed. I shall never know whether I spent a lifetime there, an hour, or a few minutes. Nothing worried me. Life, motion had stopped, or reality. I no longer worried about finding the field. Where I should sleep worried me not at all.

However there's a beginning and an end to everything and I had to leave and take up my weary search. But, never will I forget this paradise, and its shaded trees, this heaven which I have named Perfection Place.

Finding the field I bicycled in through an open gate and locking "The Knight-Errant of Englewood" up trod uptown a ways in search of a stamp for I must not allow this day to pass without a letter to Richie on his birthday. It was almost impossible to find one but finally a lady in a candy store, reading my deep-rooted desire for a stamp, sacrificed one out of her purse, her last one—and Richie had his letter!

Back to the field I decided to sleep in one of the reporters' press coops, there being one on each side of the field, but I had to wait until dark before taking my bike up for fear that some of the neighbors might misenterpret my presence and I again come in contact with the police.

Sitting on the doorstoop of the very locker and shower room we had used two years ago I had my supper, the best I've had since I left home. My supper consisted of cold pork and beans, toasterettes and a can of peaches, suggested by Richie. The empty bleachers yawn at me and the smooth, velvet turf calls for my arms and legs while a drinking fountain, bubbling nearby is a wonderful source of refreshment.

Explored the two press coops. Will use the north one which has no glass in its windows. Directly opposite is the other. They make perfect little kitchenettes. They are about 15 feet by 5 and have a door with a latch at either side. The window is an opening the length of the coop and perhaps three feet high.

Wrote that letter to Richie—an eleven page letter, and also wrote to Frank, Rob, Sister, and Jerry as the light didn't fade immediately after all.

*   *   *

On and on, weary, lonesome, heart-break miles I crawled, up hill and down hill. Dark found me still 12 miles from my goal. I was tired, dead-tired. At times I hardly cared whether some car speeding in the dark hit me or not. Often I had to run off the road to save myself. More than once my heavy bike turned over with me on these stops. My clothes were glued to my back with rain and rank perspiration. On—on—ever on. Legs giving out, arms aching, throat parched. Often, too weary to pump longer, I half fell from the seat and laying my head on my handle bars, rested. Had I been younger I would have perhaps cried. Angola 12 miles away—11—9—8—7—6—6½—4—4—3—Angola to be approached after two very steep hills.

Two miles from town, just east of Bass Lake, cars speeding both ways in the dark forced me off the road. At the very edge of the road I fell over, bike and all, and only the most desperate struggle enabled me to scramble and tug the bicycle and myself directly out of the path of a car, the driver speeding on. A Ford stopped down the road a little and a man came hustling breathlessly back to me to inquire if I had been hurt. He was relieved that I wasn't and asked about the bike. It was O.K. Time and again he asked me if I was alright and not being over-assured by my weak "yes" reluctantly went back to his car. Soon he was lost up the road. At the outskirts of Angola I stopped and ate a can of beans that I could hardly digest, I was so tired and hungry. Into Angola I crawled, was directed to the Catholic Church two miles in town and went there only to find that the priest didn't live in the vicinity but motored in for Mass. Where to turn? There was no Y.M.C.A., no Salvation Army, and I was afraid of snakes. Jail? No! New thrills now. But I could hardly walk and the bicycle strained my arms as I held it up. I came to a small school where there was located a tennis court in a little clearing. I resolved to camp out there for surely there'd be no snakes there. I chained my bike and got a quart bottle of water down the road. I opened another can of beans and eating them and drinking the water made me rather sick, I was so exhausted. I saw a fire escape on one of the buildings and decided to sleep on it out of the way of snakes. At the cement, leading up the steps, I trod on something that swished at my feet. My heart pounded madly. A snake, I am positive, for there was something big and black at my feet. If a snake it was a very sleepy, a very lazy, or a wounded one for it didn't strike, or striking, missed me. However I didn't give it a chance to think twice but plunged up the steps.

I carried no stick and, there being no lights on the street, I could not see the object below. Climbing over the railing, about a story up, I jumped. My feet stung as I hit the ground. I stumbled momentarily, sprang to my feet and raced back to my bicycle. I'd not sleep there. There was nowhere to turn. I asked a man if I might sleep in his garage but he said that would be impossible as they were not open on Sundays but I could sleep at the jail and he pointed it out just down the road. It was a county jail.

The jail then!

It was locked! But a light burned in the sherriff's office. I knocked. No one answered. The sherriff's house adjoins the jail. He has a front porch and a swing. Tired, not caring, I climbed into the swing and threw my blanket about me, chaining "The Knight-Errant of Englewood" to the railing. In less than a minute the gentle sway of the swing had rocked me to sleep. It was all very funny for shortly I jerked out of a sound sleep to see the sherriff, as huge as a mountain, towering over me and demanding what I was doing on his front porch. Half asleep I explained in the office, had my pockets examined and saw a colossal barred door close on me, a door even more formidable than that at the Michigan City jail. Up some iron steps and into one of the cubby-hole cells. Here they had mattresses! I laid down, putting a newspaper over the dirty pillow and not using the blanket as it smelled of prison.

I slept rather soundly but awoke at 5 and couldn't go back to sleep. Here they don't open up until 9 o'clock. I didn't even have my diary in my cell and couldn't even write in it. A prisoner, a slight, red-headed man with an over-prominent nose, who had paced the floor all night and all morning as I had read in story books that they do, talked with me. He was in deep trouble. He was a heavy drinker. He had been sentenced once to from one to five years for breaking the dry law, had served a year and been freed. Again he had gone to jail for a year's term and after three months a woman friend had smuggled saws in to him through the lower barred windows and he had cut his way out. That was six months ago. Since then, he said, he hadn't touched a drop of liquor until the Fourth. He had laid here sick until last night and didn't even know how drunk he had been. His home town sherriff was coming up to see about him today. He said they hardly fed him at all and the most he had gotten was half a banana cut up in condensed milk, a slice of bread and cheese and half a cup of coffee. Later he told me that someone was up then and for me to rattle on a little sliding door. I did and shortly it slid open, giving me a view of a kitchen and a woman, from her throat almost to her waist as she stood near the opening inquiring what I wanted. I explained. The bolted opening shot closed after she had told me that the sherriff would be up directly. Shortly he came to open the barred door, an uncouth and ruthless man, standing in his shirt and long, flannel underwear.

Looking back on all this now isn't so bad. It all seems like a desirable adventure, even that hateful climb into this grim little town. That seems now to be a grand conquest, a great victory for me.

But now I know how Napoleon's soldier who rode wounded to him to inform him of a victory somewhere and who when Napoleon, after reading the good news, cried "Why you're wounded man!"

Napoleon's soldier, you will remember, opened his mouth from which the blood flowed and whispering "Nay, sir, killed," fell dead.

Only the thought of how proud of me little Richie and Rob and all the rest of my friends would be, the farther I get, kept me going, I'm willing to swear.

Now to leave this detested town to its sherriff after that prisoner, poor fellow, bade me goodbye and good luck and, no doubt, continued his pacing the floor and mumbling.

Sun. July 5th: Crossed the Indiana state line into Ohio at 9:20 A.M. Good old Ohio, how glad I am to see your sweeping skyline!

Through Columbia and into Ainger I travelled. (Yesterday I had, in all, done 85 miles, my best yet, which was 25 miles better than the first day and 36 better than Friday.)

At a restaurant, a first-class place, with a huge electric fan that whizzed busily, the last rays of sunlight falling on its spotless table, and two spotless waitresses.

One started towards me with a tumbler of water but I waved it away with a shameful grin and asked for the proprietor. She led me to the kitchen where a very collegiate, young man of perhaps 31, in a chef's cap, and apron was breaking eggs into a saucer. I told him my plight and where I was headed and that I wanted to wash dishes, do something to pay for a meal. Quietly he told me to take a place at the long table and "I'll fix you up." I pathetically pointed to my dirty hands and face and asked if I could sit back there (I suppose I hold the record of being the wettest man in Indiana in yesterday's rain and the wettest in Ohio today from sweat for my clothes that dried on me in jail are soaked again). He showed me where to wash and even then I was ashamed, sitting in the restaurant for I was still a very dirty traveller and my hands, arms, and face had been burned almost chocolate colored by a broiling sun as it was perhaps close to 90 all day. He gave me two eggs, some fried potatoes and plenty of bread. I also had a rather sloppy glass of iced tea. Afterwards he said that it was alright, and that the dishes were already washed. He wouldn't give me his card but outside I memorized his address and the name of the restaurant that I might some day send some money for what I ate. I later learned that his is the classiest restaurant in town.

I then turned my sore footsteps towards the Catholic Church. It, I found, is a tiny little, red bricked church called Saint Casper's and was erected in 1895. It could be seated inside St. Martin's two middle pews. I entered, crossed myself at the holy water fountain and walking slowly up the aisle through the dim rays of sunlight that stole caressing through the stain glassed windows, and knelt at the altar railing. There I knelt in prayer, all alone, for perhaps 20 minutes. And somehow I felt all the worry and pain slipping away from me, felt the ache steal from my legs and arms. Somehow, now, I knew everything would be alright. On the side altars, so small that by stretching my arms out I could reach its length, stood sweet-peas, pansies and daisies in small jelly glasses. In the pews, there being a double row of 12 and the church seating perhaps 280 people, laid prayer books and rosarys that some had left there where they could find them when again kneeling at St. Casper's in prayer. The big altar was about the size of St. Martin's side-altars and the Church on the whole was very small with a funny little pipe-organ in the rear. It was heavenly kneeling there with only a few flies buzzing.

Thur. July 10th: The good "Knight-Errant of Englewood" with me at the handle bars hummed along the road today from 11:10 until 6 and despite excellent roads but tall hills galore and detours strutted on her way 62 miles to give me a grand total of 485 miles. Pittsburgh tomorrow!

Along the road today I got a real thrill when a car with two young men in it trailed me for almost two miles. They then drove abreast with me for several blocks, talking to me and wishing me well. You would think I was a good-will ambassador for all the smiles, friendly waves and shouts we get. My rear sign is instantly famous.

In Canton with Ashland, last night's goal, in the hills behind, I had at first decided to ride on for some miles while the light was still good but catching sight of a small stream of water I decided to investigate and wheeled my bike in along the bank of a small, gurgling, mouldy smelling stream.

Three youngsters on the lower bank hailed me and came on the trot with questions to ask. They were very nice when they heard my story and helped suggest a proper place for me to sleep and to put my things. Their names were Rocco, Alex, and Jim; Rocco, the oldest, and perhaps Italian, had a five dollar bill and wanted to send for change to give me some of it. Of course I wouldn't accept. Alex wanted to give me a dollar of his money and I suppose Jim was broke or would have wanted to help too. Rocco, who is 15 I suppose, sent for ice cream cones and we all had one. He wanted to buy me coffee—sandwiches. I went to buy some rolls and they watched my things. I showed them the pictures I had taken and also brought with me. I had potted ham sandwiches, a can of delicious spaghetti, a quart bottle of water and a bottle of orange pop, for while I had gone for water Alex, not to be outdone, had sent Jim after pop! This world is a big, good-natured, kind-hearted place and the longer I live the more I learn that everyone is good.

Just think of the simple, big-hearted friendship these three friends of mine—all I have in Canton—could anything be more perfect!

They have gone now, down to the square where Rocco says he would spend all his money anyway and they would have taken me along but I pleaded off, having to watch my bicycle. When I went to get my diary I found that one of them—Alex, I believe, had slipped 50¢ in my bag.

I have their addresses, having promised to write to them, and they to me, and I will send it back to him.

Well, here I sit now, on the edge of the bank of Canton Creek, my feet dangling over into the gurgling water! And tonight will be a new experience—my first with nature!

Fri. July 18th: Well dear diary, here I am in New York City!—My trip a success—1069 miles on the Knight-Errant of Englewood in 13 days! It's all very wonderful and exciting being a success.

Looking back now even the stout Allegheny Mountains over which I came miles and miles shrink into pigmy importance. And what an awful ordeal, what a test of my strength, stamina, and fighting spirit and what a test on the ability of my good little bike!

Once I had to walk seven miles to the summit of Mount Tuskaross of the Allegheny Chain. This mountain is the highest and is 2,906 feet above sea level. At its top the view is gigantic. One can see into three states—Pennsylvania, Delaware, and Maryland, and into 7 counties.

Philadelphia finally reached and the Alleghenys mine I was only 95 miles from New York City. At the Philadelphia post office I received mail from Sister and her family and standing in the hallway leaning against my bike I almost cried as I read their kind messages of love and hope and good wishes.

At six that morning—July 14—my 21st birthday!—the day that I left my boyhood behind I parked my bike in a small public park and crossed over to a very beautiful Catholic church, resolving to attend Mass on my birthday. An old Italian penitent, her hair drawn tight about her head, a cheap woven shawl over her shoulders, sat, telling her beads, on the top step of the church and looked every bit the character from some medieval time. From her I learned, in her broken English, that the church was the "Mother of Sorrow" Catholic Church and that Mass was at 6:30.

The Mother of Sorrow Church, promising unequalled beauty within if its perfection of line and grace of turret and steeple without be taken into consideration, falls down considerably in its extravagant promise and is dim and dusty inside and speaks the language of some aged, mournful tomb.

Up its long, mouldy aisle, like some battle-scarred, blood and sweat stained knight of old coming to kneel in prayer to his patron saint on the eve of the last desparate, the last glorious lap of his adventure, I, in my queer outfit, in my rank shirt, my faded purple sweater, my torn gym shoes, my frayed pants, thick with dried clay and Pennsylvania dust and clinging fantastically to my ankles with bicycle clips, strode boldly and threw myself on knees before the altar. There, before the sun had rose, among aged and infirm penitents, I welcomed manhood and slipped on its mantle with a slight smile on my lips and glory and expectancy, and desire for its higher combats glittering in my eyes. There I accepted manhood's trials and laurels; there I received its nobility and honor. There I was enthroned and there, in humble prayer for my ambitions that glowed golden and brilliant in the reflection of the the luxurious altar candlesticks, I recalled Father De Veaux's words— "Live clean!—Be clean!—"

With the one penny change I had in my pocket I made my offering and lighted a shiny, white candle that represented manhood, and from my pew I watched its golden flame rise and fall and promise great things, great deeds, great glories and honors to one adventurer, one knight of modern mould who had welcomed manhood as I have thus described.

Just before Mass had started I felt a light hand on my shoulder, a touch as soft as the caressing ray of a beam of July sunlight, as timid as the fall of a leaf, and turning I looked into the sad, moist eyes that had once been as blue and as clear as the sky of a little middle-aged lady whose mellowing smile, which was just a breath of wind and told of pathos beyond description, went straight to my heart. I fell in love with her.

"Are you the young man whose bicycle is out in front of the church?" she asked. Receiving my answer she told me that she had come to compliment me on my quest, that her's was not mere curiosity but deep interest, that she admired me and my ambition, that she loved to see youth ambitious, that she had had much sorrow in her life and that I had today made her forget her pain and would I say a prayer for her. For a moment her trembling, weak hand rested in mine and then she knelt in my pew.

I dedicated my Mass to her. During the hearing of the Mass I stole glances at her and saw that she was weeping softly.

After Mass my eyes were drawn to hers and she motioned me to wait for her.

At the door of "Our Mother of Sorrows" she said, "I saw that you had no prayer-beads," and she pressed her own into my hands. I looked at them and was again a boy for my eyes filled with tears. Poor, dear little woman—indeed also a "mother of sorrow." Looking at the beads I found that she had also slipped a quarter into my hand. I begged her to take them back or at least the quarter but here she showed her first bit of firmness and her insistent head shake and the ghost of a smile that touched her lips told me that my request was futile. Humbly I thanked her. "May I have your name at least?" I asked her.

She smiled, "I would like to know when you get there," she said undecidedly and then added, with another smile, "But I will know."

And with a parting smile she left me. I watched her in her little black dress with its small cape and her black hat as she descended the broad stone steps and crossed the tiny park in front of the church that stood silent in a mist of rain. Then I could see her no longer and the tears blurred the trees in the park.

Poor, dear little mother of sorrow, I feel that coming across the mountains, that all my hardships and tribulations were well worth meeting her in the dusty interior of "Our Mother of Sorrows" Church. I shall keep her rosary forever while her memory is one that nothing, neither heaven nor hell, can shake from me. She, to me, is on a pedestal far above most of us other puny human beings.

*   *   *

And then New York City and The Knight-Errant and I riding down Broadway—Broadway—Broadway of my dreams!—Broadway the fancy now a reality!

At a corner on Broadway I telegrammed "Dad" and Rob and Richie that I had arrived at New York City at 12:40 and that everything was O.K.

When I came out of the office building there there was over a hundred people about my bicycle and I couldn't get through them and they poured questions at me and shook my hand and looked the bike over and whistled through their teeth and said "Well you didn't 'Bust,' did you, young fellow?"

At the office of "The Sun," New York's oldest newspaper I stopped and while waiting for a reporter who had asked me to wait that he might interview me, I fell asleep! I awoke when he returned, apologizing for keeping me waiting and we had a most interesting talk. He was a very nice chap and gave me a dandy write-up in yesterday's Sun. In fact the story took up a whole column! He also gave me his name and address before I left, telling me to keep in touch with him.

Having nowhere to sleep, I was sent over to "The Municipal Lodging House." I expected to find something like a "Salvation Army," and imagine my surprise and my lowered respect of the Y.M.C.A. when what I discovered was—"The Bread Line!!!" (The Y wouldn't even allow me to work there, doing porter work for a place to sleep in locker-room.)

But the bread line was all very interesting, unusual and thrilling. The line extended to the pier, a matter of two blocks and was about six men abreast. There was perhaps every nationality and type of man to be encountered that evening and most of them even in their bleak condition laughed and joked and cursed much the same as most men. That evening was jammed with thrills of horror as I saw aged, infirm and crippled men form in line, wash their sick, battered, bodies under the showers or bow their wrinkled faces and greying heads over tin plates of watery stew.

The attendants were all a lower type of man and grouches strongly contrasting with the poor men they served. My bike caused them much annoyance one going as far as to call it a piece of junk. To him, it is needless to say I said some very uncomplimentary things about himself and his brains adding that to insult my good little bike which had carried me 1067 miles was to insult not only me, but the entire age of machinery! When he handled it roughly I can honestly say that I pushed him out of the way and eased my bicycle into position and was tempted to throw my fists in his direction.

In line for supper was interesting. At an ugly counter behind which savage looking men all of whom possess long faces and angry eyes and who say "foist" and "woise" one grabs a tin tray on which he goes along to collect his tin cup of muddy coffee, cheap, coarse bread of which they allow each man two slices and of which I ingenuously partook of *six* slices, and a tin soup-plate affair of watery stew in which are stirred hunks of carrots and potatoes.

I could hardly eat even the gravy, but being hungry I sopped my bread in it and had my evening meal.

Then the line again and countless questions asked by a rather jovial fellow at a window booth, and his levity was both unexpected and out of place in this grey atmosphere. I gave a fictitious name, that of Richard Wilmot, not that I was ashamed of being there—far be it!—but for fear that it might get home and they might try to help me. I was having too much fun!

Then the shower bath, and all our clothes rapped up in balls or hung on hangers and put in a large cloak room. The showers were so crowded that one could hardly move and the men all spit on the floor.

After the shower we were offered the luxury of a toneless grey nightgown, waited ages for an elevator that carried us up to the fourth floor where in a huge room that afforded about 150 upper and lower cots, we were assigned a berth. The linen was clean and the windows open, all of which I was very thankful for.

All during the night the men about me woke me with their ravishing coughs while in the morning I dressed and collected my portion of a tin plate of oatmeal in which the allotted amount of sugar and milk had been cooked and two slices of bread. I couldn't eat their awful oatmeal that tasted like stewed hay and even a fellow mate's offer of an additional two slices of bread could not be gracefully accepted as I, that morning, could not eat my own. I soon left the place. I had 50¢. Finding a generous janitor on West 8th Street who allowed me a portion of his basement for my wheel I invested 15¢ in a dozen buns that were small but very tasty. Then I extravaganzed to the extent of 20¢ for a share of a very lean, ugly, talkative barber's who however was a decent chap who collected old fruit boxes from the corner fruit stand for fire wood and finding fruit that was about to spoil and had to be thrown away by the peddler, distributed it to a few of the old, poverty-stricken ladies of the neighborhood. His motto, it was not hard to learn, was doing good for others, was that that was our aim and our purpose here. Good for my Mr. Talkative!

—Oh life you are so very interesting!

Sun. July 20th: Well dear Diary several things of interest have happened lately. At the New York *Times* office they want me to try my hand at a feature article about my trip and at the Amsterdam News they interviewed me for almost an hour. The assistant editor, a very nice middle aged man with a soft voice and a pair of twinkling eyes seems to like me immensely. I told him my desire to do a parachute jump and asked the possibility of making a jump for his paper. He smiled and looked me over from head to foot. "Ever had a pack on?" he asked. Learning I hadn't he smiled as if we shared a joke and then told me that he was to see his aviator that night and would talk to him about it. That was Friday and today, this evening at 7:30, I am to go down to the office to meet a couple aviators. Gee, won't it be thrilling if they allow me to make the jump!

You know the reporter at The Sun asked me not to go to any other newspapers until they printed the story that their paper might have the exclusive scoop on it, but after it appeared I have been stormed by reporters and a Times reporter told me that when I got over to London to be sure and go to their London office and see a Mr. Callender there. Yesterday I spent writing letters all day and I must have written close to 30!

Thur. July 24th: I got two very nice letters today, one coming from Frank and giving me all the news and the other from Roy—a particularly friendly letter.

"Aunt" Rose surely is a fine old lady. Seventy-two years old she looks but fifty-eight at the most and having lived and had a hard time, seen slavery and worked all her life, she has managed by industry and persistence alone to purchase a $7,500 home for herself and she has but a few more payments. Though she had but little education she is well read, intelligent and has a lot of common sense and mother-wit. Some of the things she told me about politics and about her following them intensely for years and years, coming from an old, withered lady, and an ex-slave were astounding.

This eve "Aunt" Rose talked and as she talked I saw the things she told me about spread to their fascinating climaxes on the white topped table before me. She told of a German spy who was here in the house during the Civil War and who they didn't know was a spy until he left and of his room with all kinds of maps in it and of his going out every single night. Then Margarette, her niece, told me of explosions here during the War but "Aunt" Rose said, "The young generation hear of the World War but they didn't see the Civil War." Then her stirring, eye-witness experiences unfolded. A retreat from the soldiers with bullets whizzing past and clipping off ears or narrowly missing—of slaves fleeing being recaptured and caused to be beaten by other slaves and chained at night—of the Union soldiers warning by firing their shells into the water near the shore of a city and of that city's trembling under the explosion—of the Union soldiers (jealous, she said, that the southerners had someone to do their work and were getting rich while they, the northerners, had to work so hard) ravishing homes, killing children, and riding their horses through fine homes.—

She's a great, a jolly, an interesting old lady!

Tues. July 29th: Sunday I rode my good, faithful and loyal "Knight-Errant of Englewood" to the train yards at 161 Street and it started back to Chicago and Richie. It arrived there Monday afternoon. Slipping back into the baggage car, alone with my wheel, as the train rumbled along underground to the Grand Central, I bid the gallant "Knight-Errant of Englewood" good-bye and laid my hand affectionately on it, caressing its scarred frame as if it had been a pet dog.

Sat. Aug. 2nd: This evening I took a walk. But this was not ordinary walking!—and life was again garbed in romance!!

I sauntered down to the waterfront mingling with its men of the docks and its waifs of the street. Narrow, disjointed streets, paper littered and straggling with urchins and in a maze at the East River shore. Foreign languages fall from the tongue with gusto. All nations mingle there, living in a mutual and understanding poverty. Spaniards, Russians, Swedes, Negroes, Chinese, Italians, Greeks—they are all portrayed there—New York indeed the melting-pot. (That the people one meets in everyday excursions along the city's streets have a variety of blood surging through their veins can readily be ascertained from their indefinite features; their striking contrasts. Noses are too long, too extremely hooked. Eyes and eye-brows are mis-matched. Nor is it any great wonder that these Manhattaners grow tall and gaunt like their buildings for they have but the barest room to grow in. There are no alleys, few back yards and private garages behind their homes are but figments of the visitor's mind, fabulous tales, not a word of which is to be credited!)   ·

Brooklyn's water-front is captivating! Melancholy and depressed with homesickness I could stay my feet no longer and had to walk—anywere—but to walk and walk!—

An utter sense of desolation had possessed me all day. The towers of Englewood etched against a blue and white sky were vivid to the memory, myriads of old familiar, smiling faces came between my eyes and the East River as I sat in my room. The "blues"—

And oddly enough I did not reason that, at home, I might possibly be as lonely, as dejected.

But the Brooklyn water-front unfolds its drama before the eyes selfishly for soon all else is forgotten in the enthrallment of sea and sky and crumbling flat-buildings still flaunting quaint, iron-wrought balconys that knew prouder days—and soft serenades whispered in the night—and vows made and broken!—

Then the streets crowded with queer, exciting, lovable people—

One sees crap games in full progress on the sidewalks of busy thoroughfares, the usual crowd of drunkards, sea-man, experienced gambler, enthused and shortly to be disillusioned novice, the red-cheeked youth without a hint of beard on his chin, the bum, the ner'-do-well, the small, round-eyed ragamuffin, and countless nondescripts.

Men curse bloodily back and forth across the street, but neither draw the bat of an eye or the frown of disapproval from young girls or white-headed grandmothers. To them it is as if they did not hear. Mothers find no protest for sons who swear before them, and occasionally at them!

Beauty is rare. Infrequently a Madonna face passes in the crowd or a pair of shapely legs encased in fine hose accompanied with swirling silk skirts and are always the source of insulting leers and blackguard glances.

Young Spaniards and Mexicans, their skin died a deep bronze, lolled over front steps and around street corners as I walked along.

One fellow particularly, with huge, bulging muscles, won my immediate admiration. At an improvised book and newspaper stand I stopped to gaze with the fascination of a boy in his early teens at the old-fashioned paper-covered novel, a gaudy picture on its cover. And these were the lesser works of Alexandre Dumas, and printed in Spanish and Italian. The mad rush of time had surely not poked its nose down these Brooklyn avenues!

A brawny little Jap bent over the lathered face of a customer in a dingy barber shop across the way, the late sun modeling his occidental features and his muscular arm, pausing with razor in hand, into something fantastic in copper. The medieval braided and twisted hair knot was on the obsolete head of the middle-aged, snapping-eyed Italian woman in a rocker at the curbing. A pretty little Irish girl with the beautiful, the insolent eyes of a Jewish mother, leaned against an ancient balustrade—

Up the street a way an old blind man fumbled with his cane along the bottom of an iron fence. I led him to the gate and was entirely disillusioned to find that he was drunk. His unseeing eyes were turned toward me, ghastly and ugly, as he protested, "I'm al' right—I'm al' right."

A street-car conductor, Irish because of his twinkling blue eyes and dialect, and on his way home from another day, walked up to the blind man and pressing a package in his hand said, "Here, Dad, here's some good tobacco." I walked on—

And all this goes on just over the hill from where proud, rich Brooklyn on its flawless green terraces looks on and bows its head. Then too, the steeples of countless churches, for Brooklyn is indeed a "city of churches," have hung their crosses high enough to see all this and to be of service to those of the inclination—and I am, after all, not so sure that there are many who do not claim some one of these churches.

A barren, unpretending Catholic church, its walls fast crumbling, stands in the center of its water-front settlement and in its scarred door I walked. There, in the basement that smells of earth and reminds one of— "dust to dust"—I knelt in one of the dingy confessionals. There I left all my sins of the past eight months.

The basement is gained access to by an iron stairway at the side of the church and at the bottom of these steps is a holy water font that neither stands upright nor is lying down. The basement is graced with a small altar that ends abruptly at the low, dark ceiling. A number of small, gilted beams support this ceiling and from the ceiling sprout several brackets of lights with bare electric globes and looking like the claws of as many crabs. There are four confessional booths and a little light.

Above a poverty-stricken but peaceful little well-kept interior composes the "church." Without mournful trees, about which small iron fences have been placed, surround the church and on the fence of each is a small tablet, dedicating it to the memory of some war hero. A withered wreath, as withered and decayed as the church itself, adorns each tablet.

Out of all this I walked finally and onto Fulton Avenue where boot-blacks were doing a lively trade and the jobless still held sway on the steps of the old city hall.

And the boot-blacks were, as usual, of every description. They ran from the shiny ebony to the pallid, half-starved, wan-cheeked boy hardly more than nine years old. And I am searching for a girl boot-black. She will have to be a game, a courageous little girl with a cheery smile but a fortune awaits her! Somehow I feel I am going to find her.

Tues. Aug. 5th: Today I had picked for that glorious adventure to Englewood, New Jersey—my Englewood's name-sake. I had to go to 125 Street where I took the ferry across the Hudson River into New Jersey. Then one of those quaint, funny streetcars you see in the East here rolled me up over a steep hill through a maze of twisting track which is indeed like a fat, lazy snake curled in the sun.

Englewood is a small, picturesque town, not as pretty, nor as ugly, as Englewood in Chicago nor as like a city. Englewood, New Jersey, is yet, for all its 61 years, but a mere little village, a village nestling placidly in a New Jersey hill not far in from the water's edge. It is restful but not, even for its beautiful homes, interesting. I was greatly disappointed but glad for "Our Englewood" that we are the superior.

I alighted at Palisades Avenue, the main road, and took up my journey afoot from there. The sun was terrifically hot. Under its shortly after noon-day glare I stood out in front of the Englewood Theatre and saw Englewood Avenue and wondered if I was a modern Rip Van Winkle coming back to find all that I knew wiped out.

I saw Englewood Avenue on the street marker and later stood on Engle Street, off from Palisades and Grand and saw "Englewood High School" engraved above my head on a white marble tablet. But how different this from what I had expected. I had dreamed on aged beauty and pictur-esqueness as in Englewood, weather worn brick in place of this new, uniform red brick, towers and gargoyles. The old school is gone and this new one, scarcely six years old, stands a rather regal little building, graced with long white columns, in the breast of a hillside while an old, wrinkled and very big cotton-wood leans against it to the left of the main entrance. A neat, well-kept and tiny campus upon which stands a new white flagpole sweeps down to Engle Street. On the corner stands the post office and around the corner the library, a pretty little building. Half a block away Palisades with its groceries, bakeries, and merchandise stores is a minor, a very young 63rd Street.

I walked up the wide, cool walk and up the school's several stone steps into its interior. A small slab on either side of the entrance corresponded with Englewood's two long figured slabs. A trophy case, filled with beautiful trophies, stood on each side of the hallway. And its trophies ushered me in saying that here too was an Englewood that was formidable, was strong on the field and track.

Summer school was out for the day and I had Englewood High to myself and prowled from basement to roof. The school is a modest little structure with a tiny assembly hall not half as large as the Lewis Champlain's, wide cool halls, and carved archways in the corridors. Everything is new and glistening and the paraphenalia of cleaners and painters stood in the basement. The school boasts but 800 students and 20, I believe, teachers. Their colors are maroon and white and their last cham-pionship in football was in 1927. Their principal, I learned, was away, but from a picture I saw that he had somewhat the same kind, intelligent features of Mr. Armstrong. His name is Mr. W. J. White. Hackensack, three miles distant, is the school's bitterest rival.

Up to the third floor I made my way, found a window open, swung onto the roof and from the highest point it was possible to climb, took several snap-shots.

Fifteen minutes later I approached a young fellow seated without and learned that he had been a student three years ago and a member of the football team. He was now working in the building. He took to me and con-sidered it his duty to show me about. He showed me the gymnasium which isn't as nice as the Englewood Community House. It has a low ceiling and two galleries, one on each side, take care of spectators. Their swim pool of which they are very proud is a tiny thing and at Englewood, Illinois, would serve as a bathtub! I took a snap of it and do hope it turns out alright. The pool is perhaps 30 feet by 9 and is 3 feet deep at the shallow end and 6½ feet at the deep end. But Englewood, Chicago, must bend her head in shame when she learns that her sister is building a new $40,000 stadium to be ready this fall. Half the money was raised by the school, the city contributing the other half.

The library contributed little to the history of Englewood High, New Jersey, other than that its origin is in the vague 80's—about 1880.

Yesterday evening when I walked down Broadway the devil must have directed my steps for I found myself at one time leaning over shelves of these 5¢ paper-covered books. Among the Shakespeares, Poe's, etc., I found a book called "How to Be a Gate Crasher." Curiosity told me to turn the pages and my eye fell on a heading—"Crashing Ocean Liners." That sold the book. I bought two others and left the store.

In my room I read it and listened to some very romantic incidents in the inexpensive and interesting thrill of gate crashing. The author, Samuel Marx, "One-eyed" Connolly, and Tammany Young are considered famous personages, and are the greatest crashers. I have often read about their exploits. He described crashing Broadway theatres, told how he did it and explained going to the biggest banquets in the Ritz, etc.

Why here was adventure—thrill—romance calling me! I too would crash something—the Paramount Theatre, one of New York's greatest!

At 3:30 I stood in front of the Paramount, book in hand, and reviewed my procedure—the Englewood adventure was history now.

"I honored it with a visit on the glamorous opening night, when only celebrities of national importance were expected to attend. There is a stage door entrance and elevator to offices and dressing-rooms, located on 44th Street. A fire escape and stairway are also handy, if you do not prefer the lift. Go to the ninth floor, where some executive offices are located, and no questions will be asked by the elevator man. Find the exit door that leads to the balcony and you are in. Take any seat. Since the opening night, which I hugely enjoyed, I have used this method of entering many times. It is not only cheap, but eliminates the dread horror of standing in the perpetual line that is always waiting for seats at the Paramount."—I read.

The famed stairway and fire escape was found and nonchalantly ascended—and another adventure was mine. On the 9th floor I discovered the balcony, an exit door and worked my way down a carpeted stairway, hurdled a velvet roping at the bottom, reading a sign "Do not go above these stairs"—and stood in the balcony of the mighty Paramount!!

The show *was* good.

After the show I was ambitious. Why not a dinner a la Samuel Marx? Walgreen's welcome mat has always been cordially extended. Walgreen's then! There I ordered and ate a delicious baked ham sandwich on lettuce and rye beside which lay a long slice of pickle, mustard clustering its top as trees cluster the top of the Alleghenys; a slice of blueberry pie which is my favorite; and a malted milk as only Walgreens makes them. The bill totaled 50¢ and tossing all scruples and conscience to the winds I tucked it in my pocket and leisurely partook of my meal which I had timed perfectly as it was but 10 after six!

After my meal I merely sauntered to the notions counter, picked out a 15¢ file, paid for it at the counter, and walked out! A 50¢ meal for 15¢—not bad!

The file should make Stan an excellent souvenir present—he with his perpetual store of puns should think up some very *pointed* and *sharp* things. That is why I selected a file!

Sun. Aug. 17th: Well here I am back home, my dreams all shattered and broken at my feet. And I must smile—and lie with smiles. Oh those last two hours were heart-breaking in ugly old Brooklyn and New York. And then the bus and two whole days and two whole nights of coming at top speed toward Chicago. I never realized that from Chicago to New York was such a great distance until I came home on the bus and saw it labor on—on—on—saw landscape of everlasting trees and valleys sweep by. It didn't seem such a terrible distance coming on the bike although it *was* tiring.

Tues. Sept. 9th: A scene here.—And, oh, I am so—I hate it all. All my life I have been unwillingly brought into them. And I have never been happy. I am searching for and have always searched for something—and I do not know what it is I am searching for.

I don't know why they wouldn't leave me alone, leave me in New York, let me live my own life!

But the ruling Faith knows the why of all things and perhaps this shall all be wonderful strong material for me although that seems a very selfish and egotistic point of view.

Mon. Sept. 29th: Up by school this eve. Auggie is out after three months in the house of correction and tells some horrible tales. He says that every letter he received was really appreciated and read over and over. And I felt awfully sorry that I didn't write for, looking back over my trip, I can remember the heart-break of not receiving mail and the elation of reading and re-reading the letters I did receive.

Fri. Oct. 3rd: Irene came over this eve and I met her at the "L" station with an umbrella as rain beat down upon the streets of Englewood.

*   *   *

And I am disgusted with myself as a very thick-tongued mute. Why I could hardly carry on a conversation with Irene. No, this is not the brink of love. I have loved and lost but loved nevertheless.

But I could make myself believe many mad, many sweet things about lovely Irene. However after she and her mother and brother left I walked the streets angry with myself for not being brilliant, witty—angry with this life that has me so well trapped in this web, this tred-mill that dictates that I be shy, jobless—infested with the monotony of my dull, drab, hateful existence.

And only at Englewood, within the last glowing lamp-post with mother Englewood's arms about me and the fresh rain on the walks was I the least heartened.

—And it is a great life if you don't weaken.

Sun. Oct. 12th: I had a champion today. Little Susie who snuggled on the Schuster front porch was teaching me how to count in Lithuanian. "Motley is colored but he goes with white girls," she said with an elfin smile.

"What of it!" Stella, her sister, snapped with the spirit and loyalty of twelve years. Susie protested, that dear little Susie, that she meant nothing by it and had only said it.

This eve Frank argued with Louie that color didn't count in this modern age but brains. I listened but said little. As for me all of it means nothing to me for my race is the human race.

Tues. Oct. 14th: Had a spat at home this morning and left to stay away all day—to get away from it all—walked four miles—then over to Jake's where I helped him prepare the "frozen bananas" he sells at his ice cream and book store. Restless—awful restless—over to the Community House—Rob was playing basketball there. Back to 61st Street late and listened to Rob's banter there. We talked until 11:15 when I went home. Another fight. . . .

Oh it's so hard to put my feelings on paper. Yet I feel these things that are bigger than I—this life that seems to run by design rather than chance— Even writing of these sordid things hurts—hurts awfully.

And loveless, friendless, as I feel myself, with my illusions gone—my ideas and ideals of life, love, love in all its phrases, friendship gone what am I to cling to?—Hold to?—How mould my life?—To what standards?— Illusion-less—Love-less—friend-less—

I am bewildered.

Fri. Oct. 31st: Saw Tom yesterday when he followed me over to the Englewood Community House to talk with me for a while. He wore a dark coat and a black and white scarf which were very becoming. Tom's not working; nor is anyone in these terrible hard times that have hit Chicago now. I hate being without work, means, independence, but my pity is bought by the thousands of poor unfortunates out of work who have families to support this winter.

Fri. Nov. 7th: Darn dull existence. No work. No fun. No advancement. No nothing.

Sat. Nov. 8th: It takes a large cemetery in which to bury all of our dreams, doesn't it?

Mon. Dec. 1st: Down to Art Institute to see Mr. Burkholder, secretary this A.M. about letter concerning a letter I wrote Mr. Frank G. Logan. He interviewed me for Mr. Logan, an old friend of his, who asked him to, and Mr. Burkholder says I made a favorable impression. It was about my work, my letter, and going to college. Mr. Burkholder made mention of a scholarship to Beloit College in Wisconsin, but I have my heart set on the University of Wisconsin.

Saw Miss Cross this afternoon.

1 9 3 1

Sun. Jan. 11th: This afternoon I went down to school as it was planned yesterday and played touch football with Rob and Kobe. Art, the McBride brothers, Johnny and Roy, George, and Benjie were also up there and played. We played until dark. It is needless to say that it was great sport or that I enjoyed it more because the ingenious Rob was along.

Surely the other fellows, those who have been and are his friends (Art, Kobe, etc.) know what exists between us. I wonder if they know how happy and carefree it is just being with each other. Like love—only stronger I think.

Rob is getting as much from me, I am sure, as I get from him. I'm giving as much as I receive. For you know, dear diary, that when I give I give wholly. Half measures are no virtues of mine. I love with all that I possess. I would go the limit for my friends and count not the cost for there would be no cost.— And I do like Rob—mightily.

I hope that this shall be the real, the lasting, the ever-lasting thing.

Thur. Jan. 15th: Well that awful affair of a year ago—last January when Frankie got cuffed around by that man up at Englewood and I did nothing although Frank was defending me, has been wiped out.

This evening at something to five o'clock Turk and that brother of Billy's were trying to stuff red pepper in George's (Sam's cousin) mouth. Finally they let him go and James' brother told him not to get tough. "No, I can't, not with you," George replied, referring to his size.

"Aw let him alone. He's smaller than you," I told James. He flew off the handle, wanted to know if I was telling him what to do, dared me to wait there until he returned.

I waited. He returned with Billy and instead of finding out what it was all about I was surprised to find that Billy was there for trouble. They intended jumping me.

Well! I defied them. Told them that that would be cowardly. Billy warned me that I'd better shut up or his brother would get mad. Mighty brave they were! I offered to fight them one at a time, but no, the other James told me that he'd jump in. Suddenly Billy swung at me. I ducked and cracked him in the face and with the same movement started pulling off my coat. Billy struck me several times when I was trying to get out of it. From the corner of my eye I saw the other James make for George and land a blow in his face. I went after him, Billy after me. They had me against the barber's window. The James who had gone after his brother had me around the waist and was using foul tactics, trying to rupture me. I pounded him in the neck, meanwhile trying to keep Billy off.

A crowd had gathered. A young reddish-headed man I know by sight who is perhaps 28 years of age held Billy off. Others separated the other James and I. Suddenly I was aware of that tall dark southerner, the James' step-dad, having appeared. You will remember, dear diary, that I had previously had words with him in Jake's store. I was glad to see him with a certain fiery malice, for I knew that if he stepped into it I would manage to land him a damaging crack. My red-headed champion and he were arguing, my friend saying that his interest was fair play.

The crowd had separated all of us combatants and I was looking away when Billy's brother suddenly rushed at me and hit me full on the nose. My nose bled immediately. It didn't hurt, nor was it damaged even to making it sore now, but I swear that I'll have my revenge on both of those brothers. I'll catch them alone and "leather" them good—an expression used in the paper about boxers "leathering" their opponents and one Rob is fond of jesting with. The crowd, damn them! held us apart again, though someone told me James hit me and ducked a mile away.

I almost wish that fight had gone on. I have confidence that I could have handled those cowards with some damage to myself. Fairly, of course, I would, I don't believe, use unfair tactics, were I mobbed.

After the fight I stood there, chilled to the bone, my teeth chattering. It was bitter cold. I got into my coat, made sure that no blood was on my face as no one home must know about this, and prepared for home.

My champion stood by me. I thanked him and he asked me who that noisy bunch was. He said he'd heard them before.

Home I went immediately here to my room and sat for half an hour, my teeth chattering. I was hot and cold in turn. Ate nothing. Bea was over and Mother went down to sister's with her. Thank goodness for that for it left me to myself.

Never fear, dear diary, I shall have my revenge. I hate fighting, street fighting, but it is with an almost savage joy that I await my turn which I know shall come!

Thur. Jan. 22nd: Met Rob up at the E.C.H. gym this afternoon late and walked home with him. He gets to look more like Lon every day!

Wed. Feb. 25th: This observation on Alice's leaving—Women may love (a man or their children) but women cannot be friends. They know not the first thing of the meaning of friendship.

Tues. April 28th: A plan of having Mr. Julius Rosenwald, the wealthy philanthropist, invest in me which I have been working on for over two weeks fell through today. I offered a percentage of every book I ever write, or myself at the age of forty-five as an experiment of science by contracting cancer or any disease—"for at forty-five I would have lived—would have had my writing—would have had a beautiful friendship in my life." I reasoned in a letter to the Rosenwald Fund. I know that Mr. Rosenwald would have been interested but he is sick in bed and cannot even read his own mail. Therefore I had to write to and see his employees and—failure.

Oh the plans I had planned—the dreams I had dreamed—but they shall come true—I cannot fail! I shall win!!

*   *   *

Why is it no one has ever understood me?

Wed. April 29th: Have invented a plan by which I can make a comb with which women can comb a curl into their hair.

Sat. May 23rd: The little jokes of friendship are treasured through the years, and give it a vocabulary of its own.

*   *   *

Dear, dear Rob! How loveable is his personality. Laughter comes easy to him. And true our friendship is already endeared by countless little jokes that are our own. Rob is so quick, such a wit. Many are the jokes I could set down here that he has originated or that I've been a partaker of. (Who robbed goofy after I'd said "Goofy Rob"; "O." "What do you mean by 'O'?" "Just plain O." Is this the other side of the street. [Rob] "I call my dog Ginger." [Me]—"Why?" [Rob]—"Because he snaps." I call my dog Punch because he's a little licker. I call my dog Fido because that's his name. I call my dog flea because he bites. My dog can talk. Ask him what he had for breakfast and he'll say nothing. Only today when the janitors and a bunch of other fellows were playing baseball up at school Rob said, "They've got good clean-up men on those teams." I asked him who. "The janitors" he replies.)

Oh I haven't by any means set down the best jokes—some escape me, some don't look as good in writing as rolling off the tongue of Rob the humorist. Nor can I hope to capture his inimitable way of springing them, his intonation, the occasion of the jokes—

How true it is that we may admire the wit and intellectual power of a friend, we may lean upon his sympathy and sound judgment, yet it is his moment of giving way to unconsidered mirth, his sudden drop to sheer nonsense that endears him to us.

*   *   *

Met Rob on Normal Avenue this afternoon and we repaired to the school yard handball courts where we played handball. This eve we played baseball and then sat along the side of school until close to eleven o'clock when I walked him to "our corner."

"So long Rob."

" 'Bye Mot."

Sun. May 24th: It seems that fidelity to an ideal, the abstinence from (how can I put it?) things sexual is an abnormality, a sin rather than a virtue. Accusations—Suspicions—

*   *   *

It seems a shame that so many youngsters in this neighborhood, kids in their teens—thirteen—even twelve—are chasing after girls—not loving them with the idealistic silly and yet beautiful way youth has of doing things but with passion as their sole aim and desire. Is it not awful that these boys have no ideals, no aim in life?

Then this neighborhood. That bunch at 61st Street lighting one cigarette on the butt of another, allow kids of 10 and 12 to hang around them and pick up their cigarette butts and cursing, making vulgar remarks about and even yelling after women and girls passing on the street, ducking behind the "L" to drink wine or even sometimes whiskey, shooting craps in the "L" exits where men and women coming from work have to pass around them at their game. They have no pride, no shame. They curse endlessly, constantly spit all over the sidewalk and try to be as tough as possible. They steal books, candy and cigarettes from Jake—oh a rotten bunch and yet I don't suppose one of them would do a really mean, low-down thing.

I am older than Rob and past the age where my environment can possibly influence me and yet I don't care to associate much with this gang. True I've never known Rob to gamble with them, curse, tell dirty jokes, drink, or even smoke but you can see what they will do to him in time.

It is up to me to see that he doesn't fall to this. And I will stick to him through thick and thin. I will win him from all of it—for my good and for his good because he will always be my friend and someday he'll thank me. I've decided that if I can't have him for my friend why I don't ever want a friend. It's up or down with him. But up if possible.

Then too there's his home atmosphere. His mother is a loving and devoted mother, a little Canadian woman. But his father, an Italian, is rather the tough type from things Rob has told me unconsciously while we joked and talked. Richie has already fallen somewhat to this home atmosphere, but Rob won't!—I won't let him! He hasn't fallen yet. But he gives as much in friendship as he takes and here is where his danger lies. It is not impossible that he should absorb as much from that gang as he gives of his personality.

He has never lacked love or friendship or companionship as I have. His qualities are those that I wish were mine. True he is young yet and needs development and it's up to me to see that he gets the most out of life that

that smile should never be erased from his face. I can remember myself at his age. I, at that, wasn't so unlike him.

Ever since I was a little kid of eight or nine I've wanted to be a great writer and to have a great friendship in my life—to be a Damon and have a Pythias in my life to have someone to run and play with, to wrestle with, to laugh with, to walk arm in arm with.

There was dear old Louie for a brief flash—and Morrie—and Will— and Tom—But never before an all-consuming friendship like this. This should last through the ages. This should shine eternally—should be everlasting. Our lives should be woven together, cemented—our names should be synonymous of friendship—

"I know not whether our names shall be immortal. I know our friendship shall."

Mon. June 22nd: This morning I called up a Mr. K. W. Miller of The Commonwealth Edison Company as I had written Mr. Samuel Insull, millionaire president of the Commonwealth and he had turned my letter over to Mr. Miller. The latter asked me to come down to his office this morning. Of course I did.

Mr. Miller, a rich man, was the nicest man I have ever met. He was so friendly and sympathetic and I had always believed the wealthy to be indifferent to us duffers. He had the kindliest, friendliest brown eyes that I have ever seen and they twinkled understandingly, companionably. Have you, dear diary, ever seen brown eyes that twinkled! Well neither had I until to-day. I thought that only blue eyes could light up in that particular way. His smile too was one that lighted his whole face. I've never been as thoroughly aroused by a first impression in I don't know how long.

Mr. Miller was about 33 years old. Tall, well built, faultlessly groomed and his office was large and luxurious.

He liked me as much as I liked him. I could see that in his smile, his attitude to help.

Mr. Insull had asked him to look into my invention for him. It was, Mr. Miller informed me, really out of his line as they did research work in light and power, but he looked over my model of the comb and had me explain it to him. He called up several men in the building (different departments) for information. I was quite amused when he, in explaining once said, "The inventor is here in my office." The inventor!

Finally he took me to one of the head men in the particular department that looks into electrical inventions of the type I am working on. This Mr. Hudlin was, as Mr. Miller also, an inventor and about 42 years old. Earnest and competent but rather loose in his manner and habits. He was very kind and told me about inventions of his own and that I should expect rebuffs; that even inventors with good ideas were rebuffed. He also said that the company hardly sold enough curling irons to keep them up, that woman psychology was a thing hard to beat, and that it dictated that the woman go to the hairdressers as her neighbor did. "But I don't entirely blame them. We have our peculiar little prides," Mr. Hudlin continued.

Mr. Miller was on my side. He often interrupted in my favor or suggested to my help. It was plain that he was my companion. I could see that easily when we were both seated opposite Mr. Hudlin in the way he hunched his chair near mine and in the way he threw back his shoulders.

I had already suggested that I could possibly sell it as a novelty comb to be sold in five and ten cent stores rather than an electric comb if that failed. Sell it as a comb to keep women from combing out their permanents, to retain and encourage the curl in their hair. Mr. Miller now suggested that Mr. Hudlin's eyes shone with the anticipation of sales in that way. There's something there alright. Something that will catch the eye. If there were a lot of those combs on a five and ten cent counter, just the idea of the curly teeth would sell them.

Well, Mr. Miller had me come back to his office, showing me the main sales floor of Commonwealth on the way.

"I want to give you a break if I possibly can," he told me and continued by saying that he thought there was a lot in my idea and asked me what I wanted to do—sell as a novelty or go ahead with the electric side of it. I told him novelty and also that I had no pull at all and wouldn't know how to go about seeing anyone who might be interested and that I hadn't expected really that Mr. Insull would answer my letter. He said that Mr. Insull was very careful about things like that and always looked into them. He also told me that of course ideas for a lot of absolutely silly inventions such as perpetual motion often came in but that I had something.

Then he took me in an adjoining office and introduced me to a Mr. Ryan. He and Mr. Ryan together had several addresses of comb manufacturing houses for me.

Finally, after perhaps all of an hour and a half with the nicest man I've known on first acquaintance, I left with my addresses.

Mon. July 20th: I'm absolutely fed up! Accidentally knocked a plant off the porch while rocking. She called me all sorts of rotten, vulgar, river-front names—cursed for half an hour. I was angry and told her so. She raved. She and the old man told me if I wasn't careful I'd have to find a new home. I told them I was, away from here, and asked them why they didn't leave me alone. *Oh why didn't they*! A place to sleep and food—how often they wash my face with that. And I try not to be an expense. I won't let her buy me only what I need. A pair of shoes, two pairs of pants, two shirts—in a year. With all the romantic ideas of home, home is oftimes hell and almost any place else is better sometimes. Romantic bosh!

I often find myself repeating and thinking of Micky's words—the philosophy of friendship. "Intimacy," he said, "breeds contempt." Often, alas, too often it does and we find out how rotten we each are.

Sun. July 26th: I've lived all these years with my hands to my eyes. Put your hands over your face and what do you get. Oh such a wonderful picture! I made a god of myself. I colored everything to my own desire. It was a beautiful world. Draw your hands down and what do you get?—Disillu-

sionment. I have put my hands back over my eyes but ever so often life tears
them down.

Fri. July 31st: Mentally I died tonight. I must have committed suicide. I
was so disgusted with human beings and their fallacies that that was the
only course out—mentally at least. And it was topped by "Mother." She
hurt poor little "Punk's" feelings and although he was hungry she wouldn't
give him a bowl of "Gumbo" when she knows he is crazy about it. I told
him to come over on Fridays, that we had it then. When he came I told him
we had it, she told him we didn't and treated him pretty nasty. This cli-
maxed a mood of mine of several days duration and it was then that I
rushed out, toward the school grounds and destroyed myself.

*   *   *

Thank God July '31 is over!—
Ahead—August 1931—unseen into. Its surprises and happiness of
which I am certain to start with dawn—

Wed. Aug. 19th: Another illusion was shattered today: —is pregnant.
Oh God!—Are there no decent people in the world. I've tried and am
still trying to find decent people that I may put them in my life and make it
decent too. I am sure that I am gambling right on Rob. I've tried hard to be
decent, minorly I've sometimes failed but I believe I have been fairly decent.
I've never seduced a girl. Always love and friendship and happiness I've
held supreme. Ever I've been seeking it. Please God, let me have Rob, let
him be everything I think him. Please let us be happy in our friendship.

Wed. Aug. 26th: Went to print shop to see about the posters for the Curly-
Comb and found that to get only six posters made would cost $20—and me
without a cent!! Where will I get the $ so that I can send all the information
and advertisement to Walgreen's?

*   *   *

(I'm in an awful rotten family. An awful rotten family. I know it.
Indecent—ignorant—crude.)

Thur. Aug. 27th: Happy Birthday Rob!! Your 16th my dear pal.
Many—many more!! And may we share all the rest together: You and I—a
friendship rivaling that of Damon and Pythias!!

Fri. Sept. 4th: I learned another sordid chapter of the family today.
Even to write these things down makes me feel cheapened in my own
self-respect.
I recognize no one in this damnable family as being related, regardless
of how distantly, to me. I stand and am alone—alone—
I am shivering to the marrow of my bones yet.

Sun. Sept. 6th: Wrote an inspired letter to Walgreen's about the comb.

Tues. Oct. 6th: This eve when coming home from 61st at about 5:30 a man whom I didn't recognize called to me, grasped my hand firmly with both of his, and said, "You're Motley, aren't you? I'm glad to know you son and I want you to know that I like you and have heard a lot about you. It doesn't matter an iota to me if the pigmentation of your skin is different than mine and it mustn't matter to you. If everyone felt that way we'd have a wonderful nation wouldn't we? Unfortunately everyone doesn't feel that way. *But always remember that you're as good as any man and there isn't anything you can't do.* You know me don't you?"

I had to admit that I didn't.

"Well," he said, "My boy and my girl are crazy about you. Theresa— You know Theresa. I'm M——, Harvard '94, a Pennsylvania man and 24 years a judge in the municipal court. You must come over and see them. Nobody can enter my house if he's black—from the inside. But I want you to come over. I don't give a God-damn about a person's color. It's what he is within that counts. I saw you pass our house on the opposite side of the street when we lived on Stewart and saw you speak to Theresa and saw her wave at you. I asked her who you were and she told me. 'Why don't you have him over sometimes?' I asked her. 'he's a colored boy, father,' she said. 'I don't care; that doesn't make any difference to us,' I told her."

I had on my purple jersey with the 33 on it. "How'd you get that? You earned it—didn't you?" and picturesquely saluted me and was gone . . . but he followed me home, really, his arm around my shoulders.

Wed. Oct. 7th: Walgreen's definitely turned down the "Curly-Comb" today. To say I'm horribly disappointed is whispering it. Oh how hard I've worked and tried—the fatigue of mind and body and soul. The aching for something better than this awful, this dull, this hum-drum existence. Oh where are all my dreams, my hopes, my air-castles, whither flown?

But I can't lose—*I will win.* I am waiting in weakness—I shall walk in power.

Liggett's Drug Stores, Inc., are my next hope. The moment I got the bad news from Walgreens I started a letter to Liggett's.

Sat. Oct. 17th: Rob wore my Purple A.C. sweat-shirt—you know, dear diary, the one from old Purple A.C. basketball days and so now the cycle is complete—Louie, Rob, and I have worn that sweat-shirt. It was torn almost completely off of Rob on our opponents' desperate tries for him but I'll keep it forever. I'll never wear it again. I'll never wash it and I'm going to keep it just as it is for a souvenir. Always it will remind me of the two greatest pals a fellow ever had and of my own athletic days.

Rob, in it, and with a helmet pulled down over his head, was a striking image of Louie—Louie as he looked when we were Sophs at Englewood.

Fri. Dec. 4th: Is it because good is so passive and evil seemingly so active that the latter seems to overwhelm the former? I'm sure that it must be positively fascinating to be bad—really bad.

Sat. Dec. 5th: At times it seems to me that it's quite obvious that birth is the beginning and death the only purpose of life. I know it's a very gloomy outlook but sometimes that mood, especially lately, seems to, at times, overcome me. And it seems that the only right of birth, of life, is the right to die. The question then is, is death a deterioration or the dream come true? Sometimes I believe that possibly death is a deterioration that finally overcomes us for at birth we are probably more perfect than we shall ever be and as young children very, very happy. And then there is a series of disillusionments, rude awakenings, and hurts that can never be cured. It appears that we are all fighting against evil from birth and like a dark shadow, the lengthening curtain of nightfall, it bears down closer, closer over our lives, scarring our friends, companions, relatives, neighbors—shattering our ideals, taking the fairy's wand and Lancelot's shield and Galahad's great nobility and finally getting us. I've felt the presence of this shadow strongly here of late. Will it conquer? It has taken so much I cared for and I wonder if I—flesh and blood—can fight it—if my heart and my soul are strong enough to ward off this evil or will I too in time fall in one of the many ways, the hundreds of ways a man can become sordid and ugly. What has man left when he feels his dreams and ideals crumbling—crumbling—

Does decay finally succeed in every life and then does the God who is all wisdom—all thought—all all—draw the shroud in mercy?

Go to bed gloomy!!

Tues. Dec. 8th: It's a silly, benighted old idea but if I could tonight sell my soul to the devil I would. What matter what should become of my pinched soul if I could be happy here and now—boundlessly happy—and have everything I wanted. Think of all the people I'd make happy, the poor, the helpless. And my friends!! My friends!! And I'd have Love and Friendship. Fame—Money—Power—Health always—Fine old age. It would be worth burning for!!

But I wonder if in so forming a pact with the devil one would have to have one great ruling sin, evil, in his life? So be it. But could faithfulness and sincerity in the right usage of Satan's gift in this life entitle one to everlasting servitude to the master monster later? I don't suppose. I really believe in a devil, but it is all so interesting. It is such an entrancing surmise!!

1 9 3 2

Tues. Feb. 2nd: Have decided to sell the "Curly-Comb" from door to door. Went out this morning and sold only 52 combs all day—and on Michigan Blvd., too! Everyone seems to be broke.

Sun. Feb. 14th: Have sold only 122 combs. Have lately invented a football game which is played with specially printed cards. I call it—"Card-Table Football" or "Card-Table Quarter-backing." I invented it last Friday in a few minutes. The idea came suddenly.

Wed. March 16th: Worked for Miss Rathjie today and made $1.75. Mr. M—— came over to see me this afternoon. He's really set on my going to Pennsylvania University. He, in the good old days, played football there for four years, at Harvard three years, and at Georgetown for two years, he told me; and, although, he said, I am small, he thinks I can make good. He said the school offers nothing but that he's an alumni and one of those men who try to fool themselves into thinking they're still young and sit in the stands and yell "Rah! Rah! Rah!" He likes me, likes me a lot. He said his children like me. He said that he can get me a scholarship to Penn. and that I'll have a library job—that he doesn't want me waiting on tables. He said this would include my room and board and spending money. He said he's having yearbooks sent to me.

Would I be a fool to turn down this offer? It's true, he said, that schools still buy athletes, especially football players. But my heart still says—Wisconsin!—Wisconsin!—Wisconsin!—and being bought for my football ability isn't really honest according to my meagre standard.

Mr. M—— said that Mr. B——'s daughter, Margaret, who had been married for a year or a little longer, was dead and that he had been to the wake. I said, knowing Margaret, that that was too bad, but he asserted, "No, it's not!—Considering the man she married."

Then he explained that at the wake, as at all places where mixed crowds gather, the three cardinal subjects of conversation came up: those of the present depression, politics, and the color question. He said that one particular obnoxious person introduced the race question.

Fri. March 18th: Sometimes I feel as if there isn't any such thing as love;— that love is only a myth—a fairy tale a mother once told her child when the world was new and a fable that has come down through the ages like "The Three Bears," "Little Red Riding Hood," "Jack and the Bean Stalk."

Thur. March 31st: Eleanor comes over continually. She seems to like me and wants me to make love to her. I don't like her and just can't. Today I finally got my football medal from her.

Sat. April 2nd: Have started training for football this fall and am doing roadwork every night up at the Englewood track.

Sat. April 9th: Rob has decided to give me a little of his time again instead of spending all his time in pool rooms and with the rowdy 61st Street gang. We were together batting a ball this aft. I was glad, of course, to have his friendship again.

   Even Junie, Art, and Kobe have quit the 61st Street bunch as being too low for them. As for myself I have failed utterly and a final set-back to my plans for money and power and happiness was dealt me yesterday. Should Rob fail to be less the wonderful, the sterling man I believe he was meant to idealize it will be my failure, my defeat. If I could have, or even if I could yet get the money for a car, a trip and other ways and means of offering Rob a clearer sight of a clean, happy youthful existence and future usefulness I believe success can be snatched out of an evident drubbing.

   My world has come to an end many times before and one time more or less shouldn't count much, but this has been the cruelest losing of a dream I've had. If I don't come out of this, if I degenerate from here on, please, dear diary, you, if the world turns against me, be true—as true as I have tried to be to my loves, my friendships, my ideals.

Thur. April 21st: Well it's happened again—again I've fought 2 to 1! and been licked. This time it was Johnny and Roy. Trouble had been brewing since last night because of nasty remarks Johnny sent to me in messages by young, cross-eyed Hickey. They were the type of remarks no fellow who considered himself a man would stand for. He and Frank have been acting especially wise here of late anyway. Well tonight Johnny had a whole gang of fellows with him including Turk (Warren) and Frank. He got particularly obnoxious until I could no longer stomach it. Walking up to him I asked him if he remembered the time, some months ago, he slapped Red, the younger and smaller kid than him. "Well," I said, "Here's that slap back with my compliments." And then it started—Roy and Johnny—and I—and the mob closing in—Turk with his club—waiting—

   I stumbled over some bushes and losing my balance fell, as one of the McBrides pushed me. Both of them pounced on me, tearing my sweater and shirt and hitting me on the head, face and neck, and kicking me, while I myself tore a snag in my trousers when I stumbled. I also have a badly swollen eye which doesn't, however, hurt at all. And, worst of all, I didn't get in one telling blow. And you should have heard the shriek go up from that bunch of ragged kids ranging from 9 to 17 years old.

A well liked fellow, this Motley!!

Mon. June 27th: It would, I think, be fun to be a failure and a hobo—but an intellectual wanderer of the world able to laugh at life and realize that everyone is mad—including one's self.

We spoke of the layman and their limited knowledge. Alex believes in sin too, he feels that if the urge to sin is there, gratify it. We both agreed that women—just aren't—that as companions they don't rank—have no sportsmanship.

I told Alex (although I was carried away at the moment and it is against my ideal of Round Table Chivalry) that for some men, especially those who are imaginative, romantic, adventurous, it is best that they find a dear friend, two friends, or three, and live with them, but sleep with a woman when it is necessary. There the companionable and passionate are gratified and a degree of happiness or at least contentment and comfort is maintained.

We agreed that love is only an illusion—that love of a man for a woman—is merely a means of maintaining the species—that love, when that type is spoken of, is really an ugly, passionate, beastial thing.

It is my firm belief that every fellow who has reached the age of 18 should have read:

(1) All the fairy stories [in early life] he could lay his hands on: (2) Robinson Crusoe; (3) The Story of Arthur and The Knights of The Round Table; (4) A Story of Damon and Pythias; (5) The Three Musketeers; (6) Any really good story of athletics and school life such as those from the pen of Ralph Henry Barbour; (7) The Count of Monte Christo; and (8) Walpole's ''Fortitude'':—

Everybody who has read these books has, then, the vital ideals of honor, courage, chivalry, loyalty, imagination, and friendship. A boy who has read these should have a far better chance of being a real man.

Sat. Oct. 22nd: This eve I went over to Fred's house and sat talking to his mother and dad, his aunt and uncle. Perry and Marve were in the house playing a baseball game and Fred was out in the barn (where he has a chemical set) with Babe, Cliff, and Al.

I was in the house about two hours and until about 9:15 when Fred came in and went upstairs immediately. Marve told his mother that someone in the barn had vomited by the door. Finally it was discovered that it had been Freddie. Mrs. H—— and I hurried upstairs. Fred was as pale as a ghost—and talked nonsense when his mother almost tearfully questioned him—something about his looking like a monkey—that he was alright but just wanted to go to bed.

It later developed that Babe had brought over a bottle of wine and that with the fumes of the Bromine and other acids and chemicals they had been fooling with they had all become rather dizzy. Mrs. H—— gave Fred some hot milk—he failed to hold it in his stomach and twice vomited.

Someone called up on the telephone and Mr. and Mrs. H—— had to leave in the car on an important piece of business.

I stayed with Fred. Turning off the light I stood by the foot of the bed, my chin in the palms of my hands. A dull, listless rain fell with monotonous moanfulness beyond the large windows that gave the room a sad grey mantle. Fred tossed back and forth on the bed and my mind went tossing back and forth too—the team—what it had meant to me—what it was coming to—Fred whom I had depended upon—that chalk talk—practice this morning which I had turned from with disgust and walked home—Roy always giving his best—Eddie to whom the team means a lot—Jerry not trying at practice—what was the use of it all—

I was brought back to the present by Fred vomiting again.

Then quiet—quiet again except for the springs of the bed occasionally and once a half groan from Freddie. From his pillow, out of the bleakness of the room, came his voice—"I'm going to quit the team. I was doing alright until tonight. I'm the captain and am supposed to set an example for the others. I'm going to quit Monday."

"You're not a quitter, Fred," I said.

Silence—The rain dripping—dripping—the stir of the bed springs—

"I'm a fine one. I don't deserve to be captain."

"Didn't anyone ever make a mistake before?" I asked.

"Will you do me a favor, Mot?—Make Roy or Jerry captain."

"Will you do me a favor, Fred?—Try to go to sleep."

Sun. Oct. 23rd: This eve we burned a flare and then all went up to the show. Roy and I finally wound up at the Harvard as we had seen most of the other pictures.

Roy is a prince of a fellow. The more I see of him the better I like him and I see him every day. He thinks he owes all his football ability to me. He gives me the credit. He has told me so several times. Oh, I've helped him a little but he deserves all the credit in the world. He's worked hard—he's tried, he's fought—he's played hard—and it's always been his best—his level best.

And he's the chap they say is conceited and a Kodaker—a grandstander. Well I'll take two like him every time!!

Roy gets hurt an awful lot. It seems that it's his ill luck to have something happen to him every game. I believe he has rather brittle bones and he doesn't weigh a whole lot. But he always comes back for more. A lot of the fellows say that he can't be hurt as bad as he appears to be, that he is merely kodaking a bit. They have their opinion and I have mine and in mine Roy ranks ace high.

I have to smile every time I think of an incident of yesterday afternoon. I wanted Roy to go to 63rd and Blackstone with me (a plot of mine that we might see All-American) and he didn't want to go as he said he wasn't dressed for it. He thought I was mad when I said "Oh, so that's the kind of guy you are!" We were sitting on a window sill of one of the old Lewis Champlain Buildings by the track and I was hurling stones out upon the track.

Suddenly Roy said, "Do you want my jersey?"

Why, I didn't know what to think, to say or do. I was dumbfounded.

"Why? What do you mean?" I asked.

"Well, you're sore at me," he said, "I'm not like those other guys. I'll give you my jersey."

"Oh, Roy, I'm not sore at you, you big nut!" I replied, "and even if I were, it wouldn't make any difference with your playing. You'd play if you deserved to play."

"I know," he said, "But it wouldn't be any fun if you were sore."

Isn't he swell!! A fellow like that gets you!!

Sat. Nov. 12th: Oh God! I'm sick and tired of it all. My very soul cries out to toss it all to hell and get away—anywhere—but as far as possible from this place—Home!! The irony of it!! All that one should love and cherish should center about the home, but with me—no!! It has ever been this way. Arguments. Discontentments. Drunkenness. Sin. Shame. Hate. All festering here like a Canker. The happiest moments that I have spent have been away from here. The other day I cried like a baby unable to check myself though I clenched my fists, grinned and repeated to myself "Nothing Matters! Nothing Matters!! Nothing Matters!!" But the tears like stabbing swords ran down my cheeks and shamed me—a football player—a man—a stoic—blubbering like a kid.

1 9 3 3

Sun. Jan. 1st: And now as the new year and I stand apart a little and look each other in the face, I find a friend. Strangely enough I don't go into this year as into others but with confidence and with the feeling that I know what is going to happen. And I do know that this year I shall have a wonderful summer vacation after which in September I shall go to Wisconsin to live and work so that I may gain my citizenship and enroll at the University of Wisconsin in September 1934 as a citizen of the state. And, if I can get a job with the hours so arranged, this fall and next too I shall work with the Freshman football team at Wisconsin in preparation for my three glorious years. These things I know.

*   *   *

And as for aspirations? I have but one desire this year and that is to become a football machine and to improve and improve all the time.

Mon. Jan. 30th: This eve late (in fact until after one A.M.) Mr. and Mrs. H—— and I sat in their kitchen and talked.

Mrs. H—— said, "Your brother is married to a white woman, isn't he?" She went on to say how many mixed marriages she knew of and spoke of a couple handsome colored fellows she knew who were married to white girls and how jealous the girls were of them. Mrs. H—— has had several very good colored friends.

"I bet you won't marry a colored girl, will you?" she asked.

My answer was in the negative.

I tried to explain myself. To tell that I don't feel that the colored people are a part of me. I've lived in this neighborhood all my life. My friends, my everything have been white people. I don't look down on Negroes but I'm not one of them any more than the Prince of Wales is. I don't feel at home with them—I—oh it's hard explaining—but I'm not prejudiced against them or any race of people or any religion—I try to keep open-minded on all these subjects. But I do like to think that my people are the human race, my creed the creed of humanity. However I am white, always shall my friends, my associates, my neighbors—Oh the more I try to explain the more muddled I get and I don't want anyone who might chance on this book in the future nor do I want myself—my inner self to feel that I am practicing malice against anyone or anything—nor that I am prejudiced—or narrow or a snob.

*　　　*　　　*

Mrs. H—— said, "It's too bad I haven't a daughter, Willard, but I haven't."

Sun. Feb. 12th:　Well they've kicked my poor little puppies out. The other day when I left home I locked them in the coal shed where I had to keep them instead of in the basement where it is warm. I don't know why I locked them up but it was lucky that I did for when I came back brother called me aside and told me that the old man had poison mixed in some meat and was going to give it to them as soon as I turned them out. Oh no, he'd never poison those poor little hounds if I knew anything about it. I would have gladly left here first. God, I don't see how anyone could kill a poor, defenseless animal—and above all a dog—man's truest friend. The old man was raving when I came in and demanded that I open the shed. It was shortly after six and he had to go to work at seven. I went upstairs until he was gone.

Brother let me put them in one of his flats and is going to let me keep them there until the cold spell is over, for the very night I put them up there it turned cold and the next day it was -19, one of the five coldest days in the history of Chicago. I put a lot of rags in the flat for them, but they, poor little pups, only seven months old, must have been awfully cold, and the minute they urinated it froze to the floor.

I've got to see my little puppies through. How I don't know. But I will. Although I love many people and things I honestly believe that little Pidge and Touchdown are the only things in the world that truly love me.

Sat. June 17th:　Today is my dogs' birthday. They are a year old today—are Pidge and Touchdown. I bought them each a pound and a half of hamburger, piled it on a pie plate moulded into the form of cakes and stuck a pink candle into each. I also bought Touchdown a harness for 50¢ and shall have it stained red as he is going to Wisconsin with me. I shall get Pidge one a little later when I get some more money.

Mon. July 3rd:　Was sitting out in front of Charlie's house with him when Teresa M—— came along, lovely as a picture in a flowered dress a tiny basket of macaroon cookies under her arm. She is selling them and stopped. Both Charlie and I bought a bag for 10¢. I had earned 40¢ today and in the end invested it all in macaroons as well as a dime Charlie owed me. He bought three bags. She had started out with 10 bags, sold one before she met us and eight to us.

We went in Charlie's house as he wanted to eat. Teresa and I sat on the sofa and talked and laughed and compared ideas. She is growing into a very charming creature, soft brown hair with a golden tint combed back from her divinely broad childish face which is ever all smiles. She hints of E—— and looks more like her than any girl I've ever seen around here. Then, too, she has eyes like Richie.

Sun. July 30th: Well dear diary with these lines I begin book 17—and the last book of this period of my life—the series of boyhood—for I have been nothing but a boy since first we took up our ways together. Remember how a bewildered, friendless boy I first asked and received your friendship when in my under-class days at Englewood. With you I have shared all my joys, sorrows, aspirations, dreams and lost days. Together we have thrilled to the companionship of Louis and later of Rob and Rich. Together we have adored E—— and changeless we still see the entire embodiment of love and romance in her.

Oh we've gone barefoot together and been broken hearted together, my staunchest friend, and now that boyhood grows into youth (a stage I hope I shall never outgrow—perpetual youth—) I leave these familiar scenes to go unknown to Madison Wisconsin where I hope that within the walls of that dear college there I shall find the happiest moments, most joyful experiences and finest companionships of life that may long endure a youth as idealistic, optimistic, and dream-ful as the boy. I now am at a stage and age when most fellows are worldly-wise men.

I heartily take up the adventure for I shall be absolutely unknown and alone. I shall have not a single friend there, know no familiar street—Like an adventurer of the middle-ages, I, in search of knowledge, athletic prowess, companionship and happiness, shall strike out.

Of course I doubt ever meeting or having a friend as fine and loveable as Louis nor shall any love save E——'s ever possess me. But they tell me the college life is a happy one—a care-free one.

And life moves on—It is only fair and right that I go on now and gain that that I need to make life successful for me—It is high time I received that I consider necessary to make me the immortal author my heart and soul says I am destined to be.

Too long I have lingered here around too familiar scenes and friends—Life has paled and grown dull—Acquaintances have soured—I have nothing—absolutely nothing I want.

Long I have wanted to flee from it all—get away—challenge with bared sword this thing they call fate—This destiny they paint as a deadly and malicious demon who but by chance or luck smiles on few and is far more given to scowling.

I have an all-consuming belief in myself—I know what I want—I know that I shall get it—I know that only by assailing and constantly besieging that that I want shall I conquer it.

And *I will* get everything, large and small, that I want. There isn't even the tiniest doubt with strength enough to float a dandelion seed in my mind. Later, possibly as boyhood gives birth to youth I shall in this book describe all my ambitions for the next ten years to come at the conclusion of which time I shall be the Man-Laureate, renowned, admired—loved!!!

Mon. July 31st: Touchdown is coming along astoundingly well in his lessons. On the command of "Line Up" he "lines up" on his rear legs in a sitting position. The next job from that position is to teach him to bark on a command of "Signals."

He can also jump through a hoop, lining up before and after his leap. He does the hurdles, too, three to date, lining up before and after his jumps.

Touchdown's ambition is to be mascot for the Wisconsin football team.

*   *   *

The fellows up at 59th and Wentworth are an evil-minded bunch—but just human after all! Pete, a rather handsome Greek who looks 21 but is only 15, Roy and several of the others go to a joint run by a mulatto prostitute and the things they tell you with vain braggadocio and man-of-the-world unconcern makes your hair stand on end. Even the kids 13 and 14 *know an awful lot.*

But, all in all, I don't find them an awful bad lot. Then, too, they're immensely interesting.

Fri. Aug. 4th: Kidding the fellows about going to Wisconsin, I told them some time ago that the Coach wanted me to room with him. Now I tell them that the President also wants me to room with him and that I'm having a hard time deciding!!!

Tues. Aug. 15th: Raising my female dogs teaches me exactly what a mother goes through with girls. "Touchdown" would rather be sired now than have anything else. But her schooling comes first. She must go to school with me, be mascot of the team, learn all her tricks—then I shall see that she is satisfactorily mated. Perhaps at that time on the strength of her beauty and intelligence, of being mascot for the football team, and of her tricks her puppies will be in great demand.

Thur. Aug. 17th: I had the most disillusioning experience of my life to-day . . .

I went to the store for some meat and at the corner of 59th and Wentworth saw a priest. Naturally when he glanced at me I spoke to him. On my way out of the A. and P. with a pound of rice I observed that he was standing near the store and right where I would have to pass him. He spoke, saying that he was new in the city, was waiting for someone on the "L" who was late, and had come to Chicago for the fair—The World's Fair.

When I started across the street he said that he thought when I spoke that I had recognized the collar and asked where I live, and on learning said he had some time to kill and that he would walk a block or two with me. This I considered surprising but figured that perhaps he wished to talk religion. He asked my age and if I was married and said that no doubt I thought he asked an awful lot of questions. I replied that I didn't mind and he wanted to know who I lived with and if they were home. He made it plainly evident that he was desirous of going home with me, but when he learned that my folks would be there, he said that oh no he had better not as they would wonder how I had picked up with him. I told him that this would need no explaining but he seemed distressed at my pushing the subject any farther and I dropped it. This conversation carried us up to the rear of Mr. Fitzgibbon's store front on 59th Place. There he said that he would be back in the neighborhood later in the day and that he would be driving. He asked me "How would you like to go for a ride?" I answered that I wouldn't mind if I didn't have anything else to do and asked him at what time. He asked me what time I went to bed and when he started to answer my question of what time I held my breath for his answer, listening to hear if it would be after dark and knowing with some inner sense as one is often empowered that it would be. "Oh about 10:30 or 11 o'clock tonight," he answered and followed with, "Oh but maybe you wouldn't want to go for a ride." There was a silence and he continued, "I don't want to shock you—" and silence, then—"But you understand what I mean."

I don't know what I replied or how I got away from him but later I found myself alone and on my way home.

Oh my God how can he possibly—in your name—be like that. Surely if he was a man like that he should never have donned the robe. He should now desert. I find nothing to say really for I am so shocked that I haven't yet any real reaction.

But perhaps I am judging the man too harshly. Perhaps it is the beast creeping back. Maybe he fights it like hell. Mayhap he was of that nature before he took priesthood and became a priest to fight it thinking that the robe would save him.

At first I thought that perhaps he wasn't really a priest but I could smell that clean church odor, that fatherly aroma on his clothing.

How in heaven's name can he consecrate the Host—how attempt it. Why doesn't it turn to mud in his hand. How can he walk amid all that holiness, through lanes of crosses, in those good robes? How can he listen to the confessions of young boys and young girls erring for their first times. Their innocence against his colossal sin. Their heart-breaking repentence versus his ill low-scheming baseness. How dare he!!

I've tried to figure it all out but am getting nowhere. The rot that tarnished the vestments of priesthood during the middle ages and this fiend—

Ah but I cannot judge other priests, nor say that all priests have a sex life any more than I can compare Leonardo De Vinci with other bastard born, or myself with other bastard-conceived. Or myself with Negroes. Or Lou with the low Jew. Or any race of people with its lowest class. We shall then let this bastard-priest go his way and leave a God whose sacred traditions are being trampled mark His own score against our ill-companion of the afternoon.

Fri. Aug. 18th: Over to the Buckley's to see Bill this eve. Afterwards, just after dark, I went over to 603 West 63rd Street where Ruth Lockridge used to live. Now Ruth and I went to grammar school together and I remember her as the girl with the soft, long black curls. She had ambitions to write also and I took a note-book full of her compositions home to typewrite them for her. This was over 8 years ago and tonight I meant to return them having run across them while cleaning out some of my things in preparation for going off to school. She still lived at the same address according to the phone book so I took myself there.

The building is famous for its gruesome history and is called "Holmes' Castle" for it is there that Holmes killed all those women for their insurance and shot them down into the basement through a chute. There in a pit prepared with an acid substance their bodies were eaten away. The place is supposed to be haunted. It was dreadfully dark as I made my way up to the 2nd floor and seeing no light I followed the hall back to its inky-black end. There a stairway lead upstairs but my common-sense told me that nobody lived up there. Back up the hall I discovered a door near the top of the steps, knocked, was gruffly accosted, and had the door fling open to gaze into the face of a husky German. He told me that the Lockridges had moved out 6 months before. Then, he told me that the place was haunted and that upstairs of nights one could hear the canaries that once were cooped in there singing away for all they are worth. He said their favorite song is "In the Good Old Summertime." He appeared to be about 38 and not absolutely sober. I said that I'd have to come up sometimes and hear the ghosts. He said that just he and his mother lived in the whole building and through the open door I could see a rather fat elderly woman sitting in a rocking chair, her glasses back over the top of her hair. The man at the door said that his name was Schwartz and asked me, "Won't you come in?" I went in but with relief saw that he had left the door open onto the hall. It developed that he and his mother alone inhabit the building, save for the old exchange book store on the first floor. Many of the flats on the 2nd floor were offices once and where they live there are but two rooms and they have to go across the hall for water. He was an awfully good-natured fellow and stood there kidding and laughing and told me how he set his clock by means of a time table and the trains roaring past, as they are right next door to the Englewood Station. His mother sat there and laughed, saying "Goofy Ed." She was awfully proud of this big kid of a son of hers. Finally I left but with a feeling of fellow understanding and friendship for they upstairs.

('Twould be great if on going back to inquire about them I should find that they didn't live there now but had many, many years ago and were both dead now.)

Sat. Aug. 19th: Charlie brought Mrs. Rathje's old 1924 Reo home today. I put in $2 and he is going to drive Touchdown and I up to Wisconsin. (I got $1.25 for selling the car.)

Thur. Aug. 24th: Louie called me up this evening and we had a long, long talk. Dear old Louie! He graduates from his six year law course from the University of Chicago in March. Gosh time flies! It seems only yesterday, as he too said, since we played basketball and went to Englewood together.

I asked him what he was going to do when he graduated and he said get a job and probably get married.

Oh no, dear God, preserve him. Don't let him get married for years yet. Let him go with me on my three year vagabond trip around the world. Why should, why must marriage break up such fine friendships. No, no, no—he is still my boyhood pal of yesterday—just a kid, laughing and crying, rolling and tumbling at the puppy dog age. Oh I can't feature him as a married man. Let him, please do, go his way alone a while longer. Don't make him stern through marriage! Please, God, don't break his heart! That alone is perhaps the only thing I could fall out with you about. And please, oh dear God, when you do choose his mate make her wonderful and perfect, a girl who will ever make him happy. I shan't write any more, just yet, dear God, for I find my eyes filled with tears for the first time in a very long time.

P.S. Lou told me to be sure and write and let him know where I am and how I am getting along when I get to Madison.
Memories!—
Memories!—
They're eating up my brain.

Sun. Aug. 27th: Now that the bud has reached its entirety and is about to flower into youth—young manhood—I had best give up the dreams of boyhood.

Sweet, sweet dreams! Warm dreams sunned by Sol's virgin rays, dreams the like of which may never more raise their star-like eyes with the dew of boy's belief and trust yet moulding crowns for them.—

Most dreams be they those found in sleep or those visiting one's days easily escape our more tangible every day life. Dreams are so seldom possessed or realized. Most, should I try to describe them, would evade me. But dreams are not things to be put on paper, to be looked at and touched. They are bits of our souls perhaps. They, I feel, are best to be enjoyed in visions, to be thrilled, enthused, delighted with.

It has been great fun—just the dreams alone of boyhood—oh happy!

happy! boyhood and dreamhood striding hand in hand across the flight of time.

Some of my lesser drèams, less divine perhaps, I can capture in the point of my pen and transpose to the pages of this diary—these that I can find words for I shall—

My first really sincere ambition was to be a saint—To live so holy and noble a life that God would not deny me. A life, I was to live, like that of Galahad. My desire was to be the Saint For Dogs. (Oh, smile, you who later read these lines but it was a beautiful thought and ambition, I still think.) It was I who was to plead with God to give our noble and loyal little friends a soul that they would not forever be lost to us in eternity, for did not the "grown folks" know that dogs died and that was the end of them. Oh why? Weren't they a lot nobler than all men. I think I cried when I first reasoned the entire matter out.

*   *   *

I was to have a beautiful castle-like house one day that I would call "Good Hope" and a star in electric lights would shine ever at its utmost peak. (P.S. I still dream of a big castle-like house with perhaps towers like Englewood High School and huge fire places and Great Danes named— "Louis" "Mot" "Rob" and "Richie" galloping all over the place. And here are to live all together with me all of my best friends though they be 60 in number. And we shall sit around the fire laugh and talk of nights and swap stories and grow old together and grow young together. Across the front of the gate shall be that lovely poem—

> We just shake hands at meeting
> With many that come nigh;
> We nod the head in greeting
> To many that go by.
> But welcome through the gateway
> Our few old friends and true;
> Then hearts leap up and straightway
> There's open house for you,—
>   old friends,
> There's open house for you!!

*   *   *

And Rob and I had a wonderful trip in my car across Canada from the Atlantic to the Pacific Coast and through California and the American national parks. In the northern wilds of Canada we employed a half-breed guide and in our canoe the "ROBANI" explored uncharted lakes and rivers and hunted big game—deer, etc. We slept in big hotels in New York and the big cities and under the stars in the wilds. We climbed mountains—We lived! laughed! dreamed!—

Rob has, in remembrance of the trip a handsome watch, a present from me on his birthday (at which time we were in Los Angeles) on the back of which is engraved

> "To Rob
> From Will
> August 27, 1933
> Count Only the Happy Hours."

*   *   *

And some day, in dreams at least I shall have twin sons who shall be exactly like Richie and later great athletes and wonderous football stars.

*   *   *

And too I dream of someday, when my children, fair sweet Rita and E——, Louis, Willard, and Robert and Richard (perhaps so named if I should father that many) are in their youth, starting a new family.

I would tell them that we are to be the first of the Motleys and that we shall make the name symbolic of nobility, gentleness, chivalry and loyalty.

*   *   *

When dying I see the street below crowded with people—some bareheaded, some kneeling and praying for me. And the snow is gently falling over everything making all pure and white. The flakes are large, soft, and clinging like that one snow I encountered on my way home from Englewood High School one high noon, that snow that in ten minutes had blanketed everything several inches deep in a fairy-like radiance—the snow that was gentle and caressing—the most beautiful snow I ever saw. Such this day's snow would be and my wife (perhaps) (no, it would no doubt be far better that I lay my wife's head to rest) my children and friends would all be standing by in hushed silence—all the friends I had ever loved who hadn't passed on and were waiting the arrival of my train at the depot beyond life.

I am a great author, the greatest of my age, and one of my sons is to follow in my footsteps. I have one uncompleted work, my last, half finished, which he has just promised to complete for me. Under my pillow is that string of holy beads that little lady in the Philadelphia "Lady of Sorrows" Church gave me on my cycle trip to New York. Where I can gaze at it is my favorite picture—that picture of Sir Galahad (or is it Lancelot) standing bareheaded beside his white mount.

I am smiling and have just jested with Rob, Rich, or Louie (one of those I'd have saved to tuck me in the soul).

Across the foot of my bed is a blanket from the University of Wisconsin, an insignia of All-American honors and my Englewood High School letter.

I have taken up Knight-Errantry again and am rather eager to be off on this next adventure. I am happy.

Again I see that picture of the real dream I had when I was a child and that still clings to me—A blue, blue sky wealthy with stars of greatest lustre, a flower strewn hilltop and me on my back in the grass and flowers looking at the stars and sky—

Isn't dying like that a beautiful thing?

*　　*　　*

Ah but my fondest day-dream of all and one I shan't give back to boyhood is the dream of a friendship supreme to Damon and Pythias'.

I have most wanted Louie in one role. I would have been contented with Rob or Richie as Damon or Pythias.

I still dream, I still hope, I start again tomorrow for the eternal, death-defying, lasting friendship.

*　　*　　*

Thus I give up most of the dreams of boyhood—

Mon. Aug. 28th:　You know of course dear diary that it has been one of my fondest ambitions to start and build up a real, true club of good fellowship patterned after the "Knights of The Round Table." This I have never been able to do as yet but may someday. In imagination though I have been the founder of such a club called "The Knights of The Round Table" and having only the goodliest of fellows in its lists. I have been very fortunate in my life in knowing youths who I consider each a "Prince of a fellow." Naturally they are the charter members.

The Purpose Of The Club—

A social and athletic club of high and discriminating nature, seeking for its lists the best and goodliest of fellows, organized January One, Nineteen Hundred and Thirty-Three, to inspire friendship, manliness, honor, and touched by the real King Arthur's goodness and nobility; Sir Galahad's purity and beauty, and Sir Lancelot's sword and strength.

Fri. Sept. 1st:　Went over to tell Teresa good-bye today and although it is now 1:40 A.M. I am not long away from there. I got there at about 4:15 this afternoon and left at fifteen minutes past one. That's nine hours! And how joyously the time passed! First Teresa and I sat on the davenport and she thanked me for the flowers and said that the card was very sweet and that she still has it. She asked me if anyone ever called me by my first name as all the fellows and girls she knew called me by my last name and that that is why she does. Her brother Joe, 14, a clever youth who even now shows great intelligence, handed me book after book to take along with me to read. I came away with four volumes. Nick, the youth who came to a party at their house and never left, played his guitar and sang. He is a very excellent player and has a nice friendly personality. I like him a lot and of course he, like all of us, is enthralled by Teresa.

I intended leaving at 6 o'clock but Nick said that he would make some Italian spaghetti if I would stay. I stayed and surely enjoyed myself!!

After supper Nick again strummed his guitar and sang on the back porch for the Italian family upstairs and the neighbors from the several apartments nearby.

Then Teresa started a sketch of Nick which she didn't like and failed to finish. Later she made some very fine fudge and I ate most of it! It was really good! She is surely a sweet girl with a personality encountered rarely. Then too she is very pretty and reminds me of my own E——. This was the nicest evening I've spent in a long time and one I won't forget soon.

Sat. Sept. 2nd: Well dear diary now that boyhood ends today I believe it would only be fitting that I whisper to you my ambitions as young manhood—the more mature youth is to be encountered.

The next five years will be the five hardest, most severe years of my life physically, mentally and morally. There must, for this period of time be full steam ahead with no let-down at any time. I must "give her the gun" and play the part of the "little Iron Man."

I believe that in ten years time I shall be a success, that 1943 will find me a well read and coming author.

Well, dear diary, since it is with you alone that I really let go and confide all my secrets, barring no inner door or chamber to you I will confide my every ambition for the next ten years and high and mighty ones they are too. Possibly by any less understanding and sympathetic person than yourself, one less acquainted with the real "me," the man within these things will seem like only the wildest dreams of an insufferable egotist. I don't think, though, that I am an egotist but have only inconquerable confidence and belief in myself. I do believe in my genius. I do believe I have genius along the lines of athletics and literature. I do believe that I shall be the greatest football player ever to trod a field and I do believe that I shall be the greatest author of my age.

Enough then with excuses and reasons why between us, my faithful diary. We speak a simple, a common language.

I hope to star for the University of Wisconsin in football for three straight years, my sophomore, junior and senior years; I hope to be All-American these three years, captain of the team in my senior year and also the greatest captain and leader the Wisconsin team has ever had. I hope to compete for three years in basketball, being All-American there too all three years and captaining the team in my final year; I hope to run the mile and set the all-time world's record as well as be the Olympic Champion; I hope to win letters in Crew, skiing and other sports to gain more letters than any other fellow in college; I hope to be the greatest all-around athlete in the world these next few years; I hope to excell in my classes and rank Number One; I hope to take part in the plays at school, to be sports editor of the college daily, class-president one year, winner of the Tribune football trophy and considered the best sportsman in athletic competition. A large order, eh? Especially for my 142 pounds but as Napoleon said, "Impossible is a word to be found only in the dictionary of fools." And as I say, "They laughed at Columbus, they laughed at Edison, they laughed at Lindbergh, and they laughed at Motley."

My whole life centers around my making good in football. Football will keep me in school. Football will help me sell my sport stories and articles after graduation, and thus give me funds to take a year post-graduate work at Yale in English and a year's English at Oxford as well as help me along on my three year vagabond trip around the world.

After that I hope to start coaching football at Englewood for a number of years and develop the school's greatest teams as well as a little later get married if E—— will have me. Coaching at Englewood will also depend on my football ability.

Then I want to have money—to make plenty of it so that I can build that great house where my friends can come and enjoy life and live with me if they choose. While coaching at Englewood I want to write an Epic Poem idealizing football and other athletics—a Poem that will live and truly represent everything behind Alma Mater and School Spirit. Then too maybe I will have my four big Danes: Louie, Mot, Rob, Richie, and my big, open fire-place!

I realize the work, the heart-breaking toil behind achieving these things but man has ever won what he wanted and man ever can!

Adios boyhood!—On your guard youth!!—Young manhood!—the next joust is with you!!

What has been is as nothing to what shall be.

Tues. Sept. 5th: This morning I saw Doc Spears the football coach! Saw him—my future coach!—Shook his hand—twice!

Went next door to the gym at about 9:30 and waited about 15 minutes after first speaking to a tall man who asked me if I played any basketball. He told me he was the assistant coach and shortly I heard him talking on the phone to Doc Meanwell, the head basketball coach.

The first floor lobby of the gym is filled with trophies hanging from the ceiling, the walls, reposing in trophy cases. Practically every inch available is used. Doors leading off of this large room read, FOOTBALL COACH, BASKETBALL COACH, HOCKEY COACH, etc., and are the private offices of each.

In one of the trophy cases along with many footballs and basketballs enscribed with scores is a helmet of earliest vintage and on a card in front of it are the words "The Helmet of Pat O'Dea, The Greatest Kicker of All Time." Huge life-sized full photos of some of the star players in football and basketball are on the walls also and many, many group pictures. One very impressive score was the 1928 Wisconsin-Notre Dame score, Wisconsin having won 22-6.

A short husky man finally came out and asked me if I wished to see

Doc Spears. He asked my name and where I was from. He lead me past a small outer office and Spears' private secretary.

"Mr. Spears—Mr. Motley," he said. Doc Spears asked me to be seated.

The Knight-Errant of Englewood and Wisconsin's football King!! He sat at a large desk in his shirt sleeves, a sheet of paper before him on which he was scrawling football plays and formations. I laughed inwardly. Why he was no different than Palmer and me. We too worked on a sheet of paper like that employing even the same circles and X's!

He is a large man, already bulging at the sides. A fine looking man with character and friendliness in his face. He has a complexion that reminded me quite a bit of Quant. I liked him immediately.

He remembered my letter and said that Mike (Mr. Agozin of Chicago) had spoken to him about me when he was in Chicago lately. But he said that he couldn't find me any kind of work despite the strides of the N.R.A.; things here were at a standstill. He smiled, and after you have seen him smile you are all for him!!

Could I work out with the Freshman team? Why of course! He'd be glad to have me!

*   *   *

I spent the entire afternoon looking for a job. Hotels, garages, etc. No luck!

Tues. Sept. 12th: My money ran out Wednesday morning and since then I have travelled odd paths therefore dear diary this long delay in writing for you meanwhile, if you recall, were locked up in my grip at the Y.

All Wednesday, Thursday, and Friday I looked for work. Never had I wanted to work more earnestly. All day long and into the night until 10 o'clock I sought employment. Hotels, restaurants, barber shops, bakeries, factories—everywhere I went. I asked men on the street. Up to 10th floors Touchdown and I trudged only to be rebuked. These three days I had only a loaf of whole wheat bread and half a pound of bacon. The eggs, that my red-headed friend also gave me (and he has mysteriously disappeared from the face of the globe!) broke in my pocket. In two days the bread was gone and a gnawing appetite set in. Did you ever eat raw bacon? Well I did!

Nights I slept on a stone bench on the terrace of the capitol building— little faithful Touchdown and I.

Four nights that I have been here I've slept in the "Madison Home for Transient Man"—really a bread line. But it's the finest place of its type I've ever known of and I have once, you know, slept in a like house in New York. The attendants here are polite as they can be. And friendly. They all petted Touchdown and wanted to know if he was hungry and if they could get him some bones. One man escorted me to a camping cot (there are about 100 of them there for the men) as if I had paid $2.00 at the desk. There are a dozen tables with benches at which the men eat or play cards, read books, magazines, and newspapers, or put jig-saw puzzles together. One can stay here as long as one likes and the only rules are that one must keep clean and not use profane language. The kitchen is spotless white—cleaner than that at the restaurant where I work.[2] The only thing I don't like is that dead, stagnated smell that prisons and places of its sort have.

Fri. Sept. 15th: Football Practice starts today. Today I start my long crowning career. Today the Knight-Errant begins his seige for the laurel of "First in Tourney Play."

Fri. Sept. 22nd: I went down to the tailor shop this morning and found six letters waiting for me! The first one I noticed was a type-written envelope with the words <u>PLEASE FORWARD</u> typed and underscored and it had been stamped Sept. 6th. I turned it over. There was only the initial E. on the reverse side—those magic, beautiful lines. I thought it was some huge joke and suspected one of my nieces or Fred. However some something stayed my hand and I saved that envelope for last. Then I opened E——'s—This is what she had written:

"Here is my life—do with it as you will."

I have never had any fellow say that to me, and now when someone does write just those words I am unable to accept.

I cried when I read and reread your letter. It seems a pity that something every girl hopes for—to be looked up to by a man—should be thrown away so freely. I understand your position and you understand mine. And as for my telling you to become a great football star, an author, or anything of the sort—I couldn't do that. Whatever you excell in—anything—I'll just smile and say—"there's a grand fellow and I'm proud to call him a friend." For you are just that—one of the truest friends God ever made—and you're my friend.

As for the gifts you've sent me, I've enjoyed them immensely and I'll look forward to receiving any other little thing you have to offer.

I only wish I were in a position to accept all the other things you have to offer. God grant that some day you will be able to bestow them on someone who can accept whole-heartedly and with open arms.

Forever your friend—
E——

*   *   *

Oh, dear, dear diary, if you were but human that I could talk to you. I need you. You are the closest thing to me in my life. I've never felt this way before—so sad—so extremely melancholy—I can't think clearly—I don't know—but do you think that someday, someway I'll have a chance. I'll

---

2. He is probably referring to the part-time job he is seeking to replace.

wait my whole life through just to be with her five minutes at its end. Somehow I believe that there is yet a chance.

This is the first time I've really hated being part a Negro. Other times it has rather been fun—like a game—as if I were like the prince in a fairy story—under the spell of some evil witch.

Oh to think that I could fill her clear, sweet eyes with tears—brute!

But she is my friend! my friend! my friend!

Sun. Oct. 15th: Dear diary I may have to go home and take my quest elsewhere next year. Mother is paying my room rent and I can't have that, nor can she afford it. I've been everywhere but can't find work here. If I go to Northwestern I can live at home and eat at home although I shall have to pay tuition. Even so Northwestern shall be a little cheaper. I thought that by now I'd be working and saving money for school next year.

Then too Wisconsin U. hasn't claimed me as its own, enthralled me. I've given it every chance, too. This night I walked over the campus and along the lake, but nothing happened.

Fri. Nov. 17th: Well dear diary here I am back home where I've been for several weeks now my banners trailing—temporarily.

I came back by truck and on a freight train (when a man told me how to hitch one)—my dog, half a dozen glasses I was bringing to the H——s, and I.

1934

Mon. Jan. 1st: Well, Dear Diary, another. But my pen has dripped dry and I have no bright hopes or dreams for '34 nor even do I feel like writing my friends all a Happy New Year and a good morning—I just look them over to myself quietly—quietly—Nor shall I even review the old year.

Fri. June 1st: If the genie appeared to me and wanted to make me white I don't believe I'd accept. In a way it's more fun this way—being almost in incognito, on no side, able to sit on my remote hill-top and regard all humanity with a smile.

Mon. July 30th: Over to Teresa's. She and I talked from the time I came until I left at nine-thirty. I told her what was supposed to be the beginning of a story I am working on but which was really about her—and me.

Wed. Aug. 1st: Today was Joe's birthday and his dad and I were invited over. Teresa, Joe and George were there. We had almost everything to eat you can imagine, and Teresa had baked a delicious Devil's Food Cake for Joe (quite appropriate). She was exquisitely pretty today and very sweet too. She treated her dad wonderful—as did Joe, too. Judge is growing a beard and a mustache and he allowed Joe and I and even Teresa all have a shot at trimming it.

At the bewitching hour of dusk he had departed, George was out playing and Joe had disappeared. In the front room at a window sat Teresa and I was at her side. She held her mandolin, and her fingers picked out rhapsodic cords and fantasies on it. Our sportive conversation had lulled as if expecting something else—something of a serener note. I told her a story of a little boy and a beautiful woman and how this boy had always longed to kiss this lovely lady. Then I asked Teresa—"May I?"—and kissed her—for the first time.

Thur. Aug. 16th: A sudden desire struck me today to, after college, that is during my vagabond trip around the world, spend six months or a year searching for The Holy Grail. Oh not that I'd find it or am worthy of setting myself such a boon but that it would be fun—adventurous—romantic—and perhaps if it ever is found it shall be a sinner who shall find it and so be saved. Of course if I do go aseeking it I shall have to live a very fine, clear, noble life for six months ahead of time with praying and fasting.

Fri. Dec. 21st: Met Clar, with whom I played football in '28 at Englewood, in a department store at 63rd and Halsted this eve. Clar was the right end and he and I used to block to tackle together on a lot of plays.

Clar is a preacher now and of the stoutest kind. One of those preachers who travel to churches, taverns, flop houses, etc., give their sermon and then ask "testimonials" whereupon some "sinner" declares himself "saved" and tells of his past sins and his now embracing of "Jesus."

For an hour Clar lectured to me on the landing of a stairway of the store. You can imagine the Christmas crowd of late shoppers bustling past us and staring for Clar talked loud—and he waved his arms. He was set on "saving" my soul. This—his "saving" had occurred but a year ago and he was still most ardent in his enthusiasm.

I was so uncomfortable that I would have promised him anything just to get away from there. But he wanted a "testimonial" from me. "Was I saved? Had he turned me into a 'Christian'?"

I told him I was a Catholic and felt a Christian. But what I didn't tell him is my belief that real religion, real Christianity is quiet and something not on the surface, but down deep. Something like one's real emotions that one doesn't put on display and that one doesn't boast and brag of. (Will, don't let your spirit carry you away and have you ending sentences with *of*.)

I think I've found God and Christianity in sunsets and beautiful blue skies, in a sudden expression of compassion, in doing a spontaneous kindly thing, in when being with a friend feel my very heart beat warm, feel my blood pump with love for that friend because of something fine or noble he has said or done. Isn't that a bit like Christianity as Christ expounded it?

1 9 3 5

Sun. Jan. 13th: The old man died early this morning. He had been sick only a month and although very ill none expected him to pass away so soon. I cried when Touchdown died. I could find no tears for "dad" though. I'm sorry. And I'm awfully sorry for him. We didn't care for each other. We were so far removed in thought—and in method of feeling. Only once since I was a small lad was he a real father to me and that was that brief span while I was in New York. I hope he has found his God. I know God is compassionate.

Mother is taking it horribly. They would have been married 44 years tomorrow.

Death moves on swift and silent wings; its tread is stealth; its embrace the continuance of the enigma of life.

Wed. Jan. 16th: The old man was buried today. Today I saw Rita's grave for the first time. Rita—my little sister. To work after funeral.

Thur. May 2nd: Teresa came this evening at eight o'clock. The day had been dreary and it had rained. I feared she wouldn't come, especially with the weather so bad but like an angel of sunshine she came through the rain. Joe brought her over but left.

In my room we talked and she read some of my diary.

Oh I who have been hurt before had sworn so strongly that never would I again become so infatuated! I no longer dictate but yield every point to my heart and it, poor, foolish thing, is running away with itself. My brain is burning up and I don't know how I've managed to hold myself in check. Oh God give me strength to hold back. She would only laugh at me—another scalp—another trophy cup—

*   *   *

She was beautiful in a white blouse. White earrings hid in the dark clusters of her hair. Her eyes were two sharp points of humor, lively as tambourines, sparkling as white-hot coals—Oh Will, why is everything so complicated for me? Why must my heart be in one hand and doubt and fear in the other. Fear of having her now go away never to want to see me again—

This is far better. This being able to see her. This friendship with words between the lines that I dare not read aloud and which she cares not to read.

Mon. June 3rd: Sent "Shadow of Galahad" to *Esquire* Magazine.

Tues. June 4th: Over to Mrs. M——'s where I typed "November Twenty-Second" and now have it ready to send to *Liberty* tomorrow. It is now 2:30 A.M. and I have just completed "Midge" Davidson, a football story of about 4,000 words.

Sat. June 8th: Changed the title of that football story of "Peewee" Davidson and this afternoon typed it over at Teresa's.

Tues. July 16th: Completed "Horizon Chasing on a Bicycle" which is the story of my trip to New York. I shall try *Esquire* with it.

Over to Teresa's this afternoon. She was at work. Her mother is sick so I cooked supper for Teresa—pork chops, gravy and potatoes. Stayed there until after nine o'clock.

Wed. Aug. 14th: Rich over this morning. Last night Teresa told Richie that she loved him. She said that she can't sleep nights for thinking about him and that he could break her heart if he wanted to.

Thur. Aug. 15th: Rich over this early P.M. All of us went over to Tree's. We had pie and ice cream there and sandwiches later. I could read Teresa easily. She is madly in love with Rich. In the parlor she sat on the couch with him, holding his hand. She is playing us both though—burning the candle at both ends for several times she said to me "I like you! I like you!" On the couch Rich had his head on her shoulder, his eyes closed. I stooped over suddenly and kissed her. Later Rich asked me if I hadn't, saying he thought I had. We grinned about it. He thinks I am eating my heart out about her.

Fri. Aug. 23rd: The two young lovers are seated across from me in each other's arms. They seem very much taken up with each other. The game goes on merrily and Tree is doing most of the leading. She has her head on Rich's shoulder and occasionally kisses him. She is pretty tonight as every night but is being very indiscreet. Careful Tree you'll lose a heart and the game with it. Rich is rather at his ease, lying full length on the sofa and casually accepting Tree's ardent caresses—oh he's not doing half badly just now—I'd say the score is 27-6 in Rich's favor from where I sit. He is sighing little sighs and lying little lies.

Tonight I am not eating my heart out but am quite able to laugh—at life—at love—at fools in love.

Thur. Aug. 29th: Richie over. He and I with Joe and Overly played touch with the little kids in the lot across the street. Nick and Olive were here early this eve and Richie met them.

This eve Tree was over. Rich had gone out to see another girl and I had to lie him out of it. Also I hinted at some twists to make the game more interesting for him and to help her game. I think Tree is going to accept them.

We lit the two large candles, sat on the sofa with them at our feet, and smoked cigarettes as we talked softly. Tree suddenly looked at me and said, "If I did something you wouldn't take advantage of it?"

"No," I replied.

She kissed me saying "That is for my birthday." I then sat as if I was dazed and all broken up emotionally over that kiss, and I was. For a long time we were silent.

We listened to the Bear All-Star game. I warmed some spaghetti and made some tea for Tree. Her brother showed up and at 11 o'clock she went home. I kissed her good-night. No particular thrill then though.

Fri. Aug. 30th: Richie over. Tree over. They get deeper and deeper every night.

Sun. Sept. 8th: Richie was over at about 12:30. Stayed all afternoon and returned this eve. Good old Rich!

Tree met him here this eve. She is madly in love with him. We had an, to her, interesting and to me amusing conversation while he was out of the room this eve.

"You're insanely in love with him aren't you?" I asked.

"Yes," she replied simply. Tree is always frank. That's what amazes one about her.

"And I've provided you with your first love. You know you told me that you had never been in love."

Tree answered: "They say first loves never last. I'm sure this one will. I'm going to do all I can to make it live."

"Isn't love silly?" I said, sportively.

"I don't think so"—very seriously, "It's beautiful. It is beautiful."

"Yes it is. I was just being cruel. It's one of the few things that really count. One of the few things.

"You know I like you!" she said on the spur of the moment. These dashes of emotion are customary with her.

"Everyone likes me a little; no one much."

"I like you much," she replied.

"But not enough," I replied. "But you must admit that I'm acting like a gentleman about the whole thing. That I'm being true and loyal. That I'm taking it with a smile."

Her smile was admission.

I continued: "We both have Rich to think about, haven't we?"

She nodded and her eyes were misty.

Poor kid. I'm beginning to feel sorry for her. Love isn't kind. It's the worst of tyrants. It's cruel, exciting, demanding. And she, poor kid, is being completely consumed by the first flame that enkindles her heart. She's ready to sacrifice everything. Rich relates to me tonight that she is ready to go the limit. And it is he who is hesitant. Rich is swell. He never does a mean, an unkind thing. He feels that there is nothing wrong with sexual craving and the gratifying of its appetite yet he puzzles and doesn't want to do anything either he or she will regret. Then, too, he doesn't love her. Rich is my greatest paradox, my favorite enigma.

Sat. Sept. 14th: Didn't see Richie today. Saw Tree for a short while. Yesterday she wanted to tell me that she was ready to sacrifice. She wanted me to know. She asked Rich if she should tell me and finally did.

Teresa is the strangest, most unorthodox, frankest, most indiscreet girl I know. She escapes definition. And above all she is fooling herself; wants to. She's unpredictable!

Wed. Sept. 25th: Tree is married! She and Tommy were married Saturday and while Rich and I called her Saturday eve she was celebrating her wedding. Even while we waited in the car before. This needs a lot of explaining. A lot of explaining! She really went for Rich. Was really in love with him. Did she marry so that her mother could be free to marry? What happened? Where are all of her promises to Richie? And to me? She said that she would never hurt him. She told him many times when he really didn't want to hear it that she loved him. She said that her feelings would never change. What has happened? Something. I know. I shall go mad if I don't find the real reason. Did Tom try to commit suicide? He's so insanely in love with her that he might have. Or did he tell her then or never?

She will be sorry. Very sorry. And soon. Never will anyone be able to put his arms around her and kiss her as Richie did. Never will anyone thrill her as he did. She'll miss all of it. Our toasts in vinegar, our late nights to candle light, hot rolls at 2 A.M., roof climbing, all our madness and all Rich's caresses. Maybe even mine. Maybe even those that I gave with my eyes.

Poor girl. I really feel sorry for her. She doesn't use her head. She's just a little girl, an impulsive child. Those kind of people get hurt often.

*   *   *

Teresa has wittingly or unwittingly beaten us at our own game.

Fri. Oct. 4th: I have puzzled and puzzled over Teresa and can find no solution.

Mon. Oct. 7th: Went over to M——'s this morning not knowing what to expect. Mrs. M—— is moving and had me come over as she wanted to give me all of their books, for she is not taking them with her. I asked if there was anything around she wanted me to do and she asked me to take the curtains and the curtain rods down. She said "Wait. I'll get Teresa up. She's in the bedroom."

I thought Tree was at work and was surprised to learn that she was home. Took down the other curtain rods and still she didn't come out of the bedroom. I thought that maybe she was ashamed to face me after everything. Finally Mrs. M—— said: "Go on in there; she's dressed but won't get up."

I went in. Teresa was lying across the bed in her blue pajama-beach pants outfit in which she scaled the H.S. roof with us.

"Good morning Mrs.——," I said, nodding coldly. I was going to be very distant; very aloof.

"Hello, Mot," she replied humbly.

I took down the rod and then started sorting the books out of the closet that lead off from the other bedroom. I knew she'd come in there and sit on the bed as I piled the books at the foot of the bed. She did. I said nothing to her. She made some remark about a book to which I gave a cool reply. I expected her to say: "Tell Rich I'm sorry." Had she I was prepared with: "Oh no, I won't. He'd feel that it rang with insincerity just like everything you ever told him."

Or if not that I expected her to say: "Mot I'm sorry about everything." To which I was to reply: "What are you telling me for? I'm not the least bit interested. I hope you'll be happy but I don't see how anyone who lied and cheated as much as you did can ever be happy."

She said none of these things but her eyes were haunted, haunted. I went into the next room. She followed me. I went into the kitchen for something and she followed me out there. I said something to her and unconsciously the old name of endearment "Tree" that Richie and I call her by slipped out.

"Gee it's good to hear someone call me Tree," she said with a plaintive undertone in her voice.

She sat at the kitchen table, her back to the west window. She had never looked better, more charming, but I disliked her intensely for everything she had done. I made no reply and after a bit she said in a hollow voice: "Why are you talking to me?"

"Why? What do you mean?" I asked.

"You know you said if anything happened. If ever I hurt Rich."

That had me. I didn't for a second know what reply to make but finally answered: "Once a friend always a friend."

"Sit down. Sit down here," she said, indicating the chair next to her. I took it. Her foot came up on the seat of her chair, her knee at her chin in that captivating tom-boy attitude that she sometimes strikes. "Gee I'm glad to see you," she said.

"You know—" I started.

Someone knocked and a friend of Mrs. M——'s came in but went into the front of the house.

"What were you going to say?" Tree asked.

I paused for a moment, took a breath, and plunged in:

"I don't suppose," I said, "that it would matter to you if I told you that when Rich found out you were married he was drunk for two days straight, didn't go home and his folks didn't know where he was. His mother was over to my house and all over the neighborhood looking for him. And when he did go home he bawled his mother out and nearly had a fight with his father."

Oh I made quite a heroic, heart-broken lover out of my little Richie! One of the most tragic figures in all fact, history, and fiction!

Tree put her head on her knee and cried. The tears came before I had finished my last sentence and she shook with sobs. I've never seen anyone so crushed, so utterly defeated. I could feel myself choke up.

"I meant everything I said to Rich, everything I said," she said. She got up and went into the bathroom to try and compose herself, saying: "Wait a minute." When she returned her face was red and the tears still coursed down her cheeks. She tried to hide her face from me. She was ashamed of herself, ashamed of her marriage, beaten and broken. I could see that she had never had a happy moment with Tom. All my pity and compassion was her's.

She closed the door leading to the front rooms and resumed her position at the table.

"If I tell you something will you give me your word of honor that you'll never tell a soul?" She swore me a hundred times by a thousand oaths.

"Aren't I even to tell Rich?" I asked.

"You can use your own judgment there," she said, and continued: "I meant every word I told Rich. I—I'm married to Tom but I'm in love with Rich."

She continued to cry softly.

"I'm awfully sorry for you," I said.

Then she talked. Said how good it was to tell someone. Said that she now felt that she had paid her debt to her mother; that she owes her mother nothing. Simply, and without an attempt to deceive, she told:—Her mother wanted to marry. Tree was to marry and thus be taken care of. Mr. S—— (Mrs. M——'s fiance) was to find Joe employment with room and board included. George Mrs. M—— had decided to put into a home. This hurt Tree, the idea of someone of her flesh and blood going into a home. I believe this to be the main reason why she married, though she gives no excuse, no alibi, and says so frankly, states that she really didn't have to get married, although it seems that everyone is being pushed around for Mr. S——. Tree and Tommy are to take George. Tom, of course, doesn't like the idea.

Tree said she didn't herself know that she was going to get married until it happened, that she really hadn't intended to marry Tom at all.

She went on to say that she thinks of nothing but Richie. That Tom talks to her and sometimes sees her staring into space. He, Tree thinks, suspects something. She says that when Tom touches her or kisses her she feels that she is cheating on Rich.

I said that I had told Rich it used to be "our little Tree" but that it was "Tommy's little Tree" now. She said it's still "Our little Tree."

I told how Rich and I were going to send her an invitation to the 2nd annual "Caterpillar Club" just to make her eat her heart out. She said she would have come and that we were going to do that every year anyway.

She told of how she wanted badly to come over to my house, to call Rich up (our phone is disconnected), to go up on the roof, to go out to the beach.

She went on to say that her mother was marrying S—— for security but that she loved another man, a married man with a family—children.

Tree said she wanted my advice. At first I refused to give it but she insisted saying that she didn't have to take it.

Well I told her that she claimed to love Rich and that under the circumstances if I were she I wouldn't have any children, at least not for several years, that I would work if I could get a job (telling Tommy that I felt that I should do my part to keep George, as he was nothing to Tommy) and use part of the money to advance my art studies, that I would see Rich but not immediately. (She wanted to see him right away.)

She said that if she could help it she wouldn't have any children. Following this we talked birth-control and I advised her to get a couple of good books on it from the library.

She said that my ideas were the same as hers on the whole thing. About Tom I said I thought he had what he wanted, her companionship, sexual gratification from a woman he loves. Possibly I am well on my way to being an arch-villain. However now I can't feel that this is wrong. When Tree was unmarried I thought all her ideas about beauty in sexual gratification through one she loved was a lot of tommyrot. Now I feel that since her love is so deep and since she has made such a dreadful sacrifice that she is entitled to see Rich. I only hope that I can make Rich fall in love with her or that he will fall in love with her. Oh not deeply or madly but satisfyingly.

Of course we can never tell Teresa the truth about the whole affair now, though I think I was on her side all the time!

Wed. Oct. 9th: Tree is to see Richie Sunday up on the roof of school. Her idea. I have lectured them both on discretion. Tree is inclined to be headstrong. She wants to come over here to see me and sometimes to see Rich. I told her that people would talk. Say to Tommy: "Why, do you know where I saw your wife today? I think it's a shame!"

Tree replied that we were friends, that she felt that she was entitled to her friends, didn't have to give them up just because she was married.

I retorted that Tommy wouldn't feel the same way. That if I were a girl it would be different.

She says she will be discreet: she shan't. I shall have to be overly cautious and protect Rich and her.

*   *   *

I am coaching a young team of neighborhood fellows of about 16 and 17 years of age. They look pretty good. The Lions is the name of their team.

Thur. Oct. 10th: Acquainted Rich with the details last night and tonight again. Gosh how he laughed. He thinks I'm gullible after all I said about Tree being a liar, a cheater, etc., only a week or two ago. I replied that it only shows how wrong one can be. Whereas he believed everything before and I little, the tables are now turned and he laughs and says repeatedly, shaking his handsome head:

"Oh you're gullible! You're gullible!"

Sun. Oct. 13th: My Lions played and were tied 0–0 today, although they should have won by 12 points at least. It all goes back to the line. I've never had a good line. We must work that line.

*   *   *

Tree has been married 22 days today. This eve a shined and polished Rich came over, smiling and bubbling over. At 7:30 I walked him up to school to the trysting-place and restored the lovers to each other's arms.

*   *   *

12:01 A.M.: Rich was over at about 11:10. Smiling, self-satisfied, and secretive. We ate ham sandwiches. He started to talk but I told him it would keep until I finished my sandwich. He closed up like a clam. Recalled my keeping him on the bench the first half of a football game a hundred years ago because "I didn't like his attitude." He "Doesn't like my attitude" tonight and goes home with that self-satisifed, mysterious air and that maddening smile. I wonder if I shall be able to sleep?

Mon. Oct. 28th: Meeting today. No practice. Voted on a Club name. It shall be "The Knights of the Round Table" and the team shall be known as "The Camelot A.C."

1 9 3 6

Fri. Jan. 17th: Started to disappear for a week tonight. Everything was going wrong. Packed my diary books and enough paper to write stories for a week. Was going to take a room somewhere. Get away from it all. Took out my paper route and at 5:30 tramped the streets through the snow looking for a place. Sat in a hallway for an hour dead tired, could find no place. Started thinking what Rich would say, think, do. Crawled back home. Knew he'd say I was a fool!

Sun. Jan. 19th: Tree over this eve. Rich broke up with her. He told me all about it after I had walked her to the street-car (she asked me to).

He told her that it was wrong because of Tommy. That it was borrowed love. Stolen love. He even laughingly stated that he cried—that he can do so when he wants—and pressed his face against hers so that she could feel them. Rich!

Sun. April 19th: Richie woke me up at 1:20 this A.M. by knocking at my bedroom window. I let him in. He said he had plenty on his mind, that everything had happened to him and wanted to go out and drink beer. I dressed. We went to a tavern. The tavern-keeper, a portly Pole with a huge paunch who looked as if he had acquired it not by drinking too much of his own beer but by eating too well and too much, was about to close up but we slopped down three beers. Then back to my house. There he gave.

He had been over to Frances' for a peaceful evening. About 11:15 he heard someone talking very loudly in the hall below and exclaiming "I want to see Richie!" Then Frances' bell rang and Fran went to the door. Returning she told Rich that there was someone there to see him and left the door open so that she might hear what was going on.

Rich went out. There was Jean! The athletic babe he has been seeing occasionally and who has been tagging around after him. She had cornered him last Thursday and to get rid of her he told her he'd meet her at 63rd and Halsted Saturday at 10 P.M. after she was through work . . .

No one seems to know how she knew where he was. But there she was, having first rang the downstairs bell by mistake.

"What's going on? What does this mean? I thought you were going to meet me at 10 o'clock!" she exclaimed.

"What do you mean?" Rich returned, thunder struck, muddled.

"You know what I mean. And I've been waiting for you ever since 10 o'clock. Am I just an old shoe to be shoved around?"

"Aw, go on home!" Rich told her and went back up into Fran's. He had hardly closed the door before Jean was knocking insistently. Fran opened the door. Again Rich was faced by Jean. Fran's mother had been in bed but got up to see what all the commotion was about. Fran's sister and brother-in-law and father were all home and all craned their necks to see what was going on. Fran was not the least inquisitive person there, and the man downstairs lingered in the shadows below in his pants and underwear top.

"What does this mean?" Jean continued, "I wait for you all evening and find you here with another girl—after all we've been through!"

Her clenched hand went up to her forehead and she swayed on her feet—She continued—

"After all we've been through!" and then fainted,* falling prone upon the floor.

"Get up! Get up!" Rich says, unable to think, to act.

Fran's mother looks out at her. The sister and brother-in-law and father have pains in their necks now from peering behind drapes, lamps, chairs.

Finally Rich picks her up and slowly she regains consciousness but is ostensibly very weak and dizzy.

The man from downstairs comes up the steps hurriedly exclaiming:

"You sock her! You hit her! I call police!"

"I'm going to take you home," Rich tells Jean and walks her to her home only several doors down the block. She staggers all over the sidewalk and is very dizzy. They get to her house but she is unable to go in and has trouble even speaking. They sit out in front.

"I'm going. Go in the house," Rich tells her. She calls him back but he shakes off her plea with his hand, "Go in the house. I'm going."

He walks back to Fran's hoping never to see the dramatic, the athletic Jean again.

When he walks up the steps he sees his sweater and jacket in the hall! His cup! He knocks but no one will answer. He goes down to the drugstore and calls up. Fran's mother answers:

"May I talk to Frances?"

"Who is this?"

"Rich."

"No you can't! And don't you ever come here again!"

Bang.

Rich doesn't know what to do but when he thinks they're all in bed he

---

* A mid-victorian parlor game now almost extinct. [Motley's own note.]

goes back and knocks. Fran opens the door and he sticks his foot into it so that she cannot close it.

"Fran, please let me in. You've got to let me explain."

She lets him in. She has been crying but is very angry now.

He smooths it over. Explains. Explains. Gets deeper into a mesh of explanations. Fran has told him at a previous time that she loves him but he didn't tell her he loved her, saying that he and a girl named Loraine had told each other that once, had been mistaken, and had promised never to tell anyone else that until a certain thing happened. She had to be satisifed with that at that time.

Now he, as he did for Tree, puts on the weeps. (He is quite capable of crying at will.)

Cad! Bounder! Scoundrel! Villain!

She is taken in. He tells her that he loves her, away with all promises, he loves her. She cries. The place exudes with maudlin emotions, drips with tears.

(Curtain)

Rich comes to me. Blows off steam by exclaiming, "My cup! My cup!" We both are doubled up with laughs. We guffaw. He says that for a moment he almost believed that he loved her when he was telling her. We laugh. The arch-villain! The beloved gypsy!

We go on until 3:30. Then he leaves for home and I prepare for sleep with gurgling, itching, tickling chuckles.

Thur. May 14th: Tree over at 1:15 this afternoon. I made a prune cake out of a recipe her mother gave me. We kissed, Tree and I; a long held and stirring affair. Cliff came over. We got Tree's mandolin and guitar and they played for about six hours. I accompanied them on the piano on some songs.

Tree was supposed to go home at 7 but didn't go, had supper here and stayed on. She strummed again. Then we talked and finally at 20 to one Tom came for her. Mother had gone to bed and Rich, Cliff, and I sat in the parlor with Tree. Not so good. I had been begging her to go home or call Tommie up and have him come over since 10 o'clock. On the porch I said to Tom, "Come over, you and Tree, some night and play Pinnocle with us."

"Yeah, we'll play some cut-throat," he said.

That stopped Rich, Cliff and I, that squelch perfect, that retort proper. Just what did he mean by it, that dangerous statement with two meanings. Cliff, Rich and I laughed, kidded and puzzled over it for an hour and a half.

Thur. May 28th: Rich came home this evening. Old man B—— out at the cottage made unmanly advances at Rich and this evening when he sat reading the paper stooped over him and kissed him. Rich leaped up, hit him, knocking him down, picked him up again, knocked him down, and packed his things. He then demanded his pay and left, coming here for an hour before going home.

This eve later Cliff and I came here: about 10:30. Shortly Rich put in an appearance with Bozo. Shortly Bozo and Cliff went home.

Last week, Sunday evening to be exact, Rich told me not to call up at Fran's any more as her mother was sore because Fran called up here to talk to and ask about Rich.

When we were alone I asked Rich "Why aren't I supposed to call up at Fran's house?"

"Aw, her mother's sort of sore at me," he evaded.

"I'll tell you why," I replied, "Because the proud and sainted Anglo-Saxonese Miss Frances C—— didn't know exactly who I was and when she found out she was greatly and horribly shocked. You know how inquisitive I am, Rich, about everything. I wasn't going to leave any loose ends dangling and I called C—— up and found out.

"I may be wrong, but I think I'm as good as Joe, Bozo, Red, Larry, and the rest of your friends that went trailing up there, and if they didn't taint her I don't see how I could have contaminated her by talking to her over the phone. Who the crap does she think she is?

"I have breeding, a degree of intelligence, and I'm not ashamed of my batting average as a gentleman, but it appears that if you haven't that all essential white texture of skin you aren't as good as the first white pig that comes along."

I had called Fran up and she had been icy but polite. I asked her why I wasn't to call any more, asked if it was something I had said or done. (I thought possibly she was sore because I had told Rich that she was out with Bozo.)

She answered no to all my questions and kept saying "I can't say. Let Rich explain to you. Rich will explain."

I continued to pursue. She said, "It's something I found out that I didn't know."

Finally it dawned on me, the one thing I had given no thought. I asked her and she said "Yes."

I replied:

"I really didn't know whether you knew or not. I didn't think it mattered. You're an intelligent girl. Getting ready to graduate from high school. You have a mind of your own and are able to reason with yourself. Surely if Rich accepts me as a friend you should. What's so awful about it? I see no difference. Nor does Rich. I've always been a gentleman, haven't I?"

She continued that Rich would explain and I concluded by saying:

"Well I'm going to tell you good-bye. I'm sorry that you feel the way you do, and I hope you go through with the radio audition. Well, goodbye Fran."

I came home and wrote her a letter. Told her that I didn't know really why I was writing it but that I hoped that I could do her some ultimate good, show her that life didn't consist only of her family, her neighborhood, her country, her race, or even only of humanity. That I felt terribly sorry for her. That I wasn't ashamed of being a Negro, that, could I, I wouldn't deny it. That they just weren't my kind of people or the people I associated with. That I felt I was no better than they or anyone else but rather that I felt myself a citizen of the world and felt that my race was the human race. That I had no prejudices against any people, race or religion. That on the side of the Negro it must be granted that they hadn't been out of slavery 75 years and that they had progressed wonderfully. That I wasn't like those Negroes she saw up at school, that I wasn't a flat-nosed, big lipped, ignorant, pork-chop-eating, razor wielding Blackamoor. That I didn't swing from the rafters. That how could she kneel at St. Anselm's with those colored people she disliked and worship her God. That how could she imagine Christ, who was humble and consorted with thieves, prostitutes, and the down-trodden and prejudiced, be against thinking well of her. That I wasn't angry. Wasn't hurt. Just disappointed. That Rich didn't have a narrow or prejudiced thought against anyone or anything in his head. That she and he could never make a go of it. That she could never marry him now for he wouldn't stand for it if she thought I wasn't as good as she, if I wasn't to be welcomed in his home if he married. That I loved Rich better than I could a brother and felt confident he had a high regard for me.

My last lines were:

"Knowing that the friendship is all on one side I close,
                              Your friend, Will."

                    *   *   *

I sent Bill over to deliver the letter.

Now back to Rich and I in my room. I continued:

"I've known you for 8 or 10 years, Rich, and in all that time have idealized you and looked up to you. Last Sunday for the first time you came down in my estimation because you didn't give the situation the only solution it could have had. It would have been so easy. You don't love her. She had been out with Bozo the night before. Had told him she liked him and had never had as good a time with you (she didn't add that this was because you didn't act the fool, spend all your money on her and barge around in taxi-cabs). And the rottenest thing she said was that you didn't know how to dress when you went to see a girl, that you never came over to her house dressed up. You called her a cad in jest once. When she made these remarks and unbuttoned to Bozo she was really a cad.

"Then I called up about when it was all going on Sunday and after talking to you asked to talk to her. You said that she didn't want to talk to me. Then you told me not to call up there as her mother was sore about something.

"God Rich how I wish I could have been you and you I just for Sunday. I would have said 'He isn't good enough for you, eh? Well neither am I. Good-bye! And that is the last she would have seen of me. If you had wanted to talk to her I would have said 'He wants to talk to you.' And she would have talked to you or else.'' (Rich interrupted here with: "She said if she talked she would tell you right out and I didn't want you to feel embarrassed or hurt.'')

Then Rich went on to tell what had occurred. He said "What do you think I was doing sitting there letting them say anything about you that they wanted to. I told them plenty. Plenty. I told them all about you. What I thought of you. What other people thought of you. And later when Fran and I were alone I told her 'I like Will as well as I do you and certainly more than I do your mother.' We talked all about it and she cried. I went out to the toilet and when I came back into the room she was lying across the davenport her head buried in her arms. I have never seen anyone so beaten, so defeated, with nowhere to turn and no one to turn to. I sat down in a chair opposite her. She came to me, knelt down at my feet, put her arms around my legs and said, 'I know I'm no good. I'm awful and I don't deserve to even have you look at me but please believe this, however bad I am, I love you.'

"Well I couldn't walk out on her like that. And she also told me that she went out with Bozo to get even with me because she was sore with me.''

When he had finished I said "I've done you a couple of favors, haven't I? Will you do me a favor?''

"Yes,'' was his immediate reply.

"Will you break up with Fran. Tell her that you are breaking up because I asked you to. And never make up with her?''

"If you want me to,'' Rich answered without hesitation.

We talked for a couple of hours. He said much later, "I know you can't like her much Will. But don't blame her too much. I think she's true and good. A lot of it is her ignorant mother.''

Tues. July 14th: My birthday. Richie over. Then Tree. I went to the store. When I got back they were arguing about Rich having told. Poor Tree was all choked up and couldn't talk. I took sides with her. Rich didn't like this a bit although he said he wasn't sore. Tree, before he went home, held out her hand and offered her friendship.

Why shouldn't I have taken Tree's side? Rich was wrong. Tree is every bit as decent to me, and more so than Rich. She is my friend too.

Tues. Oct. 13th: Over to Tree's. She goes to the hospital Thursday to have her baby. She must have an operation because of her heart to facilitate delivery. Poor kid, I feel sorry for her and find that she is very, very dear to me.—God's finest gift—a true friend. Perhaps my only one. Johnny and I went driving this eve with Charlie and Marty (both friends of John's).

Tues. Dec. 1st: Well, dear diary, here I am on another one of these mad trips of mine. This time the lineup is John and I and the Buick. The time spent is of no importance but adventure, high, wild and interesting is our desire.

At the present moment, about 4:30 P.M., I sit in the depot at Fremont, Nebraska, catching up in my writings.

We left Chicago Sunday at 3 P.M., not having decided to leave on our trip definitely until Friday of last week.

X   X

Now for the trip—We went Lincoln highway, route U.S. 30 and had two extra tires in the car and three thread-bare tires on the wheels and one decent one. In our pockets something like $5.84. Fifteen gallons of gas in the tank and fifteen in cans.

We had our first tire trouble 34 miles from home—had three flats the first night (Sun.) and got only about 150 miles from Chicago but into Iowa—Clinton where we spent the night making our bed in the car—and a right comfortable one too!

Up at 6 after getting to bed at 2:30. The temperature in the car was 40, outside 17. Took a brisk walk about town. Started out again, John driving. Meanwhile I had my morning Chicago Tribune.

Had two flats yesterday and bought for $2.50 a tire that looked swell, carried us 50 miles and blew a hole as big as a silver dollar. We had to toss it away and creep on like a cripple. But luck, ever a friend of mine on more than nodding terms, came to our rescue and got me three additional tires for nothing, so the $2.50 purchase was profitable.

Wed. Dec. 2nd., North Platte, Nebraska, Depot, 4:40 P.M.: Dead tired John and I. Got only two hours sleep last night and that on depot benches at Fremont. Ate there, apple butter (Mrs. M——'s) sandwiches. Then changed a tire. It was cold. Asked a man in the garage near the depot if we might change it inside. He put on the light in the main garage and when we had difficulty with the rim he brought out his tools and fixed it for us. He was swell and when we thanked him profusely he shrugged our thanks off and smiling said not to forget to come by and see him when we again come to Fremont. Back to the depot to keep warm. Then at close to 12 went out to syphon gas. It took us several hours before we got 15 gallons, and at a truck we were chased and lost a five gallon can as well as its full contents. The method we are using is simple and effective. We pull up behind a car, close, lift our hood as if we were having trouble, which is, of course, a guise, sit our can down, suck on the hose and when lucky obtain a full can. So many cars however are not full enough or tilted rightly to insure success; and then too, some have locks on their tank caps. But it is in this manner only that we manage to go on and it is dog eat dog or the gentle art of getting something for nothing, a la Jim Tully. This trip shall make a very interesting story and one I someday hope to sell.

On down U.S. 30. That front tire that we put on last night was beginning to wear through as the other had. I figured that my wheels were out of line and stopped in Central City at the Dodge-Plymouth garage to inquire as to prices. The man there jacked the car up and started on it, smiling at our worried inquiries as to how much it would cost, saying only "Oh not very much."

It took him perhaps 10 minutes and when he finished I said, "Well how much do I owe you?"

"Oh—nothing," he replied.

"Gee, that's swell of you!" John enthused, "We're almost broke."

"That's what I figured," he answered, smiling.

On.

Our stomachs complained for something warm. We stopped at a farmhouse. I carried a pan, our cocoa and sugar, John two of the loaves of bread we had. I knocked and said to the woman who answered the door, "If it isn't asking too much and if you aren't busy would you please be kind enough to make us some cocoa. We haven't had anything warm since Sunday afternoon. We have two loaves of bread here that we would be glad to leave as we have more."

She invited us in, brewed our cocoa, refused our bread and fetched pictures of the new Frisco bridge, the largest in the world, and of which she, a native Californian, is very proud. Then she gave us some meat she had and when we left she shook the hand of each of us in her two hands saying, "God bless you and good luck."

What splendid people these Nebraskans are! Equalled only by the Wisconsinians! They help you, unasked; they are big-hearted, kindly, friendly. What more could anyone ask of any people or any state?

Fifteen miles from Platte we had a flat—only an inner-tube, and while fixing it John found a dime out on the lonely highway—we hold it as a token of good luck.

Thur. Dec. 3rd, North Platte, 11:05 A.M.: Sat around the depot until about 7 when we ate our supper of sandwiches and a dime's worth of coffee. Tried to sleep but were so dead tired we couldn't. Out for gas at 11:30. Tried three or four cars with no success. Previous to this a grand old westerner, Fred, about 55 years old, unmarried, living in a trailer here but spending his summers in the mountains, talked to us. He told us of his travels of going close to 1,000 miles on nothing and bringing his original 75¢ home with him. He worked it this way: He'd go to the Chamber of Commerce and tell them that he had gone broke and wanted to get home. They invariably gave him gas and oil. He directed us to the Chamber. But that would have meant waiting until morning and I was for syphoning and getting on. After our three or four flops John got disgusted and wanted to wait. I didn't. I guess I got a little sore. John refused to try to syphon so we again parked the car by the depot. I could see that he was probably right and said so. Then, as youth is ever over-confident, we were sure of succor on the morrow. So I said let's eat and we ankled down to Pierce's Cafe down the street where they dish out 10¢ and 15¢ meals. We ordered spaghetti and meat balls, potatoes and coffee. We asked the waitress, a rather plump, worldly looking, good-hearted looking medium blonde by way of the peroxide bottle if they sold cigarettes for a penny apiece.

"No we don't. Want a cigarette?" she pulled her package from her apron and gave us each one.

It was heaven sitting there eating warm food, hot liquid, smoking cigarettes and listening to a mellow orchestra playing from a Frisco nightspot.

At 1:30 we left and gave the girl a 10¢ tip. We did this because it was so impossible, so extravagantly foolish. But she had been good to us.

There was startled surprise in her eyes. I suppose she seldom gets a tip down here by the freight yards where freight-hands, trainmen, truck-drivers, hoboes and criminals make up the clientele.

To bed and slept the sleep of the dead until 8:30 this morning. To the Chamber of Commerce. Our man was out of town and won't be back until Saturday. To the Salvation Army. It was closed. To the relief station. They have no transient relief funds. Finally to see the judge of the Lincoln County Court Bldg. and asked his advice. He directed us to the court clerk, clerk of the commissioner. He was splendid, this judge.

Mr. Virgil Lewis, the clerk, said that he had been authorized until a year ago to give gas in emergency cases such as ours but that they had done away with this. But he in turn directed us to the Elks Club where he said to see Mr. De Lecy, Chairman of the commissioners. We hope for an audience at 12:30.

Jan. 15th [1937]: It's been over a month since the happenings on page 12 and memory, with all that happened, plays me a bit false. I know we got five gallons of gas in North Platte but at Pine Bluffs, Wyoming, found ourselves broke, cold, hungry, disgusted. We went to the police station, fire-house and past the Catholic priest's (as unGodly a man as I ever met) but could gain no succor. We syphoned two gallons of gas, by accident out of the priest's car, were caught by the town sheriff, old Bill Morris who wore cowboy boots and a big, big black hat and was drunk. We were installed in the city lock-up and later sentenced to terms of 30 and 60 days at the County Jail at Cheyenne, John getting only 30 days as they were to look up his record and send him back to the C.C.C.'s if his record warranted it.

Well mine is the itching pen. Of course I was not allowed my diary in my cell but at Pine Bluffs I kept it on pieces of paper, bits of bags, and at Cheyenne I wrote it on toilet paper in as small handwriting as I could. I now copy from these graphs:

Sat. Dec. 5th, Jail, Pine Bluffs: Time creeps. We have been here since Friday evening and on very light diets.

Sun. Dec. 6th: Wishing for a dog to help keep us company. Had two sandwiches (hamburger) and coffee. The turn-key gave us four cigarettes. Feel good now. This was altogether a good day. Sat on our bunk and joked. Laughed. Trotted out the old soda joke. John, who can really whistle, whistled all my request numbers and then whistled two songs that he composed. Quoted poetry. Chatted. The usual two sandwiches and coffee for supper and also some detective magazines. We saw old Bill Morris through our barred window several times today and he was either entering or leaving the tavern across the street.

Mon. Dec. 7th: Read late last night. Up early. Judge Edwards, who sentenced us, brought us breakfast and told us to prepare to leave for Cheyenne. We had hamburgers, of course. He said we move in about an hour. Asked him for news about Edward VIII. Bequeathed our magazines to the next poor inmate of these clean but dreary walls.

Later Mon. Dec. 7th, Laramie County Jail, Cheyenne, Wyoming: We are guests of the state and were incarcerated today at 12:50 P.M. being driven here in our car handcuffed together. As we were lead through the big iron doors and corralled into a row of cells the cry went up from those within, "Two more! Two more!"

Jail is a very popular place these days. There is an overflow crowd and all reservations are taken up. There are no cells for us and we will have to sleep on the floor. The jail is divided into four sections called tanks, two on the first floor and two on the second floor. Each tank has six cells and sleeps 12 men and each tank has a common corridor or bull-pen which all 12 men are allowed the freedom of from 8 A.M. until 9 P.M.; at lock-up the men have to take to their cells. Each cell has an upper and lower berth; a toilet and washbowl in the corner. John and I are in "Lower East"—that's how our tank is called.

The entire jail is absolutely clean and spotless and is done in a dull brown and silver.

Already I am rather intrigued. There are many interesting characters and I shall learn a lot about men and their manners here. Naturally every group, big or small, has a leader. The leader of Lower East we soon discovered to be Fred Nelson, a lean, good-naturedly, loud, rather attractive looking young Negro with a thin face, sharp, pinched features, a yellow complexion and a store of ready wit. He immediately took John and me in hand and made us welcome; he explained the ropes to us and had a winning way of stopping in the middle of a sentence, pulling his pack of cigarettes from his shirt pocket and saying—"Have a cigarette?"—then continuing to the end of his sentence. An old Spanish gent came to us and started a conversation saying to another inmate—"I have a couple of sons now." Then we met Buckeye—the ugliest man alive perhaps. His eyes were popped out of a pasty fat face and looked in different directions. He is about 42 and drags a lame, crooked foot after him. Shorty we noticed next. Maybe 5 foot 3 inches tall, red-faced, bald half way back, and a hefty chest encased in a red and black lumber-jacket shirt. He, we learned, follows the circus, driving a tractor or a truck. He is blunt and speaks in a husky voice. Cowboy we became aware of next. A short, dark-blonde youth of perhaps 22 with a Hawk-nose and bleak, deep-set, steel grey eyes. He wore cowboy boots and was being kidded by another prisoner. He speaks slowly to help a speech impediment and stutters helplessly when excited. He is rather quiet and weighs only about 115 lbs. His story we heard first. He walked, on a cold day, into one of the workyards on the Union Pacific Railroad. The freight-hands ordered him out. It was cold. Cowboy had a gun strapped to his waist and dared anyone to put him out. Thirty days. José is a Spanish-Cuban, thick-lipped, dark. Perhaps 24 years old.

The inmates here are not without humor or friendliness, or any of the virtues of men of honor and respect. In fact they are like one big family and take to heart the troubles of each other. They play cards most of the time, sitting on the floor about a piece of blanket and engage in interesting games of poker, pinochle and Black-Jack; and also occasionally craps. They play for sacks of tobacco, and prison inventiveness has given them very ser-viceable chips. They use the tags off of sacks of Bull Durham tobacco and have a cigar box of perhaps 250 chips. For a sack of tobacco the banker pays out 25 chips. They are laughing and joking at their cards now and one is amazed at the lack of cursing and vileness involved. In fact this jail is like a rather refined club of middle-class men. They are careless, happy, non-snobbish. And friendliness and fellowship runs high.

Fred is 24. Later in the day he told us his story. He has been here 34 days waiting trial. I will let Fred tell his own tale—"I copped a gang of stuff in a suitcase. The papers said it was worth $175 and I wouldn't have gotten caught but some colored gambler here who runs a big place and is trying to stand in good with the big shots tipped them off. I was down at Johnny Baker's pool-hall shooting a game when they caught me—Have a cigarette?—Two old big dicks came in and said they wanted to see me out-side. Well I hit that sidewalk in stride and took off down an alley with them after me shooting their guns. Man, they couldn't hit the side of a barn. Well it was night out and dark and I tore up this alley and climbed up a roof. They had all of Cheyenne's police force after me and about 25 soldiers. I went over the roofs and them after me. Man they had so many flashlights that it looked like New York City! And those cops were scared as they could be. If I had had a gun and taken a shot at them they would have killed each other getting out of the way—Have a cigarette?—They were all over that roof. I was laying on the roof laughing my can off. Right near me stood a couple of soldiers with guns and flashlights and their knees were knocking together, no foolin' man!''

Tues. Dec. 8th: I am to cell in No. 5 with José the Span-Cuban. He talks. He has been in jail seven times and has eight more days to serve of this present term. Once, though I learned this from another prisoner, he served eight years for rape. But José, the rapist, is O.K.; he treats me swell and has "wised me up" a lot. Shorty and Buckeye called me in their cell—No. 6—and asked me sly but rather obvious questions. Like many men shut up in prison for extended terms, deprived of one of life's greatest excitements, they are prone to pervertness and their inquisition was to find my status. At first I was a little angry, but anger cooled and interest in these men and their minds for the sake of my pen took its place. José too was rather queer and when Shorty said of John "I could like him—he's a good looking kid," José said to me "You're not so bad yourself." But such is life and it takes all kinds.

For the 20th time I have pleaded with the jailer to bring my little black bag to me so that I can shave. He promises but does nothing. His name is Bud.

I look like Jean Valjean. I haven't had the caress of a razor in about nine days.

For supper we had beans, a roll, bread and coffee. At last they bring my razor and I shave and bathe; then I start my diary on toilet paper and secret it in the wall each night. Wish John were here, after lockup, the nights are long and dull and sleep must be coaxed. Tomorrow is Wednesday. Letter writing day, and we are allowed to write two letters each week.

This eve I sat with Shorty and got his story. He has been on the road for 36 years; since he was 12. He says of himself that he is just a drifter, can always get a job but never will work in one place more than three weeks at a time. He has been home only once since he was 12, that time two years ago. His mother has buried him four times. "Once I was killed in a railroad wreck and they even sent my body home."

"Who's body did they send?" I asked.

"Christ knows," he replied, "I don't."

It has been grape-vined all over the jail that there is to be a "shakedown" tonight. A shakedown is a search of the cells for goods, such as razor blades, more than two blankets, more than one coffee cup. There is a great bustle. Cells are cleaned up, extra cups hidden, blankets stuffed through the bars to the trustee to be put away until after the shakedown. Here they come: The Shakedown. Bud; a city cop, big, young, handsome, tough; two deputies. We are taken out of our bull-pen, corralled and locked in a small adjoining corridor. Buckeye asks: "Hey, Bud, are you expecting an inspection by the big shots."

"Yeah. We're beating them to it."

They made a thorough inspection of each cell. Flashing flashlights, tossing out tons of magazines, confiscating blankets and extra cups.

We stood, grouped together, behind the bars watching the inspection of our cells. A convict crept stealthily up to me and revealed in the palm of his hand an old brooch with a big glass stone in it. "I've got the crown jewels of Russia on me" he whispered. This was my introduction to Reese. Reese is dark, rather handsome, with a dash of curly black hair and an aquiline nose. He's quite a clever fellow with a witty sense of humor. Has *Esquire, Forum* and the better magazines sent in to him. Later we sat in his cell and talked literature.

Jim Tully, football. He is a graduate of Georgia and played football against Albie Booth.

Monk is a trapper from the hills. He has no teeth in front; wild, watery-blue eyes and wild, limp dish-water blonde hair. Bristles of a beard show on his face. He is forever kidding or telling some wild story and his voice alone is laugh-provoking.

Wed. Dec. 9th: Said my morning prayers, tumbling out of bed as soon as they unlocked our cells. Exercised. Took my morning's shower. Early this morning some one of the inmates yelled: "Motley you're wanted on the phone!" I started. But sure enough it was so. When one from the tank above wants to talk to someone in our cell he knocks on the water pipe, linking up the two sinks. Where the pipe emerges from the tank above's floor and our ceiling there is perhaps a one inch hole all around the pipe. John wanted me. We talked there for a while and I promised to call him back tomorrow. He says he is getting along O.K. Today we were finger-printed and thus it was that I saw John for a moment as they lead him down the stairway from the tank above. He wore his olive-drabs and looked pale. "Hello John." "Hello Will."

Talked with old Padre. He's a nice old man with white mustache, dyed at the edges from tobacco. Padre got 30 days for selling a bottle of whiskey to an Indian. Padre, as the name implies, is Mexican; his real name is Martinez, and is in his 60's. Austria (or Nick, I call him Austria) is from the old country and is Padre's cell mate. They are my neighbors. Austria told about the war, the attack on Russia, about France and Italy stepping in, about the great number of wolves they had to fight, wolves so bold that they prowled the streets and the dugouts, about the meals, horse meat the size of a quarter once a day only, black bread and a tablespoon of beans—this and this only for practically every meal.

Lock-up. Lay on my bunk with the luxury of an *Esquire.* In the tank above we could hear Captain yelling and shouting wildly and preaching. He's a queer fellow in the tank above and to the west "Upper West" who when lock-up comes and the lights go off starts his mad act that continues until the early hours while the rest of the prisoners shout to him to shut up and curse at him. Every night when the lights go off we hear him yell across to some inmate in "Upper East" above us: "Oh Peterson!" in a long drawn, high pitched, humorous voice.

"What do you want Captain?" invariably comes the reply.

And then Captain always replies either: "Good night dear," or "I love you."

Everyone in our tank thinks he is crazy. He surely sounds like it.

Thur. Dec. 10th: A Negro man was thrown in tonight drunk. He was about 42. Bud the jailer announced to the trustee who enters new men's names on the blackboard: "Name's Brown." Brown: "Jack H. Brown."

Our little family gathered around him. Someone offered him a cigarette; everyone offered condolence. Brown was willing to talk: "Ah got mah W.P.A. pay an' ah went out an' got drunk. Ah don't care a damn how long ah stays here. Ah froze to death on the W.P.A. last winter. Ah saw a woman last night an' ah was drunk on top of it. That will last me six o' seven months. Yes sah! Ah told him. He asked me if I evah stole anything. Ah said 'Yes sah! Yes sah but ah ain't nevah been caught. Goin' to steal again in this damn depression.' " Later, left alone, Brown sang: "Come to Jesus with everything you need."

Fri. Dec. 11th: José uses marahauana (spelling?), hates liquor. Took my bath. Walked a mile today. When I told my cellmates that I was going to walk a mile they looked at me queerly—but I did just that, measuring off the distance of the length of our tank and estimating how many trips its length comprised a mile.

I like Hockersmith. He is in cell one in our tank and is doing the hardest time of any one in jail perhaps. He is 29 years old and is here on a felony charge. He won't be tried until April and his bond is $1,500 so he will have to stay here until his trial. He has four children and what is hurting him most is that since he came in his wife has started suit for divorce against him. He almost cried as he said that he wishes he could see his kids tonight. He is from Pine Bluffs. A farmer there owed him $5 but wouldn't pay. Hockersmith's kids were hungry so he stole a bushel of wheat from the farmer, approximately amounting to what the farmer owed him. He was caught and sent here.

Sat. Dec. 12th: Bath. Called John. Split a sack of tobacco with him that Popeye gave me. José told of marahanna. Has paid as high as $5 for it. The first time he took it he said he passed out and slept for 62 hours. The next time he tried it he vomited for three days.

Mon. Dec. 14th: The sting has gone from my imprisonment—I am enjoying it! A new experience, a new world of men and manners to study. New things to write about. Prunes for breakfast.

Captain was put in our tank today. It seems as if he was enjoying himself too much upstairs, having too good a time, making too much noise. I don't know what I expected him to look like—he has the wild dark eyes I imagined but there imagination and fact parted. He is a rather good looking man of perhaps 40. Slim, medium height, the features of an Englishman, dark straight hair part of which fell over his forehead and gave him the appearance of a boy—a bad boy. And he was badly in need of a shave. Suppertime came and he refused to eat, saying he is on a hunger strike. Also he has become quiet and subdued. The day's most pleasing experience was seeing, by pressing my face against the bars and looking down the hallway as far as I could, a rectangle patch of blue and white sky.

Tues. Dec. 15th: Last night sleep came early over a dull book. This morning I bathed then had mush and an egg for breakfast. Padre today told me that I must come to Riverton (Wyoming) and visit him. He lives alone having a small house near an Indian reservation. Today we here in prison learned from the outside trustee when he came in to bed that King Edward VIII has abdicated. I am sorry to hear this as he is a man I admire and esteem and now we have an England without him. It isn't a happy picture.

Gibbons, a young Negro of 20, loud, blatant; cocky, defiant, conceited was—like Capt., transferred to our tank today. He stole a 1936 Packard and was doing 90 miles an hour when he was caught. He has been in three reform schools and broke out of all three. They also now have a white slavery charge against him. He claims to have consumption and had a hemorrhage. He doesn't want to go to reform school but to a State Pen. Hockersmith said: "It would be better if you were sent to a federal penitentiary. You can take up a trade there. You can learn something there." Gibbons: "I don't want to learn a Goddam thing."

Wed. Dec. 16th: Tonight Capt. cleaned Popeye of all the tobacco he had with his card tricks. Everyone was grateful: Capt. is the best liked man in jail; Popeye the worst liked in our tank.

Capt. is a real character. One of the most generous persons I ever knew, considerate, humorous, witty. There is only one thing I dislike him for, hate him for at the moment: He blasphemes. He bends God's name in half with ugly jests, wicked curse words. He starts the Lord's prayer and concludes it so vulgarly so profanely that one wants to stuff fingers in one's ears and scream at the top of one's voice to shut out his dreadful, mocking or harsh words.

It is strange that he is so for he has been a Captain in the Salvation Army for years, preached on street corners, etc. And then on the other hand he has told me some revealing things about the Salvation Army. Cheap conniving, cheating tricks they who beg money on the streets and handle it in the name of the organization use. Forgetting to turn money in. Buying whiskey with it. Defrauding, immoral, thieving, lying, hypocritical.

Captain himself is here in jail on a charge of larceny against the Salvation Army. He is pleading not guilty—claims he isn't guilty—and has to lie here in jail and rot until Federal court convenes.

Lock-up. Captain's voice floated back to me from Cell One to Cell Five as he talked about the chain gang: "Punishment? They put your arms and legs in appropriate holes and have a regular beater work out on you. That's all he does for a living. You should have seen my back after one of these little parties! Oh it didn't hurt. As they say down there your feelings are just hurt."

The men listened in silence. The lights shuttered out—all but those that stay lit night and day.

Thur. Dec. 17th: Cowboy and José left today. Cowboy, we learn, owns 700 head of horse himself in Nevada but wouldn't write his folks to get him out as he was ashamed to let them know where he was. We all gave Cowboy quite a send off, Reese particularly, kidding him a lot as the Cowboy stood in his high-heeled boots, slipped on his big hat and waved back to us where we stood grouped about the barred door of our tank shouting good-byes colored with a touch of nostalgia.

Tonight Gibbons stated quite boldly that he uses dope and that he passed the time quite pleasantly in another jail where, with money, he could get all he wanted. A woman often came there to see her husband, bringing her little daughter along. While the wife and husband clung in each other's arms, kissing lingeringly, the child, as she had been taught, slipped the dope into her father's pocket. He told of another dope that looked like an aspirin pill but that they in jail dampened them and wet a cigarette with them. Gibbons wished for some tonight.

Tonight was the most enjoyable evening I've spent in jail so far. Crazy Captain Cardiff was at his best, telling stories and jokes and singing songs, all in such a loud voice that the whole jail profited—

"Well, well, well here we are all at home for a quiet evening. Upstairs we have that damn sheep-herder Blake who stole a bushel of wool and has been trying to pull the wool over our eyes ever since (this brought a big laugh). And then we have Hockersmith who broke the stock market on a bushel of wheat—and Willie—little Willie Motley from Chicago. They threw him in jail for syphoning a pint of gasoline—30 days for a pint. It's a good thing he didn't get a full can—" on and on he shouted and kidded or yelled up to Peterson—

"Oh Peterson!—"

"What do you want Captain?"

"I love you Peterson!"

Then, immediately—"Oh Shoemaker!"

"Yes, Captain?"

"Goodnight dear."

"Goodnight Captain."

It was after midnight and still the revelry kept up. As each night Capt. and Popeye shouted at the top of their lungs the one line they knew to a Wyoming Cowboy song—

"Round up the cattle and give me my cattle for Wyoming's my home."

How their voices echoed through the whole jail as they sang this line. Every night when the lights go out they break into this song and at intervals whenever they think it's getting too quiet they burst into it. I've awoken at 1 and 2 o'clock to hear that song go booming its way through jail, clashing on each bar.

Sat. Dec. 19th: Tonight we gathered before our little home on Main Street and had a Sat. night meeting. Spontaneous humor and good fellowship still reigns. Monk is swell: a real character. Spent the evening after lock-up working out next Fall's Camelot football plays.

Sun. Dec. 20th: I am absolutely happy. They claim that all we short-timers are to leave tomorrow—a Christmas present to us—that each year they let out a lot of men. It is Reese who authorizes the rumor saying he has absolute information. The news has grape-vined its way all over jail. I have enjoyed this time here—It has been a real experience. But I shall be glad to go.

I am to go!—John and I—free!—to roam!—free!—Back in the world for
Christmas.

Read most of the day. Played some Casino. John called me. Worked
on the football plays. Had a good supper. Veal roast with dressing,
potatoes, gravy, a quarter of an apple pie apiece.

Gibbons has been celling with me almost since José went. He sees me
kneel down to say my prayers each night and tonight as I write he said he
wanted me to pray for him tonight. He goes to trial tomorrow.

Hope—you beautiful angel! Hope in my heart. God on my lips. Joy in
my body. This is the best of possible worlds!

Mon. Dec. 21st: Still in jail but happy. I'm a trustee now!—The outside
trustee! I have the most envied position in jail! I have been on the street! In
the alley! Seen houses and people. There are two trustees, an outside and inside trustee. Those two men went home today, their time being up. Reese
was one of them. Red Peterson was made inside trustee; his duties to go
from tank to tank when called, keep halls and stairways clean and give the
men their razors, etc. My duties are to help in the kitchen, wash pots, peel
vegetables.

Christmas Day, 1936:   Pat could get out of jail if he could raise $10. Other-
wise, he must serve time until April 5. Captain has decided to get Pat out
and gave him the $3 he had in the office. Then he pulled off an almost
brand new pair of shoes and said he'd sell them to anyone for a dollar, Red
Peterson stuck his hand through the bars, took them, tried them on, asked
me what I thought of them and gave up the dollar by writing an order to
Bud to put a dollar to Pat's name in the office records. Then Red said:
"Captain, I still got a dollar in the office. Pat can have it." Monk "Well by
heck I got $2 and Pat you're damn welcome to it."

Captain: "Come on fellows we need only $3. We aren't going to let Pat
stay in here—you're God damn right we aren't.—Willie take this sweater up
to Upper East and see if you can get 50¢ for it."

Then Shoemaker added a dollar to the sum.

Monk: "I have a Chesterfield coat I'll sell for a dollar to get Pat out."

Hockersmith: "I have a coat I'll sell too."

Such generosity, such fellow feeling, especially in jail makes one's eyes
smart with tears—

Who wrote?—"There's no honor among thieves."

Tues. Dec. 29th: Routine day in kitchen. I don't find as much interest
down here as above in the tank. Spaghetti for supper. Got a letter from
sister. Took John a sandwich and an orange when I went up tonight. Talked
with John's cell-mate, a Mr. Craig. He is doing 30 days for riding the
freights. He said he saw us at the depot in North Platte. John remembered
seeing him but I don't. He is an electrician and for years worked in

Hollywood mostly at the M.G.M. studios. He says Myrnna Loy is as pretty as she is on the screen. Says Clark Gable is a regular fellow. Shoots craps with the electricians and is lucky. Tosses winnings to the men with torn gloves or worn overalls. He says there is always a good time when Marion Davies works a picture. She often comes on with a carton of cigarettes. Up on the ceiling the electricians will be guiding lights and gunning them down on the set. Marion Davies tosses package after package of cigarettes up to them and laughs when they miss them.

You know, dear diary, I see no difference in these men here in jail than those on the outside other than that these are a little more kind, a little more friendly, a lot more generous and have a large capacity for laughter. Swell fellows: real friends.

Thur. Dec. 31st: Bud told me today that John and I are to get out on the 5th of January. That's Wednesday! Free! Worked hard today, scrubbing, peeling spuds.

1 9 3 7

Fri. Jan. 1st 1937: There they go! The bells!! It's New Year's Day!!! Another year—1937. And strange—I never expected to welcome a New Year in jail. Yet stranger still here in prison I have discovered the secret of life—of success—learned it in jail and from a hobo:

"Never be so mad as to doubt yourself!"

X   X

To review 1936: It was at best a sorry year. The club broke up, life went stale, brother and Edith came to live with us. We took that sorry trip in the Model-T Ford, I was hurt by Fran, I found, by his own repentent admission, that Rich hasn't been my true friend—but have his vows of renewed and real friendship. My poor Tree has her baby, my poor Tree is hurt by almost everyone but me, football came and the team wasn't all I expected it to be, Fran has won Rich—I spent Christmas in jail. While this time here has been the most interesting of the year still prison during the holidays is a sad experience. Holidays are days meant to be spent with one's friends and loved ones—

So now—a year, another volume closed—I look to the new!!—On!!!—

From jail I pen it: Happy New Year Tree—Rich—Mother—Mrs. H——Jack—Fred—Marv—all—all of my friends—Happy, Happy New Year!!!

Wed. Jan. 6th: "Sweet land of liberty": I write this a free man! Man's greatest glory and finest privilege is again mine—Freedom. I was released at 11 A.M. But John's time isn't up until tomorrow morn so I am waiting for him and sleeping here in jail. Amusing—I got 60 days, John 30—and I get out a day ahead of him!!

Captain is holding sway while I write this. It is 12 midnight and the fools won't go to sleep. The jail is rocking with laughter at Captain's jokes, Popeye's songs. And above all Monk's wild cochination pierces the babble in shrieking loudness.

Here it comes!—They threw a very dark, slow talking Negro in and Captain is going to let him out: Red Peterson has handed him a spoon and

Capt. in his No. One cell near the barred door at the entrance to our tank makes noises like a key grating in a lock. He calls, imitating Bud's voice: "Moore you're going out get your stuff together."

Moore bounded off his bunk and is blubbering: "Yes sah! Yes sah!"

The jail has quieted down until not a murmur is heard and everyone is holding his sides.

Capt.: "Throw your blanket out."

Moore sticks his blanket between the bars of his cell.

Capt.: "Throw it out into the middle of the floor. Alright now throw your cup and spoon out."

The blanket sails out upon the bullpen floor followed by the cup and spoon.

Capt., making a noise against the bars with the spoon: "Stick your hand out Moore so that I can see what cell you're in."

Moore complies.

Capt.: "The door seems to be stuck. Shake it Moore."

Moore almost tears the door down shaking it.

Capt.: "It doesn't open. Stick your hand out again, Moore!"

Moore does.

Capt.: "Stick it our farther!"

Moore does.

Capt.: "Have you got your hand out?"

Moore: "Yes sah Mr. Jailer!"

Capt.: "Stick it up your ass!!"

—And the jail comes down in gales of laughter. Who said there is sadness and repentence here. My belly aches from laughing.

And now comes the time to say goodbye, to end my days in jail: We've had a jolly time here. We laughed and were never near that black hole of despair. I learned a lot about fellowship, about compassion and best of all about that king of kings—Laughter. And how to have a good time on nothing and get a laugh out of nothing and everything.

Here I have had a place to dream—to study men—a school of experience—a home—and not the worst in the world.

Mon. Jan. 11th: Well here we are in Portland, Oregon, after one hard, long grind of 770 miles from Pocatella, Idaho, without a stop for sleep. For 36 hours straight we stayed at the wheel grinding out the dreary miles, in fact we didn't even eat, so low had our funds become. And neither of us could relax and go to sleep for fear the other should fall asleep too. That way disaster lay. So we sang every song we knew and John whistled all the songs he knew and we joked and play "Remember," a game of my invention (Such as: *Remember* the day we had chili at Chili Mack's at 59th and State? *Remember* the night we drove Peggy and Mary out to the airport?)

In fact we did everything we could think of to keep awake even asking each other such questions as: Where did you go to school? What is your address in Chicago? etc.

In fact we nearly had a crash. John was driving. I fell asleep. We were negotiating an ice-coated length of highway. On either side the trees were coated half an inch thick with solid ice and looked like crystal trees. John too fell asleep and I was suddenly awakened when I felt the car leave the highway and head for the ditch. "John!" I yelled and he startled awake and grabbed the steering-wheel. The car skidded madly and turned completely around, heading back east. That was our closest call. But the last 90 miles were the hardest.

We left Pocatella at 9:15 A.M. shortly we passed the Thousand Springs, Springs that leap from the sheer walls of the hillside and which are believed to be the outlet for the Lost Rivers. Picked up a hitch-hiker and John and I made a rule to always pick up every hitchhiker we have room for.

We made Boise at 6 P.M. Ate and discovered we had but $6 left. Crossed into Oregon. Travelled Baker, La Grand. We were nearly frozen. Garages were 20 miles apart. It was well below zero. Had we had a blowout or motor trouble halfway between stations we would probably have frozen to death. At La Grand we started through the Blue Mountains. There I was witness to the most beautiful sight I've ever seen. Snow had fallen all night and driving that night we had been driving across the rugged Oregon scene through tunnels of trees and climbing higher and higher into the heart of the blue mountains. As dawn came we woke, as it were, to a wonderland, a fairyland. Everything was green and white against the lightening sky. There was the most beautiful thing I've ever seen!! It was as if one had compounded the most beautiful Xmas cards in the world into a composite picture. The beautiful Xmas Trees stood alone, in twos, in threes and in groups. The green of the trees on the blanket of the new fallen snow. The rolling hills and steep mountain heights of the background. For miles we climbed up, up, up, snaking along the edge of the mountain crest on a precarious perch of ribbon width snow clogged road until at last the summit was reached and the panorama below made one gasp at its stark beauty. Then for miles we fell—fell into the very heart of the embracing mountain scene.

John drove. One of my feet was near frozen but all I could say, while holding my aching foot as John curled around the curves at 10 and 15 miles an hour (as the roads would allow no faster going) was: "Gee! It's beautiful! It's beautiful!"

John only suspects I'm crazy—I know it.

But honestly—I am learning what beauty is—it isn't in the features of a girl—the rugged physique of an Apollo-like youth—the twisting run of a star-half-back—the lovely, haunting lines of a sonnet—God has scattered it indiscriminately over his Paradise—for Paradise is not a secluded, sequestered spot but is this entire, great world of ours—even Laramie County Jail!!

And most seriously—I like to think of having a retreat, a mountain fastness in the Blue Mountains—a place there to write—a fine place, a suit of armour and two rare swords crossed above the fireplace. And I like to think of Rich, Tree and I buried there side by side—or on the beautiful Lake Mendota, Madison, just far enough back from the shore to be under the shelter of the beautiful trees.

Sat. Jan. 23rd:　We drove on down to Santa Clara and saw Santa Clara College. Out on the highway again. A hitch-hiker hailed us. The hiker was a woman of about 42. "Hello! Where are you going?" she asked. "Bakersfield," we replied. "So am I," she answered.

"Climb in!"

Well she wasn't in the car long when we discovered that she was crazy. Two squirrels ran across the road. She said: "I own those squirrels—I have two more at home." She went on to supply the information that she had named the president. John looked at me uncomfortably. We sat in a long silence. She continued her idiot monologue. But, dear diary, you know me!—It wasn't long before I was having a lot of fun playing her game. I told her that John was Napoleon and that my name was Alexander the Great. I said: "I wanted to be Napoleon but he beat me to it and I had to be satisfied to be Alex the Great." "Oh!" she said, "I like your name better than his!"

Today we drove past oil wells and cotton fields—the first we had ever seen. Buns for lunch. Arrived at Bakersfield late in the afternoon and tidied up a bit. John let me wear his sweater which I have liked since the first time I saw it on him.

John's sister was surely surprised and happy to see him and lead us into her tiny little cottage. She is as pretty as John said she was. She fixed us one fine supper but apologized: "This isn't much but it was on such short order. I'll do better tomorrow." We had huge T-bone steaks, mashed potatoes and brown gravy, string-beans, cheese, sliced peaches and cake.

I met her husband Orvel and although he seems nice there is something about him that doesn't seem to ring true. It is close to 12 o'clock now and John and I are going to turn in on the folding davenport.

Sun. Jan. 24th:　Up at 7. To church at St. Francis' near the City Hall. Back to breakfast of waffles. After breakfast one of John's relatives came for him to take him to the airport and up with his sister's brother-in-law who is an aviator. John wanted me to go along, but Orvel said, no, he wanted to talk to me. He asked me to come outside with him. He said that I couldn't stay at his house, that I was a Negro, that he couldn't have me there in his house, especially during the day when he was away and when I'd be there with his wife, that here people stayed in their place, the Negroes, Jews, Mexicans, that his brother had told him that if he didn't get me out of there that he would kill the both of us, that his mother and step-dad were southern—and he said a lot of other things. The whole thing took the wind out of my sails. I had never run into anything quite like it.

"Here," he said, offering me five dollars, "Take this. I'm not trying to buy you off but you may need this. After all you were nice to John. Leave town today."

"I don't want your money," I told him refusing it.

"It will be better if you leave now and don't see John again," he told me in a more or less persuasive tone.

"Oh no, I couldn't do that," I told him, "After all John and I are friends. We came here together and I'm going to see him and tell him just what has happened. After all you surely wouldn't object to that."

"Well I don't think you should. It would be easier on him if you didn't—"

"Easier on him to think I ran out on him—I've never run away from anyone or anything no matter how unpleasant a situation is. And furthermore I'm not going to leave town. I have a game to play here. I'm going to write letters home from here and receive them here for a while. No one will ever know this happened. They will think that I stayed here a while."

—So John and I were both up against the same thing—prejudice. It's a funny world. However the situation is neither my fault nor John's. We like each other. We suit each other. I never ask what color my friends are, what nationality; I never ask if they are rich or poor. I never ask what church they go to or even if they believe in God: I love them for themselves.

Later John came home his eyes glowing as he told of his plane ride. I said: "Take a walk with me John, will you?"

"Sure," he replied easily.

We set out. I said after walking a long, long time in complete silence: "I have something to tell you."

"Yeah?"

"I hardly know where to begin."

Then again I was silent for a long time as we walked along aimlessly.

Finally I told him and all he could say was—"Gee, Will—I never knew—I never thought—"

I told him that his brother-in-law didn't want me to come to the house any more even and asked him to meet me in front of the post office any day between 8 and 9 P.M. He agreed.

Parked my car in a vacant lot several blocks from where John's folks live—My car shall be my home for a while. Sat and read some Robert Service poems from a small volume I brought with me. Dusk came on. I recited aloud all the poems I knew. Sang all the songs John and I sang on our way. When I came to the song "Me and the Moon" it brought a momentary catch to my throat. It was John whom I first heard sing this song and it has been our theme song. To bed in my car at 8 P.M.—Turned the front seat down and arranged my duffle bag and other things to make a fairly comfortable bed.

Mon. Jan. 25th: Await now the hour of meeting John. Later: John didn't come. I guess he couldn't get away. I waited from 7:25 until 5 after 9. Came home and looked at my hands and tried to understand why it should all be just because my hands are a little dusky.

Tues. Jan. 26th: Up at 8. Washed up in the County Court bldg. Walked streets and went into every store looking for a job but had no luck. It is noon now and I am eating breakfast—6 doughnuts. They are really rather good and fresh too though a day old. They cost me a penny apiece. Wonder what John is doing? Later: Walked—Walked—Walked—No luck. My feet ached so I sat in the library for a short while. Ate supper—4 doughnuts (I am going to live on a dime a day). Again John didn't show up. But I saw him tonight. I walked past his house in slouch hat and overcoat. He sat in the window and was talking to Orvel. Found an orange on the highway and ate it. Looked at my hands again. To bed. Blue.

Wed. Jan. 27th: This evening I waited as usual but John didn't come. God how long your days are! How black and unbearable your nights! Walked to the house and saw John get out of a car and go in. He wore his blue and gold sweater. Back "home" where I lit my kerosene lamp and hung it over the steering wheel. Read for a while but went to bed early—you know I am 2,200 miles from my friends and folks.

Thur. Jan. 28th: To mass. Got General Delivery letters from Tree and Mrs. H——. Mrs. H—— said the Ragged Strangers had a sign in their window that I was in jail. I laughed when I read that! I must write to them! Ate five do-nuts shortly before noon. Walked. Saw John's sister in a store near their house. I gathered wood and am now cooking Lima beans—1½ lbs. They shall be today and tomorrow's supper. Later: My beans are done and I have just had a pot of them. Lima's never were better. I am at peace with the world—even those who hate me. Still later: I have seen John. Walked up to the house this eve at about 7:30 and after hanging around a long time I whistled him out. He brought some of my things I had left there and we walked to my car and sat in it for a while. John seemed different, absolutely broken and dead tired. He has been working hard and showed it. I asked: "Things are the same between us, aren't they? You don't feel like they do, do you?" He assured me that we were as we had always been. He promised to come back tomorrow or Sat. I feel better than I have for a week.

Mon. Feb. 22nd: [In Los Angeles I] happened to stray along Towne Street—a short street but interesting and colorful. It is there that the bums, the unemployed, the jetsam and flotsam hang out. In a small lot roped off a woman evangelist preached to benches filled with perhaps 60 men, old and young, stooped and beaten, of all races. She was fat, surely 40, and enthusiastic over the "saving of souls." She yelled: "Raise your hands, all of you who want to come to Christ and accept the Lord." Two responses. Sheepish grins and sly looks from some—they were waiting for one thing: the free meal.

On the side, on a reserved bench, sat perhaps six women well past their youth, followers of the evangelist. One, about 50, a mop of false-blonde hair that stood up like a Zulu's grimaced maddingly at the crowd. A bulletin read: "No more beans today. They can serve you bread and coffee, first come, first served. So come early."

Under a tall palm tree that reached approximately 25 feet into the sky stood a piano. Presently a woman drummed out a hymn and sang in a cracked, amateurish voice.

I stood a while then wandered down the street away from the "Union Church."

The evangelist had competition. Three lots down (541 Towne) a sign read: "People's Forum. Self-Education Is Our Aim." A rat-faced man held sway. He gesticulated and scowled as he propounded on the government. He had more followers than the evangelist. In front of his benches stood a weather beaten stand tacked with aged signs advertising tobaccos, cigarettes and magazines. Pop and candy as well as tobacco were being sold over the rough board counter. A worn checker-board set up for play commanded a portion of the counter. Old magazines with frayed covers and yellowed pages sold for a penny apiece. But our instructor had competition too.—

Down a little ways a little old man in a thread-bare suit, soiled with tobacco ashes, stood in the doorway of a garage. His eyes continually shifted up and down the street as if vigilant for the appearance of the police on the scene . . . .

He had a grey, nicotine-stained mustache and a goatee, short, dirty teeth, a rasp for a voice and an ugly goitre-like growth on his neck. But intelligent eyes with a glint of Voltaire in their depths looked out cynically and sarcastically from behind heavy shell-rimmed glasses: He was the most interesting person among the bunch. But the bad boys always are. And most likeable.

He said: "I've been arrested 78 times and each time the judge asked me "What church do you belong to—"

He turned and pointed to a sign displaying a beautiful reading—"Your Mother loves You" and "Watch your step."

"There—" he said, "is your church. The bible teaches that your wife is your church and you are its head." He laughed.

Continuing: "These church people get you worked up, enthused—and then get your money. There are three reasons why people go to church: for social pleasures, business matters, and to go to heaven. Well heaven is supposed to be up past the sun and the sun is 73 million miles away. Who wants to go on that kind of a hike? . . . . God gave life to everything; even the bed-bugs that bite you, you suckers. When you die you're dead. You'll get no body when you lose this one. Science proves that. When a thing dies it's dead. When Christ died he was dead."

Sat. March 6th: Worked at Mrs. Smith's all morning making $1.50. Then downtown—along Main Street. Gosh I'm crazy about Los Angeles, present city of my adoption; it's so cosmopolitan. Everything can and does happen here—all people rub shoulders on Main Street: the Hawk-nosed Jew, the hurrying little Japanese lady, the big blonde Swede, the Mexican peon, beautiful-eyed senoritas, the inoffensive little Chinaman, the shuffling Negro, the laughing Irishman. Los Angeles and especially Main Street is a show-case of the world, a barometer of appetites, natures, peoples. Main

Street is absolutely intriguing. The city hall, new and glossed, and the old red-brick post office sit sunning themselves on the west side of Main, north of First Street. Off the broad steps of the city hall stepped a couple into a new world—matrimony! She wore a red hat and carried a red purse. They held hands. One could tell they were newly-weds; they were so brave and confident in appearance and looked as if they were so sure that in that world of disillusion they had just entered they were to be so shiningly different, so ideally happy. Youth! Confidence! Bravery! It, this little picture, made my eyes sting.

The sailors were in town—car-loads of them—the town was filthy with them. One stood on a corner eating peanuts from a big bag and looked like the comical relief in a deep play.

I went into Our Lady of Angels to confession. . . . A little girl in the box opposite talked too loud—"I forgot to say my prayers sometimes—"

Later I trod the streets gaily, first going to the main library (a beautiful edifice, terraced, luxuriously appointed with art decorations) to read up on Catalina Island.

At six I returned to Main.

I found the Cathedral steps and on the back of an envelope drew a chart of the other side of the street.

A cheap 10¢-a-meal cafeteria squatted ugly and active immediately across from me. In its window two men were frying doughnuts in huge vats of grease and the pastries came out crisp, golden-brown and hunger-provoking. Hand-in-hand in an endless chain ran hock shops, second-hand clothes hovels, dingy loan shark temples, eat shops, hot dog and hamburger stalls, hotels advertising 15¢ beds, shows open all night at 5¢ an admission, cafes, taverns, auction shops, a shooting gallery, 10¢ snap-shot photography stalls, a herb store, a burlesque, its crude cardboard girls going around the top of the theatre on a pivot, almost on the hem of the Cathedral's robes.

Hock-shops everywhere. The Union Mission almost directly across was sandwiched in between two hock-shops like a thin volume of poems between two unabridged dictionaries. Even the Cathedral had a hock-shop at its throat for its walls leaned against the imposing stones of the Cathedral and its display window was the most grotesque of the bunch, hundreds of 19th Century stick-pins marched in orderly rows over a faded and dusty green felt field. Myriad brooches filled a lower section of the window. Glass beads were festooned across the pane in endless rows. Musical instruments, cracked with age and tarnished green, leaned uncertainly, one against the other. Rings and watches, long discarded, bid farewell to the world from that dirty window. Even stage money, cowboy vests gaudily embroidered and beaded, sombreros, boots, daggers, typewriters and false-teeth, added to the riotous confusion of the window. Over all lay the dust of months.

Sick from the sight of so much grandeur, so much human ornamentation and triviality gone sour, I flopped down on a stool in a Chinese 10¢ eating joint. There eight Chinese and two whites handled a crowded business hour.

I ordered chop-suey. They brought soup, cold-slaw, three slices of fresh bread, surprisingly savory chop-suey, a heap of white, steaming rice, coffee, butter, water and a pudding for dessert. Meanwhile a polite waiter apologized that he had forgotten to ask if I preferred iced tea to the coffee. Total damage 10¢!!!

I barged out upon the street where swarm all races. And one is amazed at the number of Mexican faces encountered.

A little Mexican boy of about 12 catches my eye. He is in a green smock and is shining a man's shoes in a barber shop. A shock of hair as black as sin falls over his forehead. His customer is reading a paper and our little amigo is engrossed in the back page. As he reads his eyes grow larger and larger, his mouth opens wider and wider, his polish rag moves faster and faster until it dances up over the shoe and onto his customer's pant-leg. I stood there watching him and laughed loud and long. Los Angeles does that to one. Often tonight I stood laughing crazily to myself. And people passing me gave me a wide berth and looked back at me—I wanted to cry out to them— "Oh native sons of California—oh fools!—look about you, look at your California and enjoy it as I do. Discover its romance and humor, its pathos and fascination. Retard your hurrying steps. Linger. Stroll. Poke about and become a discoverer. Discover your city and its people. Laugh with me as your heart leaps. Cry with me as it breaks—

The lights are glowing. The sailors are in town and everyone knows it— the stools of taverns and cafes are populated thick with them. They come with chests stuck out and caps aslant—gay, laughing, drunk, sober, alone, in twos, or with girls. Pretty girls and girls not so pretty, thin girls, fat girls—one strolls by with three beautiful senoritas on his arms and I have to stifle a mad impulse to shout out—"Sailor, can you spare a dame?"

A blond, about 40, not unattractive but with hard lines beginning to jell into her face, staggers grotesquely past. She plucks at a man's arm and asks him where 3rd and Main is—asks him to take her there. He wears a black derby and matches it perfectly. They start off together but he is leading her the wrong way! I unblushingly follow with a Sherlock Holmes glint in my eyes. Two blocks later she complains that nature's demands for relief are upon her.

"You can't pee-pee here," he says, leading her to an alley and keeping a chivalrous outlook on the corner while she trundles into its depth. They set off again and he is leading her deep into the Japanese settlement. Here let us leave Mr. Negro and his blond enchantress.

A sailor staggers by, a piece of adhesive tape over a large portion of his forehead, his nostrils dark with coagulated blood—

The sailors and their "dames" (and short on dames) have taken over "The Silver Dollar Cafe," a semi-swank nite-club, and their riot is a mad, merry one.

I took a car home, alighting at Watts and picked "The Sonora Cafe" to have a stein of beer. The proprietor, patronage and conversation is all Mexican. I translate the Spanish Menu and study the clientele. A Mexican song goes lustily out onto the sidewalk from a 5¢ machine. A fog has come on, swept in from off the sea and so with one beer under my paunch I go home in a fog.

Sweet Los Angeles, your adopted son hails you—long may you reign— the City of Angels—and a few devils!!

First Day On the Island Santa Catalina: Avalon; Thur. March 25, 1937: I packed last night after much joshing and kidding from "Cousin Lizzie," shouldered my pack bought a bottle of White Port wine and a loaf of bread in Watts and weighed myself on a scale with my pack on my back. Scaled at 190 lbs. I weigh 147 lbs—my pack 43 lbs!

Took the steamer from Wilmington and had a pleasant crossing over the 26 miles of sea water from the mainland here on a choppy sea. Saw the mighty U.S. battleships lying at anchor and watched the sea gulls follow the ship. Met a man from "Ioway" on the boat and he told me of poor fishing at Santa Monica Beach, Los Angeles, where he had caught only 48 fish in an hour and a companion had landed a shark!

As we approached the Island—a bit of American ballyhoo: Four white girls, two being blondes, swam out to the boat and the barker aboard announced: "here come the coin-divers to meet us!"

Here's how our coin-divers talked as they dove and "pocketed" the coins in their mouth:

"Oh, gee, mister, I couldn't get that one!"

"I'm pooped, Mable. (Whoever heard of a coin-diver named Mable!) Let's swim to shore."

Shades of the Hawaiian Islands!

We anchored to music played by Spanish musicians on a little picturesque balcony over the pier. Pet seals floated out, trained like our coin-divers, on bouys, to meet us.

I was here! Cataline the romatic! Cataline the mysterious! Be kind to me Cataline, Sweet Lady!

And now a bit of history about the island:

Santa Catalina, one of the most fascinating isles of the seven seas, is really a mountain at sea and is approximately 22 miles long and 7½ miles wide at its widest point, ½ a mile at its narrowest. It was discovered by Juan Rodriquez Cabrillo, a Portuguese navigator in the service of Spain in 1542, 50 years after America's discovery.

An air of romance and mystery has surrounded it always. The origin of the early dwellers is unknown. They are believed to be Indians. Relics have been dug up that are so strange that archeologists make no attempt at interpretation. It has also been suggested that the original inhabitants were wanderers from the Bering Straits, perhaps Japanese or Chinese. At any rate they left me a paradise to roam.

After the island became known and after the first dwellers had vanished leaving relics of their period buried in the hills and hidden in caves, Catalina became the rendezvous of freebooters and adventurers. A happy and sometimes murderous crowd who lived on what the sea sent them by the way of Spanish Galleons laden with treasure and passing Catalina bound for Spain. These ships sailed from the East Indies and Phillipines and many never returned once passing the hidden caves of Catalina. From Pirate's Cove, one of the best secreted harbors of the world, swept swift boats to overtake them and ransack, rape, and burn them.

These early freebooters imported goats and let them roam the island so that, should one of their vessels become stranded here, they would have something to eat. Today, the catalogues tell me, 25,000 wild goats roam the hills and mountains much as the pirates did and in turn are a wild, happy crowd.

Came civilization—or what we are fond of calling civilization—and many changes. Now Catalina is renowned the world over for its number one place on the globe as the game-fisherman's paradise. And the flying fish, too, began to top the headlines.

The island was bought and sold several times, once for a horse and saddle. Mr. Banning once owned it. His house still stands on a hill at the Isthmus—and more about that later.

Mr. Wrigley, our own Chicagoan, finally bought it. He added deer, steer and baseball players (the Chicago Cubs). Today Catalina is called the land of perennial summer. To me it is an emerald pendant on the broad bosom of the Pacific Ocean. . . .

We had approached the isle from the lee-side, passing Blackjack and Orizaba, two tallest mountains on the little parcel of land. I gazed at them intently, curiously. Our acquaintance was to be intimate. I intended to scale them to their heights.

We anchored at Avalon-town, beautiful little village of about 2,000 people. Avalon, during the summer season, swells to up to 20,000 people, suckling an overflow of tourists. I am told that during high season all accommodation facilities are taxed to their limits and that on Sundays the sides of the churches have to be taken out and benches set up outside. But few of these tourists get farther than the Isthmus and most of the island is as wild as centuries ago and little explored. In fact some of it hasn't felt a human footstep in many years.

But enough history—I went immediately to the Cubs' training grounds to take some snaps and interview Gabby Hartnett; but the Cubs were at the hotel packing to go to the mainland for a series with the Sox.

Not to be outdone I went to the St. Catherine Hotel, flashed my press-pass, and sent a note up to Gabby Hartnett. He agreed to see me and in 10 minutes he was grinning at me and waving me into a wicker chair on the lounge patio of the hotel.

He wore a brown, freshly tailored suit with a Cubs' National League championship gold baseball hanging from a watch-chain on his vest. He was puffing a cigar.

Gabby was swell. Absolutely. He is clean-cut, talks like a very well educated man and is not as tall as I imagined but is broad as a boxcar.

He talked more about me than about himself and plied me with questions. When he found I was from Chicago he asked: "What are you doing here?"

I explained.

"Well," he said, "you came at a good time. We have been having a lot of rain but it is over now. You should have good weather. Well, what do you want to know about me?"

"Well, Gabby," I said, "I'll ask the hardest question first: What do you consider the three most important things in the world to you?"

"That is a tough one!" he replied, stroking his chin and smiling a little. But after thinking: "My home and my baseball. That's all I care about."

We talked Hack Wilson and I asked him what Hack was doing now. He said: "I think he has a pool hall down in West Virginia and is doing well enough to make a comfortable living the rest of his life—I hope so; Hack is a mighty fine fellow. He was his own worst enemy."

I asked him what he considered his greatest thrill in baseball:

"My biggest thrill came in April 1922. I had never seen a big league baseball game before and I caught the first major league game I ever saw. That day I caught who I consider the greatest pitcher in modern baseball—Grover Cleveland Alexander."

"What was your greatest disappointment in baseball?"

Immediately he answered, "The 1935 World Series with the Detroit Tigers."

"A bigger disappointment than the series with the Yankees?" I asked in surprise.

"Yes," he answered, "I've had practically all of my ambitions in baseball fulfilled but the one to be on a World's Championship baseball team. I hope to have it fulfilled before I pass out of the picture."

We talked a little longer, he saying that I would find a lot of interesting things in California. Then I left after taking a photograph of him with my cheap little camera on the front lawn of the St. Catherine Hotel. Gabby was fine, and patient, asking: "Where do you want me to stand?" and grinning a little. Who could help it?

*   *   *

Leaving the top of Mount Orizaba some unseen reveler played a game with me. He yelled "Yeah so-and-so!" (at any rate an unintelligible name). And I answered with a cheer that celebrated my fame. He yelled—I yelled—It was great fun but some serious business confronted me, for I had set myself the task of taking Mount Blackjack too. Let all the monarchs of Catalina Island fall to me!

The ridge route was a mile or more longer than a venture up the side of the precipitous wall to the top of Blackjack.

I would take the short route. How foolhardy! The longest way is generally the shortest in the mountains.

I started up following the goat path but soon it gave out. Even the goats knew better!

The mountain-side went almost straight up. Straining, shoving my smaller bag ahead, I edged on. It took me almost an hour to make 200 feet. And now there was no going back. The chasm yawned behind me.

But now I ran into real trouble and found myself stranded on a little shelf surrounding a wall of loose stone. My foot detached a rock and it fell about 500 feet down into the canyon below.

I had to leave my small bag and struggle on, my heart pounding.

I made a ridge of rock, essayed a pass where the rock is a foot wide and there is a several 100 foot drop on each side, and reached the upper ridge. But I had to go back for my other bag containing my diary.

If fear took possession of me I laughed it down with dry lips and remade my treacherous path. Going back was harder than coming up but mother luck still loved me and carried me through.

—And so Blackjack was taken. But there were no huzzahs and no rejoicing. I was too way-worn; my pants were torn, my hands bleeding. And far below on the rocks the grinning skull and stinking cadaver of a mountain goat took what little humor I might have mustered out of me.

And now the wind howled and blew so cold that my sweaty rags were like the embrace of ice against my flesh. And how the angry wind blew great clouds of mist in and about me!

Unlike Orizaba, Blackjack bore a marker and there were signs of campfires and initials cut into the wooden standard at the mountain's peak.

I meant to make Echo Lake my destination for the night but couldn't find it from my perch on Blackjack although it was presumably only two miles distance. I had no topographic map. Therefore I had to get along as best I could with an ordinary one. I started out in a direction I imagined was toward the Isthmus.

Coming off Blackjack I saw hundreds of goats below that broke and ran as I approached. Nearing a creek at the bottom of a canyon a herd of them on the other bank scattered leaving a little, frightened fellow standing behind a tree on a slight bluff. He was frozen with terror.

I opened my bag, seized my camera, and took a snap of him. He stood terrorized. We looked into each other's eyes and I fell in love with him. But he had no love for me; only fear.

Abandoning my smaller bag I leaped the creek and pursued him. He ran. I followed. He fled into a patch of cacti but his path completely through was cut off by the cruel cacti.

I made some wild promise to Fate that, allowed to bag this goat, I would willingly suffer her cruelest treatment for the rest of the day. Honest!—I made this promise and, I think, aloud. Fate gave me my wish: But she extracted her price!

Unbuckling the pack I carried on my back and leaving it in the kid's exit path, presuming that he would be afraid of anything belonging to me, I rushed back to my smaller sack. Extracting the hatchet with feverish hands I hurried to the cacti bed and cut a path through the cacti big enough for me to protrude. Just as the poor frightened kid was about to give himself up to what he considered the lesser evil—the cacti—I grasped him by a rear leg and towed him into my arms.

What awful groans of fear he gave!

But I uncorked my milk and soon had him making timid advances at my finger proving that we will get along swell when we are better acquainted. I believe I even talked to him as one would to a little baby. But I won't admit it now.

Well, baby goat was another burden—he went to the stern end of the leash and so I had to carry him too. Two bags and a goat!

I trudged on, weary of foot, broken of back, passing the Wrigley stables where fine Arabian horses are bred—they regarded me with puzzled eyes. On perhaps another mile or two to the top of a hill where I dropped all burdens. I was soaked with perspiration, chilled to the bone by the cold wind. (Don't believe the California advertisements: It gets plenty cold nights!)

I hastily threw up a lean-to, trying it on as I built it (lean-tos are tried on by lying on the ground and scratching lines at one's head and feet).

Divided my milk with Little Orizaba. (I have named him after the mountain. I am going to send him back to Mrs. H—— if it doesn't cost a fortune.) Fed him by dipping a rag in milk and he got along splendidly on it.

Drank the last of my wine. I hadn't eaten since early morning but was colder than I was hungry. Pulled a sweat shirt on over the rest of my soaked, sodden clothes and crawled into the lean-to, my teeth chattering, my legs trembling with fatigue.

> "Are you afraid of the force of the wind?
> The slash of the rain?—
> Go face them and fight them—
> Be savage again.—"

The night was really a thing of magnificence, of rough beauty. The cold, cold northwest wind roared in a giant voice and ran his chilling breath along my spine. But for all that he was a gentleman and wanted only to be friendly for great clouds came on and spit big drops of rain on my roof and he pushed them away and boosted the moon up on his shoulders. The stars peered through the cracks of my lean-to. It was a cold, cold night but not the coldest I have spent. (The night in the boxcar with Rich and the nights in the old Buick with John, en route here with temperatures reading at 32° below zero are the coldest I've known.)

And—"God's in his heaven and all's well with the world—"

My clothes were still damp in the morning but the sun took care of that. This morning I had a taste of the desert for the day was as hot as the night had been cold. I was without water, and the sun burned my scalp and parched my throat. Cacti leered maliciously and the trees leaned against the hillsides as if their strength, like mine, was spent.

I had to take rests every few 100 feet. But ahead I saw a glistening inlet of water. After what seemed hours I gained it. Inglorious moment! This wasn't the Isthmus but Little Harbor—I had come the wrong way! I had veered southwest instead of north and a little west and I had completely crossed the island at one of its widest points! The Isthmus lay six to seven miles away!

Well I made it. How I don't know. Thus I came down into this little deserted village of about 100 tourist cabins and several summer hotels. Only the attendant, old Charlie, and a young man were here.

The old man opened "The Seven Seas Trading Post" with its huge gate-like doors and cavernous emptiness and from almost vacant shelves supplied my needs.

I bought two cans of milk and a box of corn flakes. Too done in to gather wood and fry pancakes I ate the whole of the box of cornflakes. Rested. Then walked the half-mile that goes from the Isthmus to Catalina Harbor. Having crossed the island at one of its greatest widths I now recrossed it at its shortest. At the halfway point one can see the great Pacific in each direction, east and west, as it spreads its mighty wings and rears its mighty back.

I took a short walk after a few hours rest along the path that leads to Land's End and just beyond a bend came upon a little cabin at the water's edge. Two cabined boats idled in the water, each occupied by two youths spending a week-end on the water. What luxurious pleasures money can buy!

Over a hill a man with a dog and carrying a shotgun, the pockets of his coat pinned on. We talked a while and he pointed out his pet goat, tied behind the cabin and roped for him by a cowpuncher when the goat was quite young. I told him about my goat and he loaned me his nursing bottle. He is the caretaker at the cabin I saw and which is the site of the Y.W.C.A. Girls' Summer Camp.

Back at Christian's Hut (Motley's Hut now) where I have lain my blankets and will now lay myself, behind the beer counter.

Fifth Day On the Island Santa Catalina: Mon. March 29, 1937: Morning: Isthmus Cove: I am writing this in the drawing room of the Banning Estate. The Bannings once owned the island and their home, where I now sit, is now used for the location quarters of the movie stars when they are on location here. There are, in all, sleeping accommodations for 32 people. The estate sits high on a bluff, the Pacific glistening on either side. A steep flagstone walk, choked with budding wild flowers, leads up to the main entrance and geraniums grow in abundance on the lawn. Off of a patio or lounge porch a door leads into this room where wide windows gaze over the valley. Here in the drawing room is a beautiful fireplace before which sit huge pottery jars and a deep divan. A window seat stretches the length of one large window and a victrola stands in a corner. On the opposite side of the fireplace is a staircase leading to a small, overhanging balcony. A newspaper dated March 20 and addressed to Mr. Edward Burns lies on the table. The old home town paper, *The Chicago Tribune*. Under the newspaper lies a pass-key. This opens doors! I must nose around a bit! I sprung up, crossed the little patio hung with a flowering wistaria vine and where two palm trees and an avacado grow and geraniums run riot. An old lead tongued bell hangs from a rope and the patio looks out to sea and Ship-Rock (called by this name because it looks like a ship under full sail).

The key let me into the diningroom on the west wing where stood a table crowded to its last leaf.

I proceeded to the kitchen, hoping the gas would be on for then I may prepare my meals here. But there is no gas. Glasses and syphon-bottles were in great profusion, indicating that the occupants must drink more than they eat. In the pantry are those little paper pantaloons for lamb chops. I am sure that no one here ever thought of eating a lamb chop without pantaloons or if he did doesn't care to think of it any longer. Also there are cans of coffee, clams, figs, tomato juice.

Had a look into the tile bath where towels hang as if awaiting someone. Scanned the bedroom which was correctly appointed to the last detail. I will sleep here tonight! This is my last adventure that may cause me to brush shoulders with the police but this is such a delicious thrill and so full of story material that I cannot pass it up if they hang me!

I shall destroy nothing; may eat a can of something—they have plenty; and shall leave everything as I find it. But I may ring that bell!!

There is a victrola for my entertainment, soft, clean, towels in the bath; 32 beds to choose from. I shall bathe, shave, eat and sleep here. If it's good enough for the movie stars it's good enough for me.

Fourth of July Cove: Walked over here to see the man who loaned me the nursing bottle. He was on his front porch and waved and drew up a chair for me. "Sit down! Sit down!" he said cordially.

"You must get awfully lonesome here all alone," I said by way of making conversation.

"Well no," he replied, "I sort of like it. I'm sort of a lover of nature and I guess that's why I don't get as lonesome as other people."

I looked at him, rather astonished. He was as lean as a rapier, red, lean-faced, almost wizened. He had a hawk-nose and cold blue eyes that squinted. He was in ill-fitting clothes that hung about him and were none too clean. Surely not a poet to look at. More, in looks, in akin with the hoboes one sees wandering the highways and haunting the freight-yards. But it's his story; let him tell it:

"As a youth I was very bitter against the rich; I couldn't bear the thought of rich men. I was one of the first who joined the I.W.W. That was in Chicago years ago. Well since then I've known several good rich men and I pity them. They can never be sure of their true friends. Even their blood relations may be patting them on the back and wishing they would die. Sometimes when I see a wealthy man I think 'How much richer am I than he is; he's a pauper for all his money.' "

He went in, poured me more tea, and came back with an article in the March 1936 *True Story Magazine* by a Mrs. Janet Roper entitled "In the Port of Missing Men."

"There," he said, "is an article by one of my three friends. She's a great humanitarian and I don't even profess to be a Christian. She has been one of my dearest friends for 22 years. When I met her I was active, as I told you, in the I.W.W. organization in Chicago. I had been thrown out of towns and into jails and taken off ships in irons. I was very radical but sincere—I must have sincerity in a man. His views don't have to be the same as mine. I'll respect his opinions, I'll argue with him—argument makes one strong—but as long as he isn't a hypocrite I'll admire him, whatever his belief. Once I find a man a hypocrite I'm through with him. There can be no more regard or friendship there.

"Well this woman had me bring her all of our pamphlets—you've perhaps seen them scattered over the streets. And she'd read them and we'd argue good-naturedly. She'd smile and say: 'You'll change. All youth is like that.' Well I have changed. I see how much more to be pitied than laughed at I was. I don't go out to save the world any more. But I was sincere at the time and I still respect the opinions of my youth and still see the good but impossibility of the I.W.W. organization. There's a saying, 'If a man hasn't some socialistic tendencies before he's 30 something is wrong with him and if he has any after 40 something is radically wrong with him.' That's quite true."

Seventh Day on the Island Santa Catalina: March 31st, Wed.: Cherry Valley: I walked over to Cherry Valley on Cherry Cove this morning at about 11 o'clock and talked with Captain Rix.

"So you want to write," he said, "I'm interested in you, my boy. Tell me what you read."

I named some authors and after a bit said: "I find Mary Corelli's books especially interesting."

"Stay away from her, at least until you are older," Capt. Rix answered, "She's emotional, melodramatic, and sometimes badly written."

"I like her style, her large vocabulary," I protested.

"Oh, she's very profuse," he replied.

He was fixing an aerial and I helped him. Afterward he had me come in and he fixed coffee and sandwiches.

"I'm very much interested in your people, but I'm not in touch with them. It is especially difficult being an alien; you see I'm still a subject of England. Some of our great men are Negroes. A lot of white men will say no—no—no! But even the hardest boiled will say: 'Well I knew a Negro once'—only he'll say 'nigger.' Perhaps the only one he knew. Some of the colored women are supremely lovely. The most beautiful creature I ever

looked at was a Negress who was half Spanish. I particularly admire what is
known in the south as the 'high yallah.'

I'm not a rake or anything of that sort but I love to look at pretty
women. There's nothing like a beautiful woman, but when she hasn't any
brains I'm through with her. It's like possessing a beautiful picture.''

We talked books again and he strongly advised me to read Arthur Ben-
nett's "Old Wives Tale" and to by all means learn it by heart. And to read
H. G. Wells' earlier works to get in touch with the English people and their
way of talking. And Conrad.

Capt. and I carried on until 1:30 P.M. He had this to say about writing
tonight:

"Tell yourself that you are working on a blank subject. Your reader
knows nothing. You've got to tell him everything. You've got to rub in the
facts that matter, over and over again. Your readers don't read; they just
skim over. Think of them almost as children you are trying to teach. Make
it clear. A word will do it; two words will do it—but one word will do it
better. You are writing to a lot of people who can hardly read; many of
them. But your reader is at least sane if he cannot read. But don't credit him
with more than that; that's his limit. When I say they're sane I merely mean
there is no immediate prospect of their relatives wanting to shut them up.

"Don't do as I do—sweat all day writing two sentences—Get it
down!!!"

"If you can't pass an examination about your characters, their ages,
their habits, their peculiarities, you don't know them. If you are an artist
too you should be able to draw them; if you are an actor you should be able
to speak like them. Know them. Let them live inside of you. They are
friends. They will help you.''

Twenty-First Day on the Island Santa Catalina: Wed. April 14: Cherry
Valley: Sitting there by the sea I made a surprising and disconcerting
discovery: I am madly in love with Tree. I know now that I have been kidding myself all along when I told myself that I wasn't in love with her any
longer but that we were just the world's best friends. I know now that I went
away so that I wouldn't again fall in love with her now that she is married
and loves Rich. I know that I have loved her from the beginning. When I
brought Rich on the scene it was only because I couldn't have her—she
didn't love me—and because I hoped that at least these two people whom I
love might find something in each other. Even when Rich and I compared
notes and both pretended that it was only a game I knew and he knew that
we played no game. We knew that he loved her and I knew that I loved her.

Now I want to go home. I want to see Tree—as much as I can. Talk to
her—Sit with her. Our candle-light. Our hot Parker House rolls. Our frozen
fruit salad.

Some evening I am going to propose to her. I mean it. I am going to
say: "Tree I have something very serious to ask you. Will you marry me!''

She will say: "Why, Mot! What do you want me to do—poison Tommie?''

I'll answer: "No, seriously, Tree—Will you marry me—but with these propositions—If anything ever happens to Tommie and if Rich is married."

And she will say: "It's a bargain, Mot!"

And we'll shake, but I'll really be holding her hand. And she'll know it; and smile; and let me.

*   *   *

And what fun I'll have when I tell Rich: "I'm an engaged man! I'm engaged to be married!"

Los Angeles Again: Fri. April 23rd: Walked to Watts this afternoon and met the brothers, Auguste and Felix, on the street. We renewed our friendship. Mailed some shells to Mrs. H——. Wrapped Catalina Island ash-trays from the Banning Estate for Rich, Fred, Bessie.

Wed. April 28th: Each day we bring arm-loads of roses into the house. Outside the garden is crushed with them. But for all of them, for all the fine weather here, for everything good here I wouldn't give Chicago up nor would I trade one dirty little alley in Englewood—and there are plenty—for the whole state of California. I am more or less like those roses outside that wouldn't do nearly so well if they were transplanted. I suppose home, the place from which one comes, that native soil is where one's true heart always is.

Thur. April 29th: Went with cousin Lizzie to a small church near here to hear some Negro spirituals (the first I've ever heard) sung. On a little stage sat the singers: Young, old, light, dark, black. Children of 5, 6, and 7. Old black, shiny women of 40-50-60-70 dressed entirely in white. One little boy in the group looked like a white boy and could have been white anywhere he had wished.

In came a white girl of about 22 who looked to be a movie actress, she was so alluringly made up and dressed. Her boyfriend sat through it all with her and smiled in spite of himself.

Fri. April 30th: Basketball with Auguste and the fellows tonight and he invited me over to his house tomorrow.

Sat May 1st: Worked for Mrs. Moody. Called by this eve for Auguste. He was called in by his Dad a minute and returning said that he had put his cigarette out and hadn't finished his smoke.

"Doesn't your father know you smoke?" I asked.

"Oh yes. But I never smoke in front of him. When I haven't any cigarettes he always buys me some. And when he smokes he always offers me one but he knows I won't take it. It's out of respect that I don't smoke in front of him. You know how your father is. He runs everything. He never talks to you much. You respect him and you look up to him. But your mother is different. She is frank with you. She talks to you and explains things to you. She kids and jokes with you. You know she loves you and you love her. I pull out my cigarettes and smoke in front of my mother. And sometimes she smokes with me,'' he explained in his entrancing accent.

A friend of Auguste's drove by in a Ford and took us up to 103rd Street. There we met Gus' brother, Felix, and Manuel, another Mexican fellow. Off we went together and at 1 A.M. we had drunk several bottles of beer, several bottles of pop, and played several games of snooker pool at the two poolrooms at this end of Los Angeles. I had never played snooker before and never played in a poolroom. I felt like a chump and easily managed to lose every game. Gus bought a pound of unshelled peanuts and we walked 103rd street shelling them and catching them in our mouths. Went into "The Jungle Tavern" for a couple of minutes where a three piece orchestra (I am being polite when I say orchestra) held sway.—Well it was noise anyway. The dance floor, at best, would have been a poor basketball court and the walls were garish with paintings of various jungle animals— one couldn't, out of respect, call it a mural. Next we went to the "White Spot" and Gus fed nickels to the "music-machine" so I could hear the Mexican singer, Lilya Mendosa, he had been telling me about. And she *has* a voice.

We wandered homeward along about 1 A.M., Gus and Felix singing and trying to teach me the words to "Lupita."

"Tengo a mi Lupe con su bocita—"

and

"Alla En El Rancho Grande!"

We met still another Mexican—Garbie—and sat on the curb-stone at Gus' corner and talked until 2 A.M. It ended up in a Spanish lesson for me.

Wednesday is "Cinco de Mayo" (the Fifth of May), a grand Mexican holiday, and we hope to go down to the fiesta at Olvera Street or to a little Mexican town 9 miles from here for the celebration. My Mexican friends' last name is Cruz and instead of being called Auguste at home and by his friend he is affectionately called "Tino."

Sun. May 2nd: Oh these Mexicans are fine genteel people. I know of no in- cident to the contrary in my dealings with them. They are as polite, even to the lowliest peon, as the nobility of any race. They are always considerate of the other fellow's feelings and welfare and often generous to a fault (so it is with Tino). The last tortilla must be shared. Little jokes and happiness and friendship must all be halved. Auguste is like that. And Felix. Manuel. Jasper. Ylario (pronounced E-lah-ree-o and meaning Larry in English. I must use it in a story sometime without the Y—it has a nice sound when the "lah" is made very long and full. And looks good in writing or print too: Lario.)

A true illustration of this inherent Mexican virtue is this:

Yesterday at the Plaza a crippled Mexican of about 30, walking on a peg-leg, reached the drinking fountain almost simultaneously with me. He stepped aside and with the expressive Mexican gesture—the friendly and courteous wave of the hand—yielded his place and said with a slight smile, an admixture of the humble supplication of the peon and the magnanimous grace of the lordly: "You drink first."

So it is with the Mexican nature.

However it is said that they either love or they hate and that they are great thieves. Well I don't know about this—though I do know that all races can be thieves. And I do know that the Mexicans are mannerly. Thoughtful. Courteous. Polite. Even shy. And they never stare. They never seem to see a slight, an indiscretion, or an evil. Nor for that matter anything that isn't meant for their eyes, and I am thoroughly convinced that were a person to walk the streets nude no Mexican would raise an eye, lift an eyelid.

And, too, they carry themselves with pride and poise. The elderly men are almost all skinny, wizened as if centuries of toil had worn their flesh down to the bone and as if they had been pressed to the ground for ages. The youths, though generally slim (one seldom sees a really husky or fat youth or young man) are as straight as Roman spears. They carry their heads up and their eyes straight forward. Their high cheek bones and reserved nature gives them the appearance of pride, but pride without pride's arrogance. And they're positively handsome, mostly due, I believe, to their gallant carriage, their brown, dreamy, aloof eyes. In fact, to see them is to see so many young princes of noble blood. And whether dressed in an old blouse and overall-pants or in the most select fashion they always give that princely impression.

The girls are ravishing! I've never seen an ugly one. There's always something in their favor. Their eyes. Their hair. Their breasts. Their teeth. Even the plainest has something in her favor. Generally it's her skin. I have yet to see a Mexican girl with a blemished skin. Dusky—soft—smooth.

However their beauty is like a morning in spring or a rainbow, radiant, perfect—but quickly spent. The women become heavy and coarse and weary surprisingly early in life. Nevertheless they carry a certain attractiveness with them to the grave.

And Tino is swell! Swell! My kind of people! Kindly. Friendly.

He's not as good looking as most of the Mexican fellows nor as typically Mexican. His hair isn't nearly as dark nor as curly or are his eyes dark, passionate and dreamy. He has grey-brown eyes. Hazel perhaps.

What is fascinating about him after his personality is his accent. And sing!! He and his brother both have good voices and Tino was in the high school glee club in Arizona and also here in L.A.

And gosh! He sings one Mexican song after another in a beautiful, soft, modulated voice.

He's good on American songs too.

Tino and I in Chicago. Tree, Cliff, Rich. The guitar and mandolin—my front porch—what a dream!!

Felix and I walked up to the library and lay on the lawn idly pulling up grass. And talked: girls, fellows, California, Chicago. And then girls again.

Once, as we lay there, I grew silent and Felix asked what I was thinking about. I smiled and said—"Oh nothing."

I didn't tell him that I was thinking about how Rich and I used to sprawl in my back yard and pull up grass and talk.

Later we met Tino and at about 9 he and I went over to his house.

His dad had the kerosine lamp in the kitchen and was drunk, so we went in Tino's bedroom and sat in the dark and smoked cigarettes before an humble little adobe fireplace. (How I wish I had one in my room at home! Tree and I are one when it comes to loving candles and fireplaces.)

And as we smoked I sat there and thought of Tree and how we used to do the same thing.

Late in the evening I asked Tino casually: "What do you consider the three most important things in the world?"

At first he laughed and said jokingly: "Wine, women and song!"

When I laughed at his sally he suddenly grew serious, said:

"Golly that takes a lot of thinking! (What a delightful accent he has!)—He thought a long time; I kept silent. Then he said: "Health, will-power, and God I'd say. Health is important. You've got to feel good. Will-power—will-power to do the things you want to do, to succeed and to resist bad things. Yes, I say health, will-power and God. Will-power covers everything in you and God covers everything. And most of us have all three when we are born—" he added softly his hands held out expressively, his face wrinkled in a grimace, half-smile, half helpless perplexity.

It's always enjoyable to sit in a dark room and talk. To anyone. It's as if the persons who are talking aren't really present but that their souls have come out to converse.

Mon. May 3rd: Well I feel as if I had just come out of a world of freaks and madmen! And with me I have brought the title, plot, and characters for a book I shall call "They Who Blaspheme."

I have been on Towne Street standing listening at the "church" there. And I never before saw such mad antics and fanatical blubberings struck in the name of God—a farce unworthy of the name of religion—pseudo-trances, church songs sung in popular, jazz-time rhythm, gibberish in a supposedly God-given but strange tongue.

A young minister with a sardonic grin, hawk-nose and deep set eyes stands ready to preach and his "sister" and "brother" biblical orators stand about him with their hands on his head, his shoulders, his back, and all the time shouting "Amen!—Praise the Lord!—Halleluja! —Glory to His name!"

And there was the rather nice-looking blonde of about 32 who sang "He's the Lily of the Valley" and had it been sung in a foreign language and had I had my eyes closed I would have thought he was singing some "blues" number in a cabaret.

And the woman who played hymns on a guitar in cowboy rhythm—Anything to catch the customer.

And the man to whom God gave the socks and ties and the davenport.

And the big 240 lb. Amazon blonde of about 45 whose hair stood all over her head and who looked like Mrs. Cohen and not unlike an African Zulu-zula and said "woild" for world.

And the little German woman of about 54 who sang old-fashionedly with one finger in the air, wore a little bonnet and a sentimentally sweet smile and generously sprinkled her oration with "vitch—ven—vonderful," etc.

And the piano player who smiled his big smile and seemed so swell and human and about the only balanced person there.

And the fool penitent in the front row.

And the drunk in the back seat next to the sneerer. And the bread-line tickets. And the girl with the tight dress and wobbling rear who went down the alley and visably divided the audience's attention.

Then, as to characters, I will introduce Capt. Cardiff, my blasphemous friend of Laramie County Jail, may eject Judge M—— for a chapter or two, but in a splendid way and will probably put Clar Johnson in it.

I may even have Jesus, returned, in the book, walking among the people of our day, misunderstood and seeing his words so wrongly used and his gospel so badly treated. The book will be profoundly written and spun around the idea: "If you want to steal something steal it in the name of God" and—more hypocrisy, lies, fanaticism, evil and blasphemy is committed in the name of God than in any other way and religion is a saleable commodity like automobiles, washing machines, lawn-mowers.

Mon. May 17th: Well this has been a big day and proved, at its end, the old maxim: "It's a small world after all," for just a half a block from Olvera (Olvera where I go at every opportunity!) I met old Craig with whom I was in jail in Cheyenne and who was John's cellmate. It was rather pleasant seeing him—like someone from home.

This morn I arose at 6:30 and hitch-hiked to the South Pacific Commissary Department. But no work yet. On my way to the Union Pacific office, as I approached the Santa Fe Station on Santa Fe and First I saw that they were preparing to shoot a motion picture. Half the tracks of the depot were littered with all sorts of lamps, lights, cameras, cables, wires, and other paraphenalia. I gathered with the crowd. About 50 men were busy rigging things up: Building a wooden runway alongside of the train for the camera and sound truck. Police were roping off a section to keep the crowd back. Electricians were testing lamps, carpenters hammering nails. The director and his satelites were doing several things at once, a crowd was swiftly gathering. I asked a hanger-on what picture they were shooting. "Barbara Stanwyck, Ann Shirley, and John Boles in some picture," he told me.

Under the big lights stood Barbara Stanwyck's and Ann Shirley's stand-ins while technicians were getting the lights right, rolling cameras into position, and tape measuring distances. The stand-ins were chewing gum as fast as their jaws could go and the blonde stand-in for Ann Shirley was a homely little runt I thought.

"Barbara Stanwyck is somewhere around, that's her car over there," my informer told me, indicating a huge Cadillac, license 3838 standing near-by with two women in it. Soon they got out of the car and walked across to the cameras. They were Stanwyck and Shirley.

I was never so disillusioned! Barbara Stanwyck I had always pictured as rather small and slim. Well she is a big woman—tall, heavy—almost husky—especially around the shoulders. Her hips were as big as if she had borne six children and her stomach stuck out a trifle too much. But she has a beautiful face and legs; large and shapely. Later I was to see the very freckles about her nose and eyes when I stood not three feet from her. But she has a captivating smile, is gracious, and a hard worker for she had hurt her leg, walked with a decided limp, and later in the day looked as if it were torture to stand upon it. But she went on without a murmur. At every op-portunity though she sat in a chair which was brought to her or took direc-tor King Vidor's proffered arm and walked to a chair assisted by him. There she would sit relaxed until her next take, often bumming a cigarette from an electrician or a carpenter.

Ann Shirley is a slight little thing with common grey eyes, uncommon and lovely hair of an indescribable hue of copper and a nice set of teeth she is fond of showing. She too is a hard worker but as to looks I have seen any number of girls and women more attractive and prettier than either of these movie stars on the streets of Englewood.

The police kept hustling the crowd back and a cop was telling one woman firmly that she'd have to move back. I looked up—and who was the dummy ordering on but sweet, comical Edna Mae Oliver. She was smiling kindly and meekly obeying.

She stood facing me, almost touching me, but not looking at me.

"Hello Miss Oliver," I said.

"Oh hello there!" she answered with an exclamation point and as if she knew me adding—"what company is this ?"

I told her.

"Who's working?" was her next question.

"Barbara Stanwyck, John Boles and Ann Shirley," I replied.

King Vidor had seen her and came up, put her arm under his, and said: "I just saw you, Miss Oliver! Come over and have a seat!"

"Oh I can't!" she explained, "I'm down to catch a train. I'm off to Europe."

And she strode away, gallant old lady, swinging along on her long skin-ny legs like a girl in her teens or a six foot youth. She was, I thought, more like she appears on the screen (though not as ugly as she is made up for the movies) than Barbara Stanwyck or Ann Shirley.

Well I stayed half the day watching them take and retake a scene that took hours to shoot correctly and will be run off in less than two minutes: Barbara Stanwyck is Ann Shirley's mother and comes to the train to see her off. Anne gets on board after kissing her mother goodbye, they talk at the window, Barbara runs along beside the moving train, watches it disappear, and stands, her gloved fingers to her lips, her eyes filling with tears.

Dialogue: "You'll write to me, won't you?"

"As soon as I get there."

"Have a good time and don't think about me. And wear your blue dress."

"Goodbye mother" (throws kisses).

I saw so well as I had crawled under the restraining ropes and stood hob-nobbing with the sound-men and electricians and acting as if I belonged there.

So I got an eyeful. And a star's life is hell! They work for their money. They earn it! All day in the sun taking the same boring scene over and over. It was awfully dull watching it.

Meanwhile the "poor" extras—15 or 20 of them—sat in the train reading and talking all day as the train pulled out and backed up. And they get $7.50 a day! After each "take" there is from 10 to 15 minutes of re-adjusting of cameras, lamps, microphone, then the "retake."

I approached a desk which held a typewritten script. There I got all the details. The picture is called "Stella Dallas."

Barbara's personal maid sat on the sidelines—I talked to her and asked what was wrong with Barbara's leg.

"Oh the poor dear hurt it yesterday while riding one of her horses. And now she has to work out here in all this heat. And she's such a dear thing. So sweet to work for."

I was leaning against one of the back tires of Barbara's car during the morning when she limped over to it alone to rest for a while when she wasn't needed. Gallantly I opened the door for her and closed it after her. She smiled at me and said sweetly: "Thank you."

So two more desires have been accomplished—to see the filming of a picture and to see some of the stars. Both proved dull, disappointing, disillusioning. But had it been Garbo! Myrna Loy! March! Baxter! Laughton! Del Rio!

Sun. May 23rd: Spent the bitterest moments of my life last night. Marve wrote that Fred had heard, two days ago, that Tree was dying. Oh God!!—I wired home immediately, telegramming to mother: "Heard Tree dying. Find out. Wire Western Union. Hitch-hiking home if true."

Fri. May 28th: A letter from Mrs. M——. Tree has been given blood transfusions. I've got to get home. I'm going to hitch-hike. I told Tino and Felix so tonight I told them goodbye in their dingy little room. They shook my hand warmly and there were tears in their eyes. How kind they are—these new friends. How important I feel and how grateful.

Felix followed me out and walked a ways with me. Finally he said, "How much have you?" I told him that I have a little money. I haven't and didn't have a penny. He said: "Here's a dollar. (Poor fellow, he worked 12 hours for that dollar today and he and his family are as poor as they can be.)

I wouldn't take it. He followed me two blocks down the street—insisting that I take the dollar. So I took it. And carried it crumpled in my fist; clutched in my fist while all sorts of emotions chased through me. In this manner I came home and packed.

Mon. May 31st: Can't they understand that there is a thing called friendship and that it can exist between a man and a woman just as well as it can between two men or two women? For what she has said I hate "Cousin" Lizzie. She has said that I am a fool to want to run home to a married woman—and a white girl, at that. (Oh God *when when when* will people find out, when will they learn, that little things like color, creed, race mean nothing!) She has said that I am getting like ――― about married women. That when people are sick what they need most is money; that I should stay here and if I have to do anything I should send her folks some money. *Money!* Tree wants me. She wants to see me. I love her. She is my best friend. I am her best friend. Can't anyone understand that? Can't I scream it and make them understand? Oh Tree you and I understand. Why can't others?

Fri. June 4th: Letter from Rich. He says he goes to see Tree a lot, that she is coming along fine and should be out of the hospital by Christmas. Now I can rest easier and stay at the Marble Inn until I have enough to go home on; maybe drive back in my car in a month.

Fri. June 18th: I am still at the Marble Inn though looking for something that pays better.

Tonight two couples came in—a Mexican girl and youth and a colored fellow with a white girl. The fellows sat at a table but the girls had to go to the toilet. The toilet is outside and people have to come through the kitchen to reach it. These girls, not knowing the way, started out the entrance door and it was my duty as a cad and a bounder to show them the way. When I caught up with them they were going through the patio. The Mexican girl, visibly drunk, put her arm around me in the patio to steady herself. Being, as Rich puts it, a man, like himself of rather shady character, I slipped my arm around her. Her lips were red and smelled of wine. "I'm so damn drunk," she said, and added quickly, "You must think I'm terrible!" I answered some inanity which seems so appropriately the thing for a man to say to a maid when the moon is high and the maid not entirely repulsive.

We gained the toilet door and my duty done I turned to go back. But she stuck her head out the door and said "Kees me!"

She didn't have to ask me twice. The man in me stood up and barked! She was soundly kissed!

I waited to get her telephone number, but her boyfriend came out. He applied first his fist and then his foot to the door, cursing angrily and was finally admitted. Inside he gave her hell and I listened, the writer in me now at work.

Inside Mr. Roberts asked me if I was working outside tonight.

At their table the two couples found nothing to get along about and after the Negro had slapped the face of his girl twice and soundly and she had taken it as a chastized child would (making me think that he has had his way with the girl and been to bed with her—Thus works my evil mind!)— they got up and abruptly left.

At the door the little Mexican hot-pepper turned to Roberts and me and said:

"Forgeeve us!"

Sun. June 27th: Took Jesus to church!—Funny as it sounds. Sam, another Mexican (Mexican-Irish) went with us. St. Joseph's, then to Olvera Street and breakfast at El Paso, the small and cheap Mexican restaurant on the southwest corner of the Plaza.

Jay and Sam truly enjoyed Mass. They hadn't been in several years, they told me.

At work tonight I learned that Mr. Roberts has two menus—one for the white trade; one for the colored:

"What menu do you use if a colored man comes in with a white woman?" I asked.

"White menu!" he said, "He should have known better, he should have known better. He should have stayed in his place."

"A white man with a colored woman?" I pursued.

"White menu!" he snapped.

"What if Mexicans come in?"

"Oh the Mexican's the same as the niggah!" he replied.

Mon. July 5th: Learned the truth about my car today. Jay took it from in front of the Jermica and ran into another car, doing $65 damage to the other car. He had been drinking and (legally) was driving a stolen car. And driving without a driver's license. Tino told me all about it. Jay is in real trouble and he is going to have to pay for my car. I feel sorry for him, but I'm not going to be a sucker again. Felix gave me some good advice tonight:

"Don't trust anybody, Mot. Especially people you haven't known very long. No matter how friendly they are. Don't let anybody make a fool out of you. Not even your best friend. Well maybe you could excuse your best friend once—a fellow like Rich. You could look over it then. But if it happened again, no matter who it was, just forget about him. Put him out of your life."

Tues. July 6th: Congratulate me, dear diary. I've played the fool again; again I've been made a sap of. Up until tonight I grumbled and talked in a thunderous voice about seeing that Jay paid for the damage he did to my car or went to jail. But I guess I really didn't mean it: I would have felt worse than Jay.

Tonight he came to me and talked very earnestly. He said: "I'm going to talk to you right. I'm sorry about your car. It was all my fault and I shouldn't have taken it. I tried to sell my car (a Model-T Ford he has). I tried every way to get the money and I lost my job. I told my father about the trouble but he couldn't help me because we're on relief. I feel awful about it, too. I go to eat, I get the food out and I can't eat a thing. I start thinking about everything. Look (he slips his finger inside his belt and shows me how loose his pants have become on him from three day's worry)—I lose all that weight. Honest, fellow, I try to get the money. I owe that man $35 damage I do to his car. I owe you $5. I will go to Fresno and work in the grapes and send you the money. Honest I will, guy. I want you to believe me—"

His eyes were earnest, he talked fast, his voice was pleading, and I'm soft anyway: I agreed. I shall probably never get the money. If I don't I won't feel disappointed and if I do I'll feel greatly surprised. But I am, more or less, putting faith in the inherent honesty of the Mexican race.

Sat. July 10th: "Cousin" Lizzie becomes more unbearable every day. I refuse to stay here much longer. She hates white people, she hates Mexicans. Today she said I should be ashamed of myself "taking up with some old Mexicans."

Sun. July 11th: Down to the Plaza where I went to Mass at the old Mexican church "Nuestra Senora—"

Over to Olvera where I bought a straw sombrero, a typical Mexican hat made there on the little street. (¿Le gusta mi sombrero?) Wish I had enough money to take Tree and Rich each one. Also Fred.

Like a gypsy caravan the city has moved to the beach. There, where Manuel took Felix and me in his coupe this afternoon, were stretched gaily colored beach umbrellas, motley sun tents and blanket lean-tos of various colors: bright yellows, greens, oranges, reds, blues. Americans, Mexicans, Japanese, and Filipinos consorted on the sand. And there was a sprinkling of sombreros like mine; also music. Where you find a Mexcian you will find music—generally a guitar. That's what I like about Mexicans: they let themselves go. Ah!: The gay, loveable, reckless, happy races—the Mexicans, the French, the Spanish, and sometimes the Irish.

The Japanese girls, I note, are very pretty and have good shapes.

If you want to see tousled curly black hair on boyish heads or black shoulder length hair like a whirl of velvet skirts or a cloud of smoke, go to Brighten Beach, Terminal Island!

Riding home in Manuel's car, the radio turned to "the station of the stars," a feeling of complete relaxation and enjoyment settled over me.

Wed. July 14th: Over to Pershing Square from two to five listening, listening. How many of the habitual characters of the park I saw! The old man, barefooted, in white overalls, flowing white, shoulder length hair. The usual three or four communistic workers. The girl I described before who looks like a prostitute and who is called "Mary" in the park. She loves to talk to men and sat preaching to three or four until a good sized crowd had gathered and finally took leave, saying: "I love you all."

One man listener: "I don't want a gal that loves 'em all. I want one who loves only me."

I stood with four distinctly different youths and we argued with a radical who wanted to tear down religion in general and the Catholic Church in particular; wanted to divide education and the colleges; wanted to tell us just what is wrong with our country. He had, at his finger tips, the solution to everything. He was Russian, of course.

His listeners were:

(1) a handsome, slim, dark-haired youth of about 19 with smokey blue eyes that could have easily been called dreamy and were heavily lashed.

(2) With him was a mediumly husky dark youth of about the same age with limp bronze-blonde hair falling over his forehead and a mouth that smiled easily and mischieviously. They were both working their way through the University of Southern California.

(3) A German youth (I am presuming at his nationality: He looked German) with a quiet sense of humor, deep set grey eyes, high cheek bones, a square face, wavy brown hair and a habit of pressing his pipe-stem against his lower lip. He was very well dressed. Wore a sport coat—very splendid pants of a different but harmonious color. He was about 27.

(4) The other youth was a copper-colored, curly-haired tall lad of about 24 who grew quite angry at the heckler's tirade against the Catholic Church and swaying from his heels to his toes to thoroughly underline his big points, he, quite brilliantly and with great emotion, defended the Catholic Church, pointing out the wonderful education the Church gives its priests and that the priests and nuns have nothing of their own.

I was very proud of him. Later I talked with him alone and learned that he is a neighbor, a resident of Milwaukee, has been here 10 months, has hitch-hiked over a great portion of the country and now haunts Pershing Square.

Mon. July 19th: We were given a cabin and pulled the car in alongside of it and unpacked. Night was coming on. At about the same time five American youths drove in in a coupe and started unpacking at a cabin two doors down. Soon as they were unpacked they came down and visited with us. They were five young fellows and immediately took me on. Especially one gangling youth. During the conversation, discussing people, he said: "I don't like niggars, though. They're no good." I replied, smiling inwardly: "No the damn niggars are no good."

I felt no resentment; only amusement. I wonder what *I* look like. Well I'll have to keep my hat clamped down on my head for should he see my hair he will surely know what I am and would be embarrassed.

Sat. July 24th: Beetville: 11:10 P.M.—Poker and crap games go on all about me. On Main Street, in the cabins. (In the middle of Main St., in fact.) Pay is changing hands. Chilo won $9 in a poker game and told me that he always prays before he gambles. Strange!

I shall pray tomorrow before I play 20 or 30¢ on Chinese Lottery when I drive into Fresno.

The Suicide Crew won a case of beer tonight for loading a new record in trucks.

There are 970 acres of beets here to be topped and loaded.

There are three of us here from Chicago and they call us all "Chicago."

There is a lad of 16 here, small for his age, nice looking and soft looking. A classroom looks his limit, but he says he started weeding beets when he was 5 and topped when he was 8. I asked: "Aren't you tired of it," and he surprised me with: "No, I'm just getting used to it." He wears a boy scout shirt and is from Nebraska.

Tonight we talked of a strike. I am its leader and we are to strike for 40¢ an hour and ice in the water they bring us.

Sun. July 25th: Up early. Made a table for my cabin. Then Frank and I drove into Fresno. We ate at a Chinese restaurant—T-bone steaks! Wrote 5 letters, 3 cards. Did my shopping for next week. Met Bennie Gonzales, a member of our Suicide Squad. (Frank is on the Suicide Squad, too.) We talked strike. I am to raise my voice and growl—¡mañana!—It promises fun.

We met other fellows from the ranch and drifted into a Tavern. Everyone was treating. I had about 10 beers and also 3 milk shakes (because of a pretty waitress!) during the day.

Thur. July 29th: I awoke and found Spanish words leaping in my mind. Truly I am learning swiftly. But some bad news—the boarding house is going to close up. Fierro has lost his contract at the Ranch and some contractors from Sacramento have moved in to do the work—cheaper. Senor Guzman and his family with most of the workers here are moving on to a small ranch approximately 2½ miles from here.

Frank and I have decided to head up the coast en route to Chicago. Bennie the little Mexican of 44 is going with us as far as Chicago enroute to his home in New York.

Wed. Aug. 4th: Got two second hand tires. Made good time to 107 miles short of Salt Lake City. Across the weary Great Salt Lake Desert. Learned that Ben had only about $2 when we left Beetville, having lost the rest of his salary in a poker game. He didn't tell us until today. We are in a fine pickle and shall be far short of Chicago when we go broke. I had $27 when we left; Frank about the same.

In Elko, Nevada, where I went to buy a little token for Inez in a Curio Shop the attendant, an old, grey-haired but robust man, said when I picked a little beaded article:

"Do they make a lot of these in Hawaii?"

"I'm sure I don't know," I replied.

"You're Hawaiian, aren't you?" he asked.

Later a man asked me: "Aren't you Mexican?"

Thur. Aug. 5th: Carbuerator wrong. Had it adjusted for 50¢. Made poor mileage. Poor Bessie is doing her noblest best and all I ask of her is that she get me to Tree and that as quickly as possible.

Got to Salt Lake City. Broke. Only $1 left: On to Evanston, Wyoming, looking for ranch work. A man: "What are you?"

"A Negro."

"I didn't think so—you're so good-looking." I'm glad that I have the capacity of being amused without an attendant vanity.

Drove out to the edge of town—which wasn't a long drive!—gathered wood, cooked spaghetti. We slept in the car near the depot.

Mon. Aug. 9th: Job-hunted. Nothing doing. Ben met a Mexican youth who had a dollar and wanted to get to Denver. We offered to take him. Ben and I each sold a beet-knife for 25¢ each and bought gas to go to Denver on.

Denver is an old city filled with bums, it appeared. We headed for "Skid Row" and there meals were advertized for 5-10 and 15¢. For 5¢ one can get pancakes and coffee.

I am in the car with Bennie now. Frank is out walking—probably ditching us so that he can go and eat.

Tues. Aug. 10th: Well here I am this day in Denver, broke, listening to the quiet voice within that is constantly bringing me impressions and ideas for future stories. But even more prominent is the suffering and constant prayer to God for Tree: hundreds of times each day I whisper to Him:

"Please take care of Tree. Please see that she isn't dead and that she won't die. It doesn't matter what happens to me just let Tree live. Take care of Tree—that's all I ask."

Ate a 5¢ breakfast—two pancakes and coffee. Very filling. But I can't reconcile myself to coffee and cigarettes. I will be glad when I get home and drop acquaintance with both.

Walked all over town, visited all the free employment agencies but no work.

On the corner of 18th and Larimer a troupe of young girls—15 to 26—the Denver Crusaders they called themselves—sang and preached and gave testimonials.

Same old routine.

An old man of about 45, a cigarette in the corner of his mouth, a felt hat pulled over his face, booze on his breath, said to me:

"Look at them. Something lacking in every face. Look at the expressionless stare in their eyes. Can you tell me they're normal? Find me one face in the bunch that is normal. Do they look happy? It gives you something to think about."

He was right.

One of the evangelists shouted: "Jesus is coming! He's coming real soon!"

The voice of a big blonde youth of about 24:

"Yes, He will be popping up any day now."

Another voice: "Go up and see if you can bum one of them. Hell you couldn't get a cent!"

Another voice: "I preached for 12 years and stayed drunk all the time."

In the crowd I noticed a blonde youth with the deep-set eyes of a poet or a fanatic and he trembled visably as he listened to the singing and preaching.

Walked. Walked. Walked.

This evening, hungry, I happened upon "The Society of St. Vincent de Paul." The window sign said:

> "WORKING MEN'S CLUB
> FREE READING, RECREATION—
> EVERYONE WELCOME."

I entered and talked to the quiet little German-looking man at the desk. He said of course they fed there and I could get a meal.

They feed in the kitchen, 14 men at a time at one long table. I was late but several attendants warmed me up a meal—Soup, two slices of bread, spaghetti, stew, cabbage, boiled potatoes. All the coffee I could drink— three cups were forced on me. Generous lemonade pitchers of cream stood on the table and beside them bowls of beets and half pint bottles of cottage cheese.

Wed. Aug. 11th: Walked until 1 A.M. Looking for a dish washing job. No luck. Piled into the car with Frank and Bennie and attempted sleep until 6 A.M.

Looked for a job until 1 P.M.

In my walking I came to a rather handsome but grim building on 28th and Downing that had the look of an orphan's home. Behind a tall wire fence I saw two small children and a young boy. They were in a sort of flower garden. I supposed it was a home for orphans.

The boy was about 12, very innocent looking and had a hoe in his hand. He was tanned and a very handsome boy. He smiled at me with the reserve and shyness of adolescence.

Stopping by the fence I asked:

"Are you the gardener here?"

"I'm in here because I'm *bad!*" he replied, putting particular emphasis on the bad.

"What did you do so bad?"

"I stole a bike," he answered simply, truthfully.

"You're Mexican, aren't you?" I asked.

"Yes."

I stood by the fence talking to him for about a full hour. He is 13 years old and got 30 days in the reformatory but served 17 before he was sentenced. Of course those 17 days won't count. He won't be out until the 29th of this month.

"When was your mother here to see you?" I asked.

"Oh she doesn't come to see me," he said.

I asked for her address, telling him that I would have her come to see him but proudly he refused, saying: "No if she doesn't want to come to see me it's alright. Anyway I cry when I see her."

"We all cry sometimes," I told him, "Sometimes just inwardly. But you shouldn't be ashamed if it makes you feel better. Do they feed you good?"

"Oh I guess they do, only it doesn't seem like it. There's nothing to do in there but sit and wait for the next meal. There are only three more kids in there and they won't let us talk loud or play games. And they make me wash walls and are always after me: 'Joe comb your hair. Joe wash those pots. Joe you've been here long enough to know what you're supposed to do.' I'm going to run away from here. It wouldn't be hard to get away from here."

Smiling, I talked him out of any such notion, persuading him to take his punishment with a stiff upper lip and come out of the reform school a clean, finer boy and remember that he had only a little more time to serve.

Once, during our talk, he asked: "Did you ever steal?"

"Well once I got in trouble," I told him.

He told me that the Cor-betta Ice Cream truck drivers keep their money in a compartment under the seat and that he had three times pillaged the trucks for money—$14, $55, $24.

"You don't want to be a crook," I told him.

"Oh, gee, I know it. But when they put you in here it doesn't make you any better. It makes you worse."

Once three girls passed by and he looked at them inquisitively. But not at their figures or their legs: this will come later, in another year; perhaps two.

Poor kid, my heart was his. Thirteen, handsome with big eyes, brown, heavily fringed, tanned face, a little freckled, a mouth that trembled when he talked of his mother and the home, an elfish, half sorrowful smile that came hesitantly and then swiftly, this streak of badness in him and curse words that dropped prematurely but easily from his lips in his boyish voice. His eyes were clean and clear, his skin clean, a shy innocent smile puckered his lips.

Standing there broke I was sorry for him and sorry that I didn't have a nickel that I might go across the street and buy him a candy bar.

I *wish* I could do something for him. His name is Joe N—— and he is at the Denver Detention Home, 2844 Downing Street.

When I left him standing there by the fence, the hoe still in his hands, his eyes bright with tears, he said:

"Thanks for your company."

Thur. Aug. 12th: To employment agency. No luck. Then, unable to do myself any good I managed to do little Joe some good anyway. I went to some candy companies—wholesale houses—and plainly stated the facts about Joe, saying I was broke and wanted to take him a couple of candy bars. Finally one place gave me two five-cent candy bars and a handful of gum—free sample gum.

Went to the Detention Home to see Joe. He wasn't outside today so I rang the bell. An old lady, hard of hearing, came to the door. I flashed my bogus press card and told her that I was merely a friend when she asked if I were related to Joe.

She smiled both pleasantly and a trifle irritably and warned: "No newspaper stories! No pictures!"

She lead me down a long hall, calling: "Joe, there's someone to see you. Some Mexican, I guess."

Joe came in, shy; looking up at me bashfully.

I gave him the candy, started to give him the gum.

"What's that," the matron snapped, "Gum! Oh, Joe can't have that." She held out her aged hand and took it. "I'll give it to him when he leaves— They get it all over everything," she confided.

I talked to Joe for a little while but where we had had our confidences out by the fence he was very reticent now and often looked up at the matron, who never left the room, with ill ease.

Walked about three miles to the County and City Building where by dexterous manuvering I got Joe's home address—1229 P—— Street.

Went there. There were but four frame houses on the dirt street fronted by eight strands of railroad tracks on the other side of which stood the bleak rears of a foundry and a paint factory. I talked to his mother (who looks like Mrs. M——) and she promised to go and see her son.

Hit the restaurants for work. But to no avail.

Sat. Aug. 21st: Tree is dead. Dead!—

Later I'll write.

[blank page]

I came home. We drove through a driving rain. As we took the Southwest Highway the rain lifted but the sky was sullen, swollen. Twice funeral processions passed us and I had a queer, an awful sensation. I let my friends off at 64th and Southpark. It was so good to be back in Chicago! To see the familiar streets, the familiar street names, the familiar licenses and street cars! I stopped at a garage and shaved and washed up. Then I went directly to Tree's house, the place they had moved to a few weeks ago—On the way I stopped at St. Bernard's church, went in, knelt, prayed—oh prayed so hard for Tree. Promised God that I would try to write the greatest book yet written in His praise, in His name.

Then I went to Tree's. Soon I was to kneel at her bedside and talk to her! Hold her hand!

There was no one at the house. I rang the front bell. No answer. I knocked at the back door. No answer. I rang the front bell again. No answer. I thought Mrs. M—— had gone to the hospital to see Tree. Coming out of the door a young boy, a strange boy, said to me:

"They aren't at home."

"How is the girl that lives in there?" I asked.

"She's dead!"

Dead! Tree dead. Dead. This was the bitterest moment of my life, the blackest day. And to learn it from a stranger.

"Dead!"

"She died Monday," the boy said.

Tree dead and buried. Never to see her again. Never to hold her hand again. Never to hear her say "Oh Mot!" again. Never. Never.

My poor, dear Tree this I swear. All my life I shall remember you—always and forever and revere you in my heart. You loved candles, as I do. Remember how we used to burn candles at my house, you and I, and watch together in the dark as they burned. Our voices quiet friends that walked shoulder to shoulder, hand in hand, head brushing head in the gloom of my room. You shall have your candles. As long as I live and as long as I am home (and later when I can be sure of it, when I am away from home) a candle shall burn day and night in your memory. I shall have a wall-niche built and the candle shall burn there for you, to you, to us. Death cannot end what was between us: It shall go on forever and when I die Tree, please—God willing—come to me and take my hand and say when I look surprised as you said in your room when you came home with your baby: "Did you expect me to change Mot? I'll always be the same." And say it with a smile, Tree; your smile.

Rich and I have been alone and talked. When I saw him when I first got back that first black day I hated him. He grinned and acted as if nothing had happened and said casually "You heard about Tree I suppose."

But tonight he and I sat alone in my car out in front and talked and though we didn't look at each other the tears flowed down our cheeks and we were both aware of each other's tears. It was late, after midnight.

He asked: "Do you think you understand me Mot?"

"Better than anyone, I think," I answered.

He said: "My emotions have been drained. I don't think I will ever be able to love again and if I don't marry Fran I'll never get married. I often wonder how it will be with Fran. If Tree hadn't married I wouldn't have been able to hold out this long. We would have been married. I often think how swell it would have been if Tree and I had married. You'd come over and cook and the three of us would sit down and eat together. It wouldn't have mattered what we had or if all three of us lived in a little shack somewhere.''

We talked about a life after this and wondered what it would be like and I told him that I have no great desire to live now. And that is true. I am ready to go at any time; ready to go to Tree. And there are years and years to wait yet until she says: ''Mot!''

I had so much to tell Tree; so many confidences to share with her.

Rich told me about the last time he saw her when she was well. He went over to see her. Her mother made do-nuts and later went out. Tree sat on the sofa and said to Rich when he sat in another chair: ''What's the matter? Am I poison?'' He sat with her and she had him lay his head in her lap. Like this they sat for an hour or longer. Later Tree's mother came home and Tree whispered to Rich to wait for her and that she would meet him at his car in half an hour. She pretended to go to bed but snuck out and met him. They drove in his car all night, skimming along the edge of the lake, and he got her home at daylight and just a few minutes before Tom got home from work as he was working nights. Rich told me that she seemed to be starving for something Tom couldn't give her. God how she loved Rich!! Dear girl. Girl that I loved.

Fri. Aug. 27th: Today is Tree's birthday. She died on the 16th. But today I went to see her, went to Holy Sepulchre and took her 21 white roses writing on the card:

''Happy birthday to 'our little Tree.' Always my hand will be lonesome for your hand.''

Mrs. M——, Judge, Joe and George went along in my car.

Within me as I stood there by the grave I talked to her and as I knelt there I didn't pray but Tree and I said the things we say to each other when we have parted and met again.

Over to Tree's house. Burned a candle tonight. Sat in my car alone tonight and thought of her. I shall never forget her, never stop loving her. Everything I ever do I shall do for her and to make her proud of me. My books shall be dedicated to her.

Sat. Aug. 28th: To me Tree isn't dead. I often pretend that she is with me. When I walk alone she is at my side and I walk next to the street. Sometimes I hold her hand. And we talk about the things we talked about before.

Sun. Aug. 29th: Over to Tree. Joe and I went to his dad's. Then we lay on the lawn at the midway and talked. This eve I met Jack and Marty and had a couple of beers with them and later chili at Chili Jack's. But there is no enjoyment in anything for me. I suppose I will go through the rest of my life looking for something I'll never find. But I must gather up the pieces of my life and patch them together as best I can.

Mon. Sept. 6th: Haven't felt like writing. I wish I could die and go to Tree.

I miss her in everything, everywhere, everyway. Of all those who attested to love her so deeply I, with her mother, alone remember with broken hearts.

Tom has already begun to go out with girls. Joe told me of several times they have been together with girls and picked girls up on the streets. Judge, who I thought would commit suicide should anything happen to Tree, goes on beyond redemption, drinking and wallowing. Joe never was greatly affected. So alone, Mrs. M—— and I go on aching and longing, loving and remembering.

Today I brought Jimmie to the house and the minute I brought him in in my arms it was as if Tree were there. I could feel her presence. I'm sure if it is possible for her to know, that she was pleased that Jimmie was here with me.

I remember writing to mother and telling her that whenever Tree came over to be sure and always give her something to eat even if it were only beans, as Tree always insisted that I eat at her house even when they were broke and had only bread and jam and only enough for themselves. Mother told Tree and says Tree said:

"That's just like dear old Mot. He's a vagabond but I love him."

Tues. Sept. 7th: Went out to see Tree. Took her a dozen Gladiola. Mrs. Boon came to live with us and Miss Rathje, her mistress, cried. I am not coaching the Camelot team anymore.

1 9 3 8

Sat. Feb. 5th: I am picking up my pen again. I haven't felt like writing in a diary. All I can think of is Tree. And still it can't be. I can't picture her dead. Away somewhere, yes. But dead, no.

The black year of 1937 is over; gone; done with. Thank God. To me it shall always be the saddest year of my life.

Recall the little boy, Joe, I befriended in Denver when he was in the reformatory. Well we carry on a correspondence. I sent in a belated birthday present of a campus coat that cost $5 in "Jewtown" here in Chicago and at Christmas sent him five shirts and a book. I like the little 13 year old fellow and he has sent me his picture (two 10¢ snap-shots). At Christmas I also sent his mother a box of candy. And Joe wrote me such a nice letter in thanks that it nearly made me cry. It is between the pages here. Strangely his birthday is on the same day as Tree's. Perhaps he can be, in a small way, what Tree was to me in a big way.

I worked at a bakery for about six weeks, being laid off the day before Thanksgiving; Beaumont's Bakery, near home, here, at 61st and Normal.

Also I have heard from and been writing to Capt. Cardiff, the ex-Salvation Army Capt. who I met in jail. I also regularly correspond with Capt. Rix from the island and sometimes send him my writings for criticism. I have been writing a series of articles about my travels:

Negro Cafe
The Boy (Joe)
Pershing Square
Food Without Religion
    (St. Vincent De Paul Society, Denver)
House Breaking for Adventure
None have been successful yet; all are out to magazines today.

Sat. Feb. 26th: Am still busy on my jail story. Expect to have the first draft finished up by Monday evening. Pershing Square came back with this: Doubt if Los Angeles has changed this much since the boyhood and youth I spent there—where are all the retired Iowa farmers? And what would Willard Huntington Wright say?—Sorry—W. S.

Sent in "City of Angels—and a Few Devils."

Tues. March 1st: Finished my jail story today and have been busy retyping it. It is about 18,000 words long. Spent 6½ hours on it today and am still busy now at 1 A.M.

Mon. March 7th: Started on Miller, the Catalina Island caretaker at 4th of July Cove. I am calling it "The Island Philosopher."

Wed. March 9th: "City of Angels" was brutally turned down: "Fair picturing in spots but over-romanticized, a little maudlin and rather posturing. Sorry."

I feel blue tonight about this one for I thought Esquire would buy it. I thought it was the best thing I'd done to date. I still have faith in it.

Got up enough confidence to start a new one for Esky: "The Island Philosopher"—have done 10 typewritten pages of it—it will be about 5,000 words and I hope to get it in the mail by Saturday. I have ditched the jail story for it.

Sun. March 13th: Am busy on a story for *Outdoor Life* about climbing Orizaba and Blackjack and catching the goat, Little Orizaba. I am calling it: "Assault on Catalina."

Wed. March 16th: Tree has been gone 7 months today and my candle has been burning a month today. "The Island Philosopher" has been sent out. Tomorrow I send out the *Outdoor Life* story—and start on "Omar Goes to Catalina Island" which shall be about my trip to Catalina.

Thur. March 17th: Went down to 8th and Halsted for candles for Tree. Walked to "Jew Town" at Market and Halsted and observed the people at the open mart there. I have noticed that there are quite a few Mexicans down there and became friendly enough with several of them to play catch with a few of them. I'd like to become friends with some Mexican youth here in Chicago and learn more Spanish from him. Think I'll go back down there next week.

Sat. March 19th: "Omar" goes slowly. Tonight I had nothing to do and 50¢ that I should have saved for stamps but was fed up on endless days of sitting so coaxed Cliff to go to 45th and Ashland with me to a Mexican tavern to have a couple of beers. We walked down there and had a beer. Then we asked the bartender if he had any tequila, the lightning-striking drink. Neither of us had ever tasted it and it is highly rated for its potency. It cost 30¢ and we ordered. It looked like whisky and was served with a chaser of ginger ale though the real way of drinking it in Mexico is artistic—salt on the back of one hand, a half lemon held in the fingers—a sip of tequila, a nip of salt and a suck of the lemon.

Gingerly we each sampled the tequila. Surprise!—It went down easily and wasn't nearly as biting to the taste although it is 150 proof. Nevertheless we got out of the tavern as quickly as possible and walked the 3½ miles home. We were rather dizzy. Two would have done the trick.

Tues. March 22nd: The two days past I have haunted the neighborhood surrounding "Jewtown" and have seen and found some interesting characters there. Talked for a little while with a Mexican youth named Joe who I intend to make a friend of mine. Went into a tiny Mexican restaurant on 14th near Newberry and had a cup of coffee and tortillas—what a treat to eat tortillas again—and they were of flour. (I prefer them to the corn tortillas.) The middle aged Mexican proprietor was a fine man and took an immediate like to me. Practically begged me to take a second cup of coffee, saying: "You don't have to pay. Et will cost you nothing." In return I offered him a cigarette. When I had finished we yelled "Adios—Hasta la vista" to each other.

Walked down around there for 4½ hours. There is a splendid article down there and I am gathering data for it though when I shall write it is the question with my pen still busy with California travel sketches. Meanwhile articles are being sent out, sent back and sent out with sickening regularity.

Mon. April 11th: Well!—The first olive is out of the bottle!—And the first one is always the hardest to get out. Got a letter from Outdoors Magazine this morning saying that they would like to use my story "Assault on Catalina" but that at the present time they are not paying cash but are exchanging merchandise in a sporting line and offered me a hunting coat, fishing coat, or a rod or some other fishing tackle. I am enclosing the letter here—

Naturally I need money but I will accept—it is a start. I expected to be wildly happy or deeply affected by my first acceptance, but instead was amused and laughed aloud when I read the letter concerning an exchange.

Sat. April 30th: Worked for Miss Rathje who moved out to Beverly Hills where she is buying a place. This eve Marv and I, with Cliff, had two gallons of beer. Later when Marv and I went to stoke the furnace an idea for a story came to me. Had a young man, a janitor with a cubby-hole basement like that one where I work, be in love with a girl but have no place to take her. He is very poor and very much in love. He takes her into the basement where she sits on the only chair, he at her feet, the light out so that no one will know he is down there, but with the furnace door open giving the suggestion and effect of a fireplace. The furnace door open with the golden-crimson light reflecting is what I want to write the whole scene around.—

Mon. May 23rd: Placed a story with *Bachelor* Magazine but here is the catch—no cash! I am enclosing the letter I received from the editor. My first reaction is admiration for the frail, 105 lb. woman who is single-handedly editing a man's magazine—and one that sells for 35¢ a copy. Naturally I need money—as badly as any poor devil who ever put pen to paper. But then, too, my article "House Breaking for Adventure" had been pushed and shoved the rounds and had almost exhausted its possible markets. In all it has been to nine editorial offices. Therefore the gamble is negligible and I have already paid $1.08 in postage for its weary trips only to have it come knocking back at my door a little more disillusioned and bedraggled every time. To have it imprinted on slick paper in an ultra-modern if floundering publication is some gratification. Don't you think? The wordage is 1,500; the material fair.

From *Esquire,* along with my "purchased" darling, came a rejection slip today which read: "Too much picturesque surface and a bit too lyrical. Sorry." This was my Calle Olvera article: "America's Most Picturesque Street." Wordage 3,000; material *good* (I think!!). I shall try it next on Highway-Traveler, a magazine with a quarter of a million readers and slick paper stuff. I think they will purchase it as they have been making some rather nice passes at me—though left-handed—by way of really "beautiful" letters complimenting my articles to the sky when returning them. At present I have a short (2,500 word) article in their offices called "Fool's Adventure" which relates my trip to California through the sub-zero weather of Wyoming, Idaho and Oregon. Marv, my friend, so friendly that he is candid with me, says that he thinks it is one of the best things I have turned out. I don't agree with him but think it has possibilities and hope it rings the gong.

All in all I have compounded 62,000 words into some 15 articles this year none of which have paid back the postage I spent on them. Nevertheless I labor on recalling that someone, possibly Captain Rix, once said: "Talent is long patience; selling long persistence."

Thur. May 27th: Answered Miss Devoe's letter and sent a biographical sketch but no photograph. Am working on the revision of "In All the World no Trip like This."

Sat. May 28th: Well I made my first sale today. This morning, in the mail, I had a letter from the *Highway Traveler* Magazine offering me $35.00 for my article "America's Most Picturesque Street." I sent it in Wednesday and had their letter today—$35.00—that's a cent a word. However had it sold to *Esquire* as I ardently hoped it would I would have received $105.00 and garnered much more prestige. When I got the letter this morning I was almost afraid to open it and held it to the light first. There was no check that I could see through the envelope but my story hadn't come back and I knew they weren't fooling. I was shaking like a leaf when I opened the envelope. However every enjoyment, every success, is small now that I have lost Tree. I wish she could know about it—I know how proud she would be of me and how happy for me.

Wed. June 8th: Al, Brother, and I went to see the Cubs take a double licking from the Giants and lose first place to them. Wrote and mailed a letter to the Southtown Economist editor yesterday telling of my proposed trip and asking if they would be interested in a weekly column of our adventures. Received my letter back today with a penciled note across the top telling me to come in and see Mr. Cleveland, the editor. I will go Friday.

Thur. June 9th: Got my check from *Highway Traveler*. I know now, after long wondering, what color magazine checks are. Got a hair cut. Gave mother ten of the thirty-five dollars and am to use the rest on the trip. Cliff and I started building a small kitchen cabinet for my "trailer" today. Will finish it tomorrow.

Fri. June 10th: Went to see Mr. Cleveland. He is a splendid man, invited me into a chair, offered me a cigarette, and talked to me as if he had known me for years. He said that he had asked me to come and see him so that he could explain—that he didn't want to write me a cold, formal letter. He said that I had an excellent idea, that from my letter he knew that I had writing ability and could put over such a column interestingly and entertainingly and that The Southtown would jump at a chance to print such a colum during the summer months but that the paper hasn't an extra cent to put out on anything. He suggested that I try one of the big city dailies and thought the Daily Times would be a good bet. He advised me to write to Mr. Richard Finnigan, the editor, a letter much as the one I sent him.

Fri. June 17th: Dear Tree—If I had one wish to be granted I would wish that you and I could sit in my room today, holding hands and talking—having one of our old time talks—a candle sputtering in a bottle—Just you and I—reminiscing—playing "Remember." If this could be so just once again then I'd be ready to die. But you are so far away from me—Farther now than the 2,200 miles I put between us just when we needed each other so badly. Please, please forgive me and when we meet again say as you said when we were first re-joined after you had the baby and with the same amused smile in answer to my astonished remark—"Tree!—You look the same; you seem the same!"—
—"Did you think I'd change!—I'll never change."
Always your friend who loves you and awaits you—
Your Mot.

Thur. June 30th: With a jest and a grin Marv and I rode into the west this morning at six on our vagabond trip through the west into California and down into old Mexico. We have started out with the old Buick laden down with food supplies, camping stove, folding car table, kitchen cabinet, and a car bed, but with very little of the material goods known as money—we have 50 gallons of gas and about $12. But we have a zest for life, a thirst for adventure—a desire to see what's around the next hill. What else is needed?
Our goal is nowhere in particular and—everywhere. Our aim an escape from dull drab everyday life—

Of course the pessimists and wiseacres did a good job of trying to discourage us. They said we were mad!—insane!—That we needed at least a hundred dollars to start on the type of trip we proposed and that that wouldn't be near enough—That we were fools to think that the old Buick could take us back to the Coast (although Bessie—that's the Buick—has proved it once)—That we'd *never* get along. That both Marv and I were too stubborn to get along together. (This is a laugh—personally I believe that we'll make ideal fellow adventurers—we both like and are interested in the same things—want to see the same places—do the same things—take life in the rough and raw—explore, take chances, climb mountains, sleep under pines, see new and strange places, adventure.)

Sun. July 3rd: Denver, Colorado:—Well here we are in Denver, the city a mile high, the city in which, eleven months ago I lived 10 days, the city where I met little Joe—"the Boy."

We arrived at ten to one this Sunday afternoon.

Denver is really a beautiful and colorful city and the approach into the city on route six from the east is a lovely drive.

Marv has seen his first mountains and is wildly enthusiastic about them, although at present we have seen them only from a great distance.

I am perfectly happy on this trip and am really enjoying it. Since way last winter I have dreamed of this—Marv and I—with me leading him to the scenes of beauty and onto the stage of life both on the raw, hardboiled, real, stark and on the picturesque and admirable style.

Marv is the ideal traveling mate and even surpasses Rich as a fellow adventurer. We have trod strange streets together, laughed at the same things, exclaimed at the same things. This trip will, I know, be long remembered as my most enjoyable and should—on the side—give me much writing material.

* * *

We drove through a part of the downtown district and over near Joe's house. Then after a short walk looking for a place to set up our kingdom we happened on a perfect camping site. I write this seated at our folding table in the "front room" of our trailer into which Bessie can be easily converted. Our lantern hangs from the ceiling. Marv, tyro author, is seated across from me writing in his diary, his forehead furrowed. We have just eaten our supper—tonight a quickly put together meal of only beans, bread and orange juice as we were trying to beat darkness. The car is parked at the foot of the boarded fence in the playground of the Central grammar school and gives us easy access to downtown Denver, Skid Row (Larimer Street to you, dear diary), and Joe's house, as well as other places of interest. The playground is perhaps half a block long and 50 yards wide. Just over the back fence is our next door neighbor, an elderly lady to whom we explained that we were camping in the school ground but would be careful of matches. She thanked us and seems nice enough. At the other end sits the school house. On one side is a small school annex building against which we are virtually parked. Outside the fence on the other side of the school yard runs the avenue and on it a trim row of low built houses. We are in the neighborhood of Mariposa and 12th Avenue.

Having secured our car on its lot we unpacked and made ourselves at home and felt rather fortunate to have Lincoln Park only a block's distance away for there we may use the toilet or lie under the trees. Our water we get from a faucet projecting from the school building.

We washed up, shaved and wrote a couple letters and cards. Then I prepared dinner—fried potatoes, fried ham butt, tea, cinnamon bread, and lettuce salad.

Afterwards we dressed up and having finished first played our portable phonograph while Marv put the finishing touches to a letter to his mother.

Then we went over to Joe's house. But the only one disappointment is that Joe is in trouble again. The day before I left I got a letter from his mother, answering mine to him for him. She explained that a bicycle had gotten him in trouble again and that he is at the Golden Reform School.

Well, dressed up, we crossed the tracks to the little shack where Senor N—— and his family of eight are scratching a bare existence. He was seated on the porch and when I said: "¡Buenas Tardes, Senor, me alegro de verle a tu otra vez!" he recognized me right away, although I had seen him only once before, and gave us a right royal welcome. His wife also came in and we talked about Joe. They had been to see him this afternoon, but Mr. N—— said that he would like to have me see him and would go up there with us tomorrow or Tuesday. He said that he had told Joe several days before that I was coming and had written that I wanted to take him to the Rocky Mountain National Park for a week or a little more. He said Joe felt awful about it. He said that he thinks this will cure Joe this time and that he had once seriously thought of writing and asking me if Joe couldn't stay up in Chicago at my house for a few months if he sent him. I would have surely liked that and still hope he can come to Chicago for a full summer at least when I get back and get to selling a few more stories. I don't honestly believe that Joe is incorrigible and think that I could do a lot for him and help set him on the right path to make a useful place for himself in the world. Then too there is a great deal of sentiment attached as his birthday is the same day as Tree's—August 27th—and I have lost Tree. In fact Tree died while I was in Denver last year helping Joe as best I could and seeing him at the Detention Home after meeting the poor little tyke quite by accident.

Mr. N——, who it developes is nearly all Indian, and whose forefathers were on the soil here when Columbus arrived, didn't want to see us go and when we finally left said he would walk a ways with us. He asked us to have a beer with him, took us to a small neighborhood tavern and treated us.

Marv and I then left for a walk into town and the beer—one beer!—

had made us light headed. But then the rare mountain air is new to us and we were evidently burning too much beer and too little air in our systems!

We walked up Larimer along "Skid Row" and Marv was absolutely intrigued by the strange types of people along the streets and the many pawn shops with their windows crowded with all types of cowboy equipment—especially the shirts. Sadly he bemoaned the condition of our purses as there are so many things both of us would like to have. He was especially interested in "The Stir Inn Jail" an unusual thing in taverns that I have already described in my diary about last year's trip.

Then we went over to the St. Vincent de Paul Society "Working Men's Club" and it was like coming home. I expected to know only Ed, the little old fashioned man about whom I wrote in my article "Food Without Religion" that I sold to *Commonweal.* However two of the old fellows who saw Bennie, Frank and me off last year and helped load my car down with food were there and we sat around talking about old times and being happy in having our courses cross again.

Later Marv and I, still a little tipsy, walked to downtown district which is really beautiful. Most particularly were we interested in the really pretty girls and young women Denver can point to with pride. They were everywhere and dressed in the latest styles.

In an elite shop window we saw a silver mounted saddle for sale for a mere thousand dollars not counting the singing Mexican spurs, tapideros, spur straps, sombrero, and bridle.

Finally we made our weary way home, Marv completely in love with Denver, and walked barefooted to Lincoln Park, through its damp grass, and back to our car to cool off our almost blistered feet.

Made down our bed and crawled in.

Mon. July 4th: Denver:—We plan to stay here today, see Joe tomorrow morning, and leave for the Garden of the Gods to camp a few days before returning here and looking for work.

This morning we walked in to Skid Row and there at the Royal Cafe where I ate a few times before we each had an order of pancakes and coffee for a nickel apiece.

Back to Lincoln Park early this afternoon we lay on the grass and wrote in our diaries when suddenly I discovered that under some nearby trees a Mexican youth of perhaps 22 was playing a guitar. Both Mexican and American songs floated up through the tree leaves. He was ringed by his youthful friends and on the fringe other older Mexicans and some Americans sat and listened in rapt awe.

Marv and I sat on the fringe. I watched his slim, brown fingers speed across the strings and entice enchanting melodies out of his guitar. I asked him if he knew "Lupita" and he played it for me first smiling friendly. When I asked for "Rancho Grande," a very light Mexican who was with him said to Marv and me "Come on fellows, come on in close and sing."

"Let's all sing," I said as we dropped on the grass near him. Under a tree sat another Mexican youth of perhaps 24—bronze faced, dark curly hair and a handsome black mustache—really a good-looking fellow. He smiled at us, nodded, and added his voice. A youngster of perhaps 17 dropped down on the grass besides Marv and looked up, smiling, at us. His face was brown, almost the brown of old but well preserved leather with a glow of deepening red under it that gave suggestion of the Indian blood of a prideful tribe. His hair was midnight black and fell loosely over his forehead in several tight curls. His lips were a coarse cupid's bow—too coarse to be the mouth of a girl but strong and full of character. To me there was in his face the remembrances of the pictures of Roman and Greek statues that I had seen in books in my first days of high school. His name is Magua and one easily imagines him below the Rio Grande wearing a sombrero and dressed in complete Mexican costume, turning browner with every sunny day.

Tues. July 5th: Garden of the Gods—

We went out to Golden, Colorado, to the Boy's Industrial School this morning—12 miles distance—to see "my son"—Joe. His dad was unable to go with us so we went alone and had a hard time getting to see him as we didn't have a visitor's permit. However after a pretty speech and a flashing of my reporter's card and *Commonweal* letter the assistant superintendent sent a boy out to get Joe.

On the school grounds, enfolded by the hills and shaded by trees, we sat—Marv and I—and talked to Joe.

Joe has changed somewhat in a year. He's harder than he was. And more restless. While we talked to him he kept pushing the soles of his shoes against the grass and complained that the men there beat them for little or nothing and that they were always made to feel that they are bad and deserving of punishment. He talked of making a break for it—of getting away. Marv and I tried to talk him into staying and said that when we come back through Denver I'd take him to Chicago with me (as his dad had already suggested such a thing to me) if his dad could get him a state leave. Some of the bitterness left his lips and into his eyes, as often had, there came a soft look—the look of a puppy or a child who is misunderstood.

Joe asked us if we would like to see the grounds and showed us around the Boys' School. At the shoe shop building a young blue-grey eyed Mexican youth of about 16 explained everything to us. He was a well informed and mannerly little youth and knew all about shoes and the shoe shop. I like him immediately and asked him how long he had to stay. He replied: "Oh I'm going home. I'm just waiting for my clothes. I've been here five months."

Meanwhile one of the lads, a friend of Joe's, asked me who I was and Joe replied in Spanish—"Mi amigo."

I feel that I've got to get Joe away from here and to Chicago—and soon—before it's too late. I feel that it was meant that I meet him so that I could have an influence on his life. I believe that I could straighten him out, get him started right. He needs a chance. He has never had anything. He's been hurt and misunderstood and like most children has felt that the only way to get even is by hurting back. If I could take him to Chicago and raise him and get him started toward a useful place in the world I feel that I shall never accomplish a more worthwhile thing. And I believe I'd get everlasting satisfaction out of it. At this minute I can see the hurt, uncertain, restless look in his eyes.

We stayed an hour and a half and then left, Joe promising to wait there for us. Back to Denver. Ate lunch at our camp site—bacon, eggs and hot muffins with cocoa after having had a 5¢ pancake and coffee breakfast at the Royal Cafe on "Skid Row."

Drove the 74 miles into the Garden of the Gods just as the sun was making a descent. Marv thought them the most beautiful things he had seen with Pike's Peak looming behind but somehow I was a little disappointed. True they are lovely with their great wind and rain sculptured towers and pinnacles strangely like gods, monks, nuns, and cathedrals in red-brown sandstone. Nevertheless with a name so beautiful they left me just a little cold.

We climbed the entrance rocks to almost their top but as night was coming on we came down to the car and found a camping site within the grounds. Then we went to Hidden Inn for a while and climbed to its tower for a view of the garden of stone. Hidden Inn is a unique building built into the rock of one of nature's figures and looks a lot like a cliff dwelling.

Ate a meal of pineapple juice, canned meat and canned peaches. Marv sang in bed.

Sat. July 9th: I've sold another story. The *Ohio Motorist* magazine writes that they would like to use "The Boy" (a story about my son) in their August or September issue. They state that they don't pay regular rates but ask me to quote them a price for it. I shall write back telling them to send what they feel fit—I need the money and will have the check forwarded to Salt Lake City. I'm indeed glad to see "The Boy" getting into print as I feel that it is good—but perhaps this is because of the personal feeling underneath.

Wed. July 13th: The little kids arrived today before we got out of bed and since Butch and Dan have to go to the country they said they wanted to have the birthday party for me today. They came back at about 2:30 with their dimes, having earned them by selling old bottles, iron and rags. Well there were Butch, the two Dans, Alec, George, and Henry—bought a big lemon cream pie and cookies and grape pop. This was the first birthday party I have had since I can remember and it surely does something to you to have little kids treat you like this. It makes you believe in things and look at the stars again.

Sun. July 17th: Tino[3] is restless. Already he has made one break for freedom, trying to "take off" several nights ago, getting caught and having several months added to his sentence. Poor kid. My heart goes out to him. Not really bad but fed up with ill-treatment, reprimands, want of the bare necessities and falling in with the wrong type of friends, his life is a problem. I fear for him, fear that he may become a crook. All he talked about was getting out of Golden—"taking off"—going. He's changing, getting tough, likes to fight, curses a lot. It's now or never that I can help him. He wants to make a break and go with us. But I don't want that. I want him to stay in Golden until I come back and then go to Chicago with me where I will try to give him a break. He said that he has never had anything, not even clothes and that that is why he steals things. He is a problem. Sometimes he seems a hardened man but always, under his outer crust, there is the little boy. Misunderstood. Tethered. Bound in. Bewildered. Crying to himself.

When we walked alone he talked to me and explained a little of this and I feel that if any kid needs a break it is he. He's good-looking, well built, smart. He could go somewhere in the world.

As we walked across the grounds he said, pointing out a kid of perhaps 12: "There's one of the kids that broke away. He got only five lashes but you should see him." He called the kid and said: "Show him your ass." The boy instantly pulled down his pants and across his behind, from his back to where his legs projected, were the ugliest welts I've ever seen on human flesh. Fully 1½ inches wide, the strap had left black and blue and sickly reddish-violet welts on his flesh. I can't explain my emotions. All I know is that there was a chocking up in me for these kids at the realization that hefty grown men had inflicted those wicked bands—and a bitterness against this reformatory. No wonder boys, released, commit fresh crimes. Cruelty and punishment weld into their being a hatred for the law. After all those kids, kids who commit petty crimes, children in their early teens and younger, are sick—not criminals—but as sick as a man treated by a doctor, and those kids should be so treated with an eye for curing—not punishing. Men who understand children should be hired, football coaches, playground attendants, athletes, kindly old men and straight young men in their early 20's. Those kids should be given new interests in life, clean, lawful outlets. They should be taught to play. Allowed to compete in sports, not brought before all the other inmates at a misdemeanor and given 20 lashes as Tino assures me is the customary number.

God I wish I were staying in Denver a few more days or knew of conditions there earlier. I'd raise a commotion that would sound to the high heavens. I'd go to the city officials and demand that something be done, refuse to leave until something was done about conditions in Golden. I'd see every "big-shot" in Denver. I'd harry the newspaper offices.

*   *   *

3. N——.

After 2½ hours with Tino we finally left—and as they led Tino back onto the grounds I watched him go, hoping against hope that he shan't have changed so much when I see him again as he has in the last year.

Thur. Aug. 4th: We drove on to Baker, Oregon, crossing into Oregon before dark at Ontario and later passed into Pacific Coast time at Huntington.

We asked about a camping site at a little ranch house just off the road and the jolly old man of about 65 said we could camp there if we cared to, so there we camped. He was quite a character—rather long white hair, shaggy eyebrows, a red, wind-lashed face and merry, twinkling blue eyes that looked like the eyes of a boy. Short, with the suspicion of a paunch and a husky, friendly voice, he seemed to be a bit of the west one reads about and dreams about—his nature that of western hospitality at its best. He brought his cats out to show to us, talking to them all the time, and introduced me to Nickabob, his part coyote dog. Then he opened a rustic little pine cabin nestled in the pines and told us we were welcome to bunk there if we cared to. Under our lantern we saw with a thrill that the ceiling was raftered with rough hewn pines, that a two-man bunk, built into the wall, was in one corner, and a large table along another wall, that the door was stout and strong as one would imagine it, and that a lone window looked out on the pines.

I cooked supper of breaded veal steak, potatoes, gravy and hot muffins. The old boy sat for a while on the bunk talking, but shortly went to bed as he was to get up at 4 A.M., so we smoked a cigarette or two, played the victrola, and rolled into our bunk.

Sat. Aug. 6th: Emigrant State Park in the Blue Mountains—
My dear Tree—

You would loved to have been with me last night. Marv and I are camping in The Blue Mountains and yesterday evening was one of the most enjoyable of my life. Early in the evening I made some biscuit bread and we ate apple-sauce on it. Then as dusk came we gathered pine boughs for our bed and built a camp-fire under the pines. When night came we made cocoa, toasted cracker and cheese sandwiches, potatoes baked in the coals of the camp-fire and frankforts roasted over the fire. Then we spread our blankets on the pine boughs beside the fire as it died to embers and curled in our blankets with a heaven full of stars over our heads and the incense of the pines sweetening the night. I read aloud from Robert Service's volume of poems called "Rhymes of a Rolling Stone," for perhaps two hours, and Marv's eyes, looking into the heart of the camp-fire, were grave and profound. As for me I pretended that I was reading to you and when at last the book was put away, another log thrown on the fire, our sweat-pants pulled on with the legs tied at the bottom and our heads on pillows at the very edge of the dying camp-fire, I pretended you were there with me. I could feel your nearness; I reached out my hand and took yours in mine. Thus I went to sleep with your hand in mine. Your head was close to mine and your lips smiling in your sleep.

I was lonesome, dear girl, for you. I was aching, my little Tree, for you. But there by the campfire I found you last night—there in the Star-Dust. . . .

Tree you don't know, can't realize how long life is without you—and how dull—nor can I believe that you have left me for good—last night under the pines before I found you at the campfire I couldn't believe it, try as I might—It seemed impossible—At home sometimes when the bell would ring I'd quicken to its throb thinking it was you again—and then I'd remember and there would be only the burning, aching throb within me. And still I can't believe it. I won't believe it. I know that someday you will come back to me. And I know, my dear Tree, that you are well and happy, but always I will be lonely for you.

As Ever,
Your ol' faithful,
Your Mot.

Tues. Aug. 9th: This afternoon, while looking for work, we secured a copy of the August–September *Highway Traveler* and there in print for the first time I saw my name under a story—for the first time saw a story of mine in print—There it was—

Calle Olvera—America's Most Picturesque Street. By Willard Francis Motley.

It was quite a thrill but whereas I thought that moment would be the most thrilling of my life, somehow it wasn't—because there was no Tree to share that moment with me.

Sun. Aug. 21st: Mount Hood is mine! I have scaled my first major peak! At one o'clock this afternoon Marv, Olie and I, in the face of a furious wind that beat at us like a lash, made the final ascent, took the last leg-weary, heart-happy step to the very summit of Mount Hood—11,253 feet!

We have over-slept and arisen at 4:30. By 5 cream of wheat and cocoa were ready and there in the bunk house we were having breakfast, commenced with cantalope. Olie sorted our equipment. Marv filled the thermos jugs with hot cocoa. I looked out at Hood and thought about Hood. Through the pines it stood majestic and lofty, crowning the horizon.[4]

---

4. Diaries for 1939 and 1940 cannot be located and may not have been written.

1 9 4 1

Wed. Jan. 1st: Another year and a new series of diaries. A new series in that the past year has brought so many new influences, ideas, perspectives into my life that I have, in the full sense, grown up. Most important is my jump from the subjective to the objective both in thought and in my writing. The year past was a full one. Most prominent was the full envolvement of my novel, "Leave Without Illusions,"[5] three chapters of which I have completed and the entire story of which is completely worked out to the last sentence. Have about 200 typed pages of scenes, dialogue and framework in a folder. Everything in the last year went into the story in one way or another. Hull House, meeting and becoming friends with Sandy,[6] gaining Mike's friendship, following him home to see and study his parents, his home life, Halsted Street, West Madison Street, talks with Peter and Beatrice, intimate friendship with Matt, Joe, Alex, Tony, Concho, Andy, Johnny, opening the door to everyone, letting them in, listening to them talk—all this has brought knowledge and information to me. Tramps down West Madison, Halsted Street, Peoria, Newberry, Maxwell were wonderful. Just walking and looking. Some of these walks were with Sandy. Impressions came in from everywhere. The neighborhood is a storehouse for a writer.

This one thing I learned last year, probably the most important thing that any writer who wants to get to the top must discover—

Some authors write at a great distance from their subjects, some very close to their subject. I want to write as a part of my subject.

In the past year I had to go on relief to get on the Writers' Project. Got some profound impressions from a relief bench. Finally on the Writers' Project in April after half a year's attempt. Then security to write, to think about writing, to go on writing . . . Read John Steinbeck's "Tortilla Flat" and became a great admirer of him. Like his writing better than that of any contemporary . . . suppers at my place, at Hull House, at the Pizzaria with Gertrude and Sandy. Gertrude a wonderful girl and Sandy just about the finest fellow I ever met. His friendship was one of the big points of the

5. Working title for *Knock on Every Door.*
6. Novelist Alexander Saxton.

year . . . In March Mike first came over. I had been watching him and talking to him on West Madison Street. Had discovered that where Tino N——of Denver was my "Nick Romano," the young boy of "Leave Without Illusions," Mike was "Nick" in Chicago, Nick from the time Halsted Street and West Madison Street influenced him until the end of "Nick." This visit was followed up with others, long talks, steaks I cooked for him, secrets he told me, sympathy I felt for him. Decided on Mrs. H—— as "Emma" in the book. Discovered Mike's brother, Carmen, a clean-cut, upright youth two years older than Mike . . . Mike goes to Juvenile Detention Home . . . Judge M—— disappears for two months. Turns up in the County Hospital with a broken hip and a fogged mind . . . Matt starts coming over with his gang—Alex, Joe, Rubin, Pete. Alex proves a fine fellow . . . I coach the Mexican football team . . . meet Mando, Miss Pell, Miss Misner and discover the neighborhood "grammar school"—Henry Booth Settlement House . . . through the rain on August 27th to give Teresa 24 flowers for her birthday . . . Sandy goes bumming, leaves his car with me . . . Matt cries over a song . . . Mike goes to the County Jail for a year . . . I have a Christmas party.

Also during 1940 I wrote a number of short stories, some of which I think are good—"The Beautiful Boy"—"The Beer Drinkers"—"The Almost White Boy."

And so, another year.

Sat. Feb. 8th: Matt by last night about eight. We drank beer, talked and played 500 Rummy until 4 A.M. Up at noon. Over to County Jail to see Mike. Conversation much the same as all the others. He had seen his picture [in newspaper] and said everyone else had also. Out home until 11:30 P.M. writing letters and putting manuscripts in envelopes. Then to "The Bench" tavern for material where I sat an hour over three glasses of beer, looking and listening to the perverts who gather there. Am looking for someone who could be "Owen" in my book. I know how "Owen" looks—his mouth, eyes, hair; but I know nothing else about him, where he works, where he lives, what his life before meeting "Nick" was like. Think maybe if I look around and listen around long enough I'll eventually see someone who might be like "Owen."

Mon. March 10th: Worked on my book again. Have decided to call it "Leave Without Illusions." Two interpretations—(1) To the reader: After having read you may not "Leave Without Illusions" concerning the good "reform" schools do; the lawfulness, honesty of the police; the "reformative value" of the reform system and the lack of real influence neighborhoods, environments and acquaintances have on youths. (2) To Nick: that now, having lived and being about to die you can "Leave Without Illusions" concerning the dirty world you lived in and "man's treatment of man"—and boys.

I had finished the first three chapters months ago (all of which will have to be re-written, tuned up, strengthened). Getting started was hard but I wrote chapter four today and night.

Tues. March 11th: Typed chapter four, then re-wrote it. Started on chapter five. The fellows came over. Couldn't work with them here this evening. Was glad to see Matt.

Wed. March 12th: Am supposed to have something written for the project and show it at work tomorrow. Spent the time instead on my book and will have to beg off of work tomorrow. Sandy by at 2. He and I are going to write an article around pictures I have taken of the neighborhood and further photos. We will submit photos and article to *Friday,* a magazine appearing weekly; one of the photo-news publications. With the idea of new pictures we went to the Forum, that quaint little place off West Madison Street, and saw Mr. Gaul, the unusual man who runs it. He says it's okay with him if we take photos. Suggested Sunday evening as a good day.

Sun. March 16th: Cold today, about 10 above with a hard wind—north. Matt, Joe, Rubin by and we were crazy enough to walk up to West Madison and back just for the walk and so that we could appreciate the fire when we returned. Sandy by at 7:30 and we went on to West Madison, to Mr. Gaul's Forum and to the Honky-Tonk tavern for some photos. Got some swell, unposed shots at the Honky-Tonk. Matt and the bunch stayed on here, playing cards. Alex also here when I returned. They stayed until 1:30 A.M. when I told them that I would have to put them out and go to bed as I wanted to get up tomorrow and work on my novel.

Fri. March 21st: Another week on the novel. Going along pretty well. This eve Matt and Pete came by. They had beer, drank and listened to the Joe Louis fight while I typed on Chapter VIII. Matt brought in a half-gallon of beer for me saying, "For inspiration." Finally I joined them. They got pretty drunk and stayed all night.

Sun. March 23rd: Did a sketch for the new Project job. Am now working with the housing project and the Chicago Housing Authority in "Little Hell" or "Little Sicily." Am to go in homes with case workers, walk around the neighborhood, listen to conversations, get the feel of the neighborhood. Sounds like a good thing. Finished the "Los Mexicanos" article to shoot back at "Common Ground."

Mon. March 31st: To work at 507 West Oak Street. Nothing much doing there. Finished an article "The Government Goes Slumming" that I was working on and then worked on part of Chapter VIII of my book. Home to 1410 and continued work on it. Finished Chapter VIII at last! It's fairly well done I think. Brought in a lot of values that I thought necessary to the whole. It was a hard chapter to write. Matt over for about an hour. Walked up to West Madison for the walk in the rain and to think about Nick. Had a 3¢ cup of coffee at the Penny Cafeteria, then back here. Have to shave now, want to read up a little on photography and then sleep.

Tues. April 1st: Sandy by my office and we went through the houses and took some pictures. Over by my house for a moment where he had written a typed page about my book (the three chapters he read for me) and we discussed changes, point of view. He is too kind in his criticisms . . . "I think this is very effective writing. It reads smoothly and easily and gets across. The scenes are so clear that the reader sees them; and he feels as if he knew Grant and Nick, and as if he had seen the others."

Thur. April 3rd: Mother's birthday. I am going to get her a half dozen pair of silk stockings on pay day. Out to the house all day. Also over to the University of Chicago Library for research work for Nick—looked through "The Denver Rocky News" for items about the Boys Industrial School in Golden.

Fri. April 4th: Finished Chapter IX and am now going to rewrite the first three chapters before continuing as I want to go out to the St. Charles reformatory first for background.

Sat. April 5th: Over to see Mike. He seems to be in good spirits all the time now. I stayed with him quite a while. He says Carmella, his girl friend, is getting fat—going to have a baby. I asked him how he felt. He said he was just mad that he hadn't screwed her—that he had respected her too much. Up all night re-writing. Took time out from 2:30 to 4:30, going at that time to the Bench for two glasses of beer—walked home from there. Dropped by Peter's where he was working. Talked a while. Then back here. Wrote until 6:30. Over to Matt's house early this P.M. for a couple hours.

Sun. April 6th: Up at 11:30 A.M. Started on the book again. Down to the two missions of Halsted Street to get permission to take photos there this week—Thursday.

Mon. April 28th: Sandy by at 8:30 this morning and we went out to St. Charles State Industrial School for boys. We "free lanced" for a while, walking around the grounds and talking to boys. One nice looking rather big kid of about 18 and who had eyes like "Nick" was sweeping one of the Cottage sidewalks. He asked me for a cigarette—on the sneak of course as they are not allowed to smoke—and I told him that I would walk along the sidewalk a way and drop some. I did. He had stolen a car and lives at Racine and Roosevelt, not far from me. Everywhere we went, into every shop, the eyes of the kids there all looked at me smoking, then up at me, wanting to ask for one. It seems a shame that they're not allowed to. Most of them at 16 to 20 years old and have been smoking for years. I managed to drop cigarettes on the grounds for them; or stamped out only the end. Mr. O'Grady, one of the big shots of the institution, took us around, showed us into shops, class-rooms, and dorms. The kids all seemed to like him and he joked with most of them. The one thing I liked about him was what he said when I asked what a particular boy was in the school for doing: "I don't know. I've been here seven years and I never ask a boy what he did. I'm afraid it would prejudice me against him."

Sandy and I had lunch in town then went out to his house for dinner. Afterwards we finished up our photo-article on West Madison Street. I didn't leave until almost midnight.

Tues. April 29th: Jack Davidson came by to show me how to run my developer and enlarger. He had to go back to work but mixed chemicals for me and lined everything up. When he left I worked with it for hours until about midnight and not only spooled a roll of film in the dark but also developed some negatives and made some enlargements—the latter not so very good. Up to the Penny Cafeteria then. Had my mind occupied on photography all day and now relaxed to think about Nick. Joe Nelson is a rather handsome Irish boy of 19 who hangs in the cafeteria and sometimes talks to me. Tonight he sat talking to me from about two until daylight—all about his life, a reform school he had been in—which bears out what I'm going to say in my book.

Fri. May 2nd: Getting along swell with the enlarger. Blew up a lot of my stuff.

Sat. May 3rd: To see Mike. Stayed talking to him for about an hour. Got a letter, air mail, from Tino's mother saying that he was in trouble; that she had put him on a bus and was sending him up to Chicago to me.

Sun. May 4th: Out south this afternoon. Tino was there. He's grown into a rather handsome youth of 17. He had had a bath, had been fed and was waiting for me. Told me what had happened. It was Easter-time. He didn't have any clothes so he broke into a store and stole a couple suits. The cops were after him and he had to get out of town. At last I'm going to get a chance to try to do something for him. The last time I saw him I felt that if something wasn't done then it would be too late. He has grown a lot harder of course but under it he's still a kid—and very shy. His eyes are the same and very much like Nick's eyes. We came down to my place. I handed him a dollar to put in his pocket for spending change. He wouldn't take it but opened his billfold and offered me the four dollars he had, saying that it was enough that I was letting him stay here and eat and sleep here. I wouldn't, of course, take it. He insisted. At last I took two dollars, put it in the drawer, told him it was there for him to use when he ran short of money. So I'm hiding a criminal from the law. So I'm the bright young man who knows what's wrong with the reform schools. Well here's my chance to see what I can do. All I've told Tino is for us not to ever lie to each other and that if ever he wants to steal something for him and me to talk it out beforehand. I told him, "I'll probably not even tell you not to if you want to. All I'll probably do is talk it over with you, point out the chances you are taking and let it go at that." He says, and I'm inclined to believe him, that he's through stealing. What I want is not to be on a fatherly or big brother footing with him but meet him on some ground of equality. Called Sandy up and asked him to come by Tuesday after work and meet Tino. He said he would.

Mon. May 5th: Gosh Tino's an ambitious kid. He had me dragging him all over town looking for a job—factories, foundaries, bakeries. Strangely enough, when I saw him last, about three years ago he said then that he wanted to be a baker, to work in a bakery. It still holds. At the house he's forever sweeping or washing dishes; and he makes his bed as soon as he gets up; this, of course, is because of the reform schools—he's been crushed. That's evident. He's shy before people and goes off into his room when anyone comes into the house. He worked so hard around here that I had to tell him he was no one's servant and that we would do the work together.

Tues. May 6th: Sandy came by. He liked Tino. Later we stood by Sandy's car, he and I and he told me that I should call on him at any time. I told him if anything big turned up I surely would. "For little things too, Willard," he said. There was a long pause then; and he climbed into his car. Gosh I like Sandy!

Wed. May 7th: I went by Matt's house today. He and Marie were there and I told them about Tino; that I wanted to try to find him a good, clean boy his age to pal around with; that I knew this was a pretty bad neighborhood and only wished that Matt had a younger brother for Tino to go with. I asked them suggestions as to some friend for Tino. They both smiled, shook their heads and said no. I asked Matt if he'd like to walk over to my place and look Tino over. He did.

Thur. May 8th: Tino and Inez have become very good friends. I took them to the Stratford tonight to see "Gone With the Wind." I didn't like it much or think that it was very well done. Too sentimental. Characters typed. Photography striving too hard to be dramatic and even, at times, statuesque.

About Tino: If I can straighten Tino out and give him a break, really see that he gets started right it would be doing more than writing books that were best sellers and lived after I am gone.

Fri. May 9th: Tino helped me enlarge some pictures today—in fact did a couple by himself. Worked on pictures all day—for the project. This morning at 5 A.M. Matt kicked on the door. He was drunk. "Where's the kid?"

he asked and told me that he had been trying to come over since ten o'clock but had gotten sidetracked. He had gotten Tino a job where his sister works. This morning Tino and I went there—it's a walk being only over on 22nd Street and half a block east of Union. Tino can walk to work. He starts Monday at $12 a week.

Sat. May 17th: Tino didn't like his job and quit today. I didn't advise that he stay because I feel that it's important that he find something he likes. He drew $11.88. Wanted to give me six dollars. I would take only 5 and put 2 away for him. Went to see Mike. Over to the H——'s tonight and drank with Fred, LaVerne and Mrs. H——.

Sat. May 24th: Selective Service paper came today. Not greatly excited because I feel that I won't be bothered in that mother is my dependent. I am also a conscientious objector.

Sun. June 29th: Well, I've taken a considerable vacation from my diary. Have been very busy on the book. Now have eighteen chapters finished. Tino is still here. He hasn't been working. I got my selective service papers, filled out the first ones and am a conscientious objector. I have been working over-time on the book, feverishly. Don't know what is to come with the war in Europe. Want to write as much of it as I can as quickly as possible. Don't know if I'll be forced to go into training, in a C.O. camp or allowed to stay in Chicago, on Halsted Street, on West Madison Street and finish my book. Don't get much sleep; only about five hours a night—the book. Have gone to see Mike every Saturday. He gets out Thursday. Haven't quite brought Nick to Chicago but should before this week is out and will then have finished what, in my mind, is the first section of the book.

Mon. July 14th: My birthday. Have brought Nick almost to Chicago. Am on Chapter XXI. Chapter XXII sees him in Chicago. Mike expected to get out on the 3rd, but won't until September. Went to see him, as every Saturday. He was in the dumps but I managed to pull him out. I have a thought—I want my character to be human, fallible but likeable. I don't want to pass judgement on them and don't want my readers to when they finish with them.

Mon. Sept. 22nd: Long time no see. Have been working hard on the book. Am now on Chapter XXV and have worked Nick into Montefiore School across the street. Finished and retyped first section which brought Nick and his family to Chicago. Tino's brother, Art, came to Chicago. Stayed for a while. He and Tino decided to go back to Denver, Tino to take the rap. However Tino is now in L.A. Met Buck and Emma. Emma, former Henry Booth Social Worker, music teacher and Indiana U. student thinks she's interested in me. Mike's time is shortly up. He gets out Wednesday. Loaned him a suit to come out in.

Tues. Sept. 23rd: Have been going to the Sawicki murder trial. Sawicki is a youth, 19, who murderered four people, one a policeman. In court he is hard boiled and cocky—a pose of course. Have been taking notes at the trial and will use some of the material in my novel. Talked to Sawicki's lawyer, Mr. Morton Anderson, assistant public defender, and after the trial he is going to have me come and see him and discuss Sawicki and the trial with me.

Sat. Sept. 27th: Mike came by this morning for a minute to bring the suit back. Said he couldn't stay but would come over Monday.

Mon. Sept. 29th: Mike over. Talked. He said he thinks he is through stealing but that if he ever feels the urge he will come and tell me first. This he told me without my suggesting it.

Mon. Oct. 6th: Mike was by Saturday. Borrowed the suit to go to a dance in. Talked about going out robbing. I talked him out of it. Matt over. Buck and Emma over. The book goes on. Nick is getting worse.

Sun. Oct. 12th: Nick is growing fast now, developing under the influence of the neighborhood.

Mon. Oct. 13th: Today was Mike's 18th birthday. He came by this morning and I bought a cake and stuck candles on it. Had taken some pictures of him and enlarged two to eight by ten size and gave them to him for his birthday.

Thur. Oct. 16th: Wrote a full chapter today and yesterday I wrote the whole of Chapter XXXIII. Am really going along at a terrific pace but love it. Work here at the desk all day and most of the night. Get four or five hours sleep only. But the thrill of creation sends me on and on.

Fri. Oct. 17th: Wrote this afternoon for a few hours. Am fixing Nick up with his first girl. Seven pages done. Am going back to it now at ten o'clock and hope to finish it tonight with luck. Mike has a job at R. R. Donnoley's Publishers. He came by for a couple hours today. I read him some of the chapter parts on making the 12th Street Store and first girls for his criticism as to truth, realism, honesty, etc. He helped a lot. Well—back to work now—

Tues. Oct. 21st: I went to Emma's for supper. Came home for a minute about 7:30. Felt in the dark for the light here where I write. When it came on I noticed that one drawer of the dresser was opened and didn't remember leaving it that way. Then looked and saw that the other was open. I looked in it. My camera wasn't there. Then I looked on my desk and saw that the typewriter wasn't there. I couldn't believe it. It didn't make sense. Only Mike knew where the key was and only he knew that I wouldn't be home. I took a quick glance at my files and felt relieved when I saw that my manuscript—over a year's work—was still there. At least that hadn't been touched. Nothing could have hurt as much as having something happen to it after living with it and believing in it this long. I went through the front room and, in the dark, felt to see if the radio was there. I can remember grinning when I did that. It was. I went into my bedroom and turned on the light. The drawers had been riffled; no doubt the idea was that there might be money there. I went back and sat at my desk. I rolled and smoked a cigarette. Mike couldn't do this. Mike wouldn't do this. I smoked another. I wasn't mad. I just felt hurt and as if I had lost something. Yet I knew Mike couldn't do this alone. His friend Johnny, who had been in jail with him, had come down here one Sunday with him to pick up the pictures of Mike I took. He must have talked Mike into it. I smoked again. Then for the first time I was scared. I was poorer than I have been since long before I went on the project. My typewriter and camera gone—$65. It seems a little strange to put these things on paper now, and as if all of them couldn't have occurred to me. But they did. Well what was I going to do about them? Nothing. If I am writing a book about a boy "criminal" and how he got that way, neighborhood friends, environment, I wouldn't now, that something had hit me, run to the police—a small segment of outraged "society" and—I believe in Mike. Don't believe he's "bad" or a "criminal."

I decided to go over to his hangout and see if he were around. Was with a rolled cigarette in my mouth but no match. A young fellow stood on the corner. I asked him for a match. He said, "Here, have a real cigarette" and offered me a tailor-made. That was what I needed. I bounced back to an honest belief in people, in their inherent good.

Over at Loomis and Taylor. No Mike. Saw Nardo dancing with a girl in the store there to juke box music. Asked him if Mike were around. "He and John went over to your house," he told me. I asked him if he'd give Mike a note for me. "Sure."

I wrote—

"Dear Mike—When you get this will you please come right over? Something has happened. I don't believe, can't believe that you had anything to do with it. But even if you did I know that you just went haywire for a few minutes. Please don't get sore at me about anything in this letter. But I thought that maybe you could help me recover the stuff. I'm not accusing anyone and even if I did know who did it I wouldn't make any trouble for anyone. You know me well enough to know that. I would be willing to pay whatever would be wanted if the stuff was returned. As you know I'm not working and wouldn't be able to pay cash or immediately. I'm not mad about anything and please don't be sore at me.

                                                                I am,
                                                                Your friend, as ever,
                                                                Will.

I told Nardo that something had happened, asked him to read the letter but that I couldn't tell him what it was all about. As he read knowing though, that he surely didn't have anything to do with it, I watched his fingers, fastened my eyes to them. They didn't shake. Nardo said, "When a guy's no good he's just no good."

I can remember saying, "That's not right, Nardo. Mike's all right. I like him and feel sorry for him."

Back home. The stuff had been stolen between 5:30 and 7:30. At 11:10 there was a knock on the door. Johnny and Mexican John. They came in sheepish. I said, "Hello, guys!" and slapped them on the shoulder, friendly. "Where's Mike."

"He was ashamed to come."

They couldn't look at me. Johnny stared at the side way. Mexican John tried to brave it out with a certain swagger.

"Sit down fellows."

"No—we got to go."

They had tossed the typewriter, covered with newspaper, on the sofa. Johnny had un-zippered his jacket and unstrapped the camera from under it. He tossed it on the sofa too.

I had a bag of cookies.

"Have some cookies?"

"No—we been drinking beer."

Incidentally, in recalling, when I looked in the empty drawer where the camera had been I saw the remainder of the box of candles I had put on Mike's birthday cake. I wondered if he had taken the camera out and I wondered, if he did, how he felt when he saw the half-box of candles.

Johnny was saying "I never bring stuff back. If I had my way about it this stuff would never be in this house again."

That was a revelation. In that moment I knew the terrific pressure Mike had been under. I suffered with him all the force and will-power he had to exert to tell the fellows that the stuff was going back. And I like him; believed in him.

Johnny said over several times, "That stuff would never have been in this house again."

So the strange night was over. I had encountered a "boy criminal's" vicious instincts; and I had found the "boy criminal" just a boy—neither good nor bad. A boy. And I liked Mike and go on believing in him. And I know that there is great good or—great evil—in Mike; that he is almost completely split between "good" and "bad." He has imagination, force, is a smooth liar, could go somewhere in the world. I hope he does. I wish that I could help bring the good in him to the surface. His problems are Nick's problems. Nick's problems are those of every "Nick" in the world, of almost every boy in a slum neighborhood.

Thur. Oct. 23rd: I was afraid that Mike wouldn't come here any more; would be ashamed to come. He came today. I offered my hand. He said,

"You don't want to shake with me," and only half-looked at me. And he wouldn't shake. He wanted his clothes, was going to work. I asked him to drop by once in a while and let me know how he was making out. He wouldn't say yes or no. He left. In a couple minutes I heard someone calling, "Oh Will!" It was Mike. He tossed his pants and shirt down to me. "I quit again!" he said; and didn't go to work.

Mon. Oct. 27th: Reapplied for the Writers' Project. Hear they are placing those who quit for private employment quickly. Went to see Morton Anderson—Sawicki's lawyer. A fine man. Sincere. Understanding of criminals—on the side of the poor, oppressed, young. Talked an hour and a half with him in his office. Went to see him about how a criminal defense case is put together for a boy cop killer. He kept someone waiting half an hour while he talked to me, taking me over all the ground. Told me to use any of his experience in the case that I wanted; to come in and see him whenever I wished. I asked if I could use part of his closing argument to the jury in Nick's defense. He told me I was welcome to do so.

Tues. Oct. 28th: Got this letter from Sandy today—

"Dear Willard—

If you need any of these between now and when you get back on the Writers' Project, take them to the check cashing place on Halsted just north of Taylor.

Don't worry about using them if you need to. Since both Gertrude and I are working and since I am still being subsidized by my family, we have acquired a mild surplus; and some of it might as well be in use for a few months as be sitting around in the bank.

See you shortly.

Yours, Gertrude and Sandy"

There isn't much I can say about that. My feelings speak through the letter. Friends are life's best possession.

Matt came by this evening while I worked on the book. He read for a couple hours then went to sleep. During that time I wrote an entire chapter—XXXVII—taking Nick on his first walk up to West Madison Street.

Mon. Nov. 3rd: Gave Nick his first jackrolling job.

Tues. Nov. 4th: Got Nick drunk for the first time tonight.

Wed. Nov. 5th: Got a notice from the Writers' Project to start work tomorrow.

Thur. Nov. 6th: Went to see the loft on Halsted near Maxwell that I'd like to rent.

Mon. Nov. 17th: Have rented the loft. Had to pay $32.50 a month—and two months rent before I moved in but I wanted it so I got it. Got first check from Project today since coming back. Only $10.95 for I put in only a few hours. Mike by a little while Saturday.

Sun. Dec. 7th: Japan declared war on the United States today.

Mon. Dec. 8th: Busy at the Loft, fixing it up.

Thur. Dec. 11th: Germany and Italy declared war on the United States.

Fri. Dec. 12th: Sandy's father, vice-president and treasurer of Harper's Company, has seen the first section of my book as Sandy left it for him to read. He wrote Sandy asking if I had an outline of the entire book, that he would like to see the rest of the book and he asked if it were autobiography. His question as to whether or not it was autobiography was very pleasing to me as that means that I am surely getting inside of Nick. Mike was by the Loft this evening for a moment. Am keeping a close eye and ear on actions and reactions of people during the war as I am planning a novel, the outline of which I will spend several years upon, on war and people in general. Think I will call it by the single word—Hate. Want to work on my novel "Life of Christ for Lowbrows" after I finish "Leave Without Illusions." At the same time, Sandy having finished his book, we want to do a novel together. I am sitting at my desk in the Loft writing this—the desk faces the window and out the window the view is very beautiful. Snow is falling. A mere flaking. I can see Maxwell Street, the end of a hot dog stand lighted up and Halsted Street going past with now and then an automobile enlivening it. And a neon sign says BUDWEISER. There's a knock-kneed pushcart with a slant-wise canvas top near a curbstone. It is black against the snow.

1 9 4 2

Tues. Jan. 27th: By Hull House to pay back part of the thirty-five dollars to Sandy. He had left the second section of his novel with me. Last night I decided to read for an hour from it and then do some writing on my own novel. Well, Sandy's novel is so good that I spent the entire evening reading it. I told him how well I liked it. Especially commenting on the way the neighborhood people—"Johnny," "Marie," "Rosita"—came to life and saying that I knew they did because *here* the author was for them, as I am for them, that here lies his feelings. And I remembered walks to West Madison, walks around the neighborhood Sandy and I have taken. Silent walks. I remembered how he looked. And he and I knew what each was thinking—and what's more—*feeling*. It comes through in his novel.

Sandy was pleased and embarrassed when I told him how swell I think his novel is. We went across from Hull House for a beer. I told him how his swell job on his novel had inspired me, how I had said to myself that I had to catch up with him, had walked down to West Madison, then to Clark Street on Madison and back home thinking out my next chapter and taking notes along the way on pieces of paper, stopping against lamp posts, tavern fronts to lean my paper and write. Then I came here and worked, finishing Chapter XLII. Wrote until 3:30 A.M.

Wed. Jan. 28th: Work. Home. Supper. Dish washing. Then took a nap. Walked to the Penny Caf and took notes there, shaping out the action for Chapter XLIII. Completed that. Back here. Am going to work a while yet although it is now 5:20 A.M. And I've got to be to work at 9 A.M.!

Sun. Feb. 8th: Today was Nick's factual sixteenth birthday; his fictional birthday is on August 27th. I had a birthday party for him, with cake and candles. Invited Buck and Emma over for breakfast at 11 A.M. and we had the cake then. I am now on Chapter XLVI. It is now 3:20 A.M. and I am turning in.

Tues. Feb. 24th: Have been transferred to the Pan-American Unit of the

Writers' Project. It is very interesting work and am getting a swell background in South American and Mexican history.

Wed. Feb. 25th:　Had to go see my draft board. Questioned about being a Conscientious Objector by the four members. Wish I had a lot of time to write about that interview and other happenings in the world but am so busy on my book that I can't take time. Therefore just notes here in the hope that I can at a later time remember and enlarge. The four was two fat cigars, a little black Italian cigar and a cigarette. Questioned—Told I would hear from them later. Hope that I will have four to six months to stay here as I would like to get the book finished or as much done on it as possible before anything happens to me. Finished Chapter L.

Sun. March 1st:　I had a visitor this morning at 1 A.M. Mike—he was down below, whistling. I let him in. He said, "Lock the door, quick!" The police were after him. He asked if he could stay, said I really ought to put him out and that he only came around when he needed me. I laughed at him and told him that that was what I was here for. He said he may have to stay a couple weeks. He was really scared. In the time from 1:30 to 3:30 when we sat talking he smoked an entire package of cigarettes, lighting one on the butts of another. He stayed all day today but late in the afternoon decided to go— suddenly—and went, promising to let me know how he made out.

Wed. March 25th:　A lot has happened since last I wrote here. Practically all of the men on the Writers' Project were transferred to a map project. I was included. Eight hour day, twenty dollars more a month. But money isn't everything. I'd have a lot less time to work on my novel, the work (draftsmanship) was not to my liking. Flunked the week's trial. Other men, who were also on trial but were trying, flunked too. Were told we'd be sent back to our project. Instead we were laid off. Have been off two weeks. Went to WPA headquarters office—raised hell—but of course under the system one has to be kicked around plenty. However got my notice to go back to work on the Writers' Project today—and return to work Friday. Draft board has also been after me. Had a couple sittings to determine my C.O. status—case has been pushed on to regional appeal board. Hope they take their time—would like to be able to spend the summer here at the Loft and believe that by mid-summer I could have my novel finished. The writing goes well, considering everything. Have finished Chapter LIX and the section all but one chapter in which Grant compares West Madison and the Gold Coast. Am going to have that finished by the end of the week and then go on to Emma. Feel that I am writing powerfully now and really putting my points across.

Fri. March 27th:　I picked up five pages of Chapter LIX that I had left at police headquarters with Judge Brande formerly of Boys' Court now of Women's Court. Had asked him to read it for criticism as to court (Boys') procedure; and for permission to use his quotes, my description of his. He said that it was surprisingly good and that I had an easy style. Suggested that I drop in at court any day and sit around if I needed additional material.

Thur. April 9th: Spent night at Peter and Beatrice's house. Stayed up all night working in Peter's room though. Am on the girl. Emma. Typed first chapter on her. Expect to devote four chapters to her before again introducing Nick.

Tues. May 5th: Matt was drunk Sunday morning 9:30 A.M. and hauled into the Maxwell Street Station by the police. I found out the same night at 2:30 A.M. Went over but wasn't allowed to see him. Yesterday I put up bond for him—$25. Today, not going to work, I went to court with him. The police tried to "bum rap" him and he had to pay the bailiff and court clerk $2 to fix it—this after they had bargained like the merchants on Maxwell Street, starting at $10, cutting to $5 and I saying, "Well we'll wait and see the judge. He will probably dismiss the case anyway,"—as he probably would have. I had been transferred to an Aviation Mechanics W.P.A. training school from the Writers' Project at only $14.60 a week and had to take it— eight weeks training. May stay there; may try to find another job. Started at Moody Bible Institute.

Tues. May 25th: Have picked Nick up again and am only a couple chapters away from his marriage to Emma. Went this afternoon to the Ziff-Davis-Alliance Publishers Reception Announcement at 450 North Michigan. Very impressive. Girls in uniform to open glass doors in whole walls of glass; executives to shake hands and say "We're very glad that you came," an inner office of leather walls, plants growing out of the ends of wooden sofas, cocktails, authors (slick to pulp—such as Cupid's Diary). Very impressive!—and somewhat comical. Matt came by tonight for a while. Outlined a chapter.

Tues. July 14th: My birthday. Am back on the Writers' Project. Nick and Emma are married, Nick is about to be sentenced to the County Jail for a year. He and Vito are robbing the L Stations. Gertrude and Sandy are on a five day vacation. Matt was by this evening. Am tying up the third section of the book—Nick's arrival in Chicago to Emma.

Sat. July 25th: Busy on the book. Go to Moody two nights a week but have been cutting classes in order to stand in Bughouse Square and listen to the speakers. At Moody I have made friends with a youth by the name of Ronald Franklin who talks to God and has seen God. He's quite a queer duck. Went out to the Harlem Air Port to see Willa Brown. Earl Franklin took me up in his plane. He did a little stunting. It was quite thrilling. Matt was by tonight about 3, half drunk. Stayed all night and until about 3 Sunday afternoon, sleeping it off.

Fri. July 31st: To courtroom to hear Mike's trial. He was actually innocent this time but happened to have waited on the corner for two youths of
16 who broke into a house and stole a lot of clothing, an electric clock, a
table radio, two guns. The kids both got probation. Mike didn't even know
where they had been. Mike got one-to-five in the penitentiary which means
at least three years which means that that's the end of him, that he will come
out a professional crook, perhaps even a killer. His lawyer wasn't too
clever. I talked to him while we awaited the jury verdict. Also talked to one
of the jurors on the street car, one of the three I felt that had held out for ac-
quittal. I asked him. He had.

Wed. Aug. 12th: Nick and Emma have gone to the woods and are married.
Am typing up all I have written as fast as I can.

Sat. Aug. 22nd: I don't feel so good. I have just come from murdering
Emma. She committed suicide by turning on the gas today. Nick served a
year in jail, came out. Emma was waiting for him. He couldn't be a
husband to her—too many men and prostitutes. At last he told her about
Owen and the others. She stayed with him, loved him; she went on for a
while. Then committed suicide. Having to do the job made me feel sad for
she was a swell and a sweet girl who had never had a break.
      Matt has joined the Navy and leaves to take his final examination Tues-
day morning.

Sun. Aug. 23rd: Matt came by late tonight and stayed all night, sleeping
here. He had been drinking. We talked, serious talk, and listened to
records. I had bought him a St. Christopher's medal and a chain for it—St.
Christopher, patron of travelers. Not that I am any longer religious or
believe in a God. I suppose I bought it from a superstitious point-of-view
and in that Matt has some hazy belief in some sort of God I thought that
perhaps it would give him beliefs in nothing being able to happen to him.
All things of the mind originate in belief.

Thur. Aug. 27th: Tree's birthday. Her 26th. Went out to the cemetery with
26 flowers for her.

Mon. Sept. 14th: I have been transferred to the Office of Civilian Defense
at Jack Conroy's request—he asked for me. Start there tomorrow afternoon.

Wed. Sept. 16th: Like the new job but have to sit in the office all day—
that's not so good. Haven't been able to get much done on the novel.

Tues. Sept. 22nd: At work I finished up a radio script for the "Calling
America" program—W.A.A.F. It goes on the air at 2:15 tomorrow—a fifteen minute script.

Wed. Sept. 23rd: Typed the final draft of the script at about 1:00 this afternoon—Howdee Meyers, who broadcasts it (it is a newscast really of civilian defense activities), picked it up and dashed down to the studio with it. At 2:15 his secretary turned on the radio in his office. I went in with Mr. Gilman, who is supervisor of our unit, and listened. It was a strange feeling to hear the words I had written just a short while before coming over the air at me. I had tried to put a little life into the script. I guess it came through a little. Mr. Gilman said that it was the best script they had had yet. This was probably to make me feel good.

Thur. Oct. 8th: Nick killed Riley. It was a brutal murder. I felt awfully sorry for him and stood off to the side seeing him kick Riley—feeling awful about it—but having to watch him do what he would naturally do and— worst of all—write down what he was doing. What could I do? Nick would have acted as he did. I stood observing—and wrote down what I observed. Also am stage managing a rain storm the night he kills Riley. It has been very difficult but I hope it is realistic and successful.

Sat. Nov. 7th: Lou and I have been to the Chicago symphony at Orchestra Hall twice. I enjoyed it very much. Nick has been caught and given the third degree. Grant has hired Andrew Morton (Morton Anderson, public defender, is the model) Chicago's best criminal defense lawyer for him. The police got no confession out of Nick. I have been working hard on the story and am up to the point where I have to impanel a jury. Every couple of days I go out to the Princeton Hotel to see Judge M—— and talk about the case, the courtroom scenes with him so that I can get my *facts straight.* He and I talk about Nick, Grant, Aunt Rosa, Morton and Assistant State's Attorney Kerman as if they were really living people. I have also again talked to Morton Anderson at the Criminal Court Building for factual material. He's a swell fellow. Have also looked over the blue prints of the Courthouse to get my rooms right; walked in on Judge Rush yesterday after court when he was calling his wife to find out what kind of cake she wanted him to bring home. Told him what my mission was—to see what the rooms behind the courtroom looked like. He was splendid—took me around explaining and even to the lockup (bullpen) where prisoners are kept while they wait trial in the court room. We went inside and stood looking at the dirty pictures and reading the names and dirty jokes.

Sun. Nov. 22nd: Andrew Morton is beating hell out of the police in the courtroom scenes. He's doing a great job (with the able help of Judge M——'s suggestions and sometimes dialogue that he suggests or quotes). In fact he's a great character and is, I think, stealing the show in this particular section of the book. He was doing such a good job of cracking down on the police while I was writing this afternoon that sometimes I laughed out loud while writing or shouted "give them hell, Morton!" which is perhaps foolish but the whole damn writing seemed less writing and more living.

That's the great thing about writing you can do and be all the things you would like to do and be in real life. You can be anyone—a great lawyer cracking down on the police, showing up corruption—or anybody else you take it in your head to be. Also you are like God. You create people, you watch them, you know what they would do under given circumstances (and in this they have free will) and you let them carry out their lives—without false moves if you know them—and in the end you neither judge nor punish them—they live; you record. This creation thing—this afternoon I was looking out my window onto Halsted Street. Across the street passed three youths, rough-reckish, pushing each other, kidding, posturing on the sidewalk. Long black hair, slovenly walk, swagger in it. Looking I had to laugh aloud. I felt as if I had created them.

Sat. Dec. 5th: The party was interesting. Art O'Leary went along too. It was an "artistic party." Girls and young fellows sitting on the floor. Plenty of wine. Classical music—played very loudly. People in little groups shouting to try and have each other understand. Profound talk—blab— about life, death, religion, the spiritual, the artistic—"art."

Wed. Dec. 16th: Nick broke down on the stand and confessed. Judge M—— hates the idea. He wanted badly for Morton to win. He said some time ago that the sooner Hitler, Mussolini, Hirohito and Nick Romano were killed the better off the world should be. He has apparently changed his mind—even about Nick . . . I feel badly about Nick too.

Thur. Dec. 17th: When I came in this evening at about 11:30 there was a little boy sleeping on the steps, half kneeling up them in his sleep with a lumberjacket pulled over his head. It was the same little boy I had seen in the hallway a couple nights ago and whom I thought was trying to steal something. I told him to come in. I went down and bought a couple hot dogs for him. He was very hungry, very dirty and very ragged. I heated some water for him and told him to wash up a little. He washed the front of his face. He said he had run away, his mother was dead, his father found a job in North Carolina in war work, his step mother was mean to him and he ran away; she washes cars on the railroad; he has been away since November 22nd. He is 13 years old.

    He slept on the couch last night. He has been here all day. Seems a nice kid, is polite, very quiet, says he was in 8th grade and he is rather intelligent.

Sat. Dec. 19th: Alfred the kid who was here has been taken to the Detention Home. Gertrude suggested that, to protect myself, I should let them know at the Juvenile Protective Society that he was here. Did, asking that the fact that I had been there shouldn't be made known to him in any eventuality as I didn't want the confidence in me he had built up broken down— that he probably thought I was the only friend he had. Was promised. Meanwhile he had written to his father who is in North Carolina. Well the

Detention people came here this morning and spilled the whole story in front of him and took him to the Detention Home. I'm sorry he couldn't have stayed here for Christmas; also I shan't forget his face.

1 9 4 3

Thur. Jan. 14th: Kerman is arguing to the jury. While I write it I can't help muttering half-aloud—"Oh! You bastard you!" If even I react to him and his viciousness this way he must be a good character.

Fri. Jan. 15th: Am working out at the University of Chicago in the Dog Surgery Laboratory as animal caretaker—feed and clean—dogs, rats, goats, rabbits. The book goes well.

Mon. Jan. 22nd: The jury is out.

Sat. Jan. 27th: Nick has been sentenced to death in the electric chair.

Sun. Jan. 28th: Sandy has sold his novel! Swell!—The best news I've heard in a long long time.

Fri. Feb. 5th: Grant has decided to throw everything up and come live on Halsted Street. When I finish this chapter I'll be only two chapters from the end of the book! I'll have 111 chapters when I end.

Thur. March 18th: The novel isn't finished yet. I have been unable so far to see the warden of the County Jail to get my facts on the electric chair and executions exactly right, but am to see him this Saturday, our appointment having been postponed from last Saturday. I have a new job at the University now. I am a laboratory technician, Bill Johnson having quit. The job is six days a week but with a ten dollar raise. I now make $125 a month. There is draft exemption with the job.

Sat. March 20th: Went to see the warden. Still feel like puking from his discourse on the efficiency of the chair, the record of only six seconds to strap a man in and start the juice burning through him, his wall of 25 photographs of the men who have died in the chair since he has been warden—these photos being in his office on one side of his desk where he can see them. Sickening too is the half-inch square diamond on his finger that he works to death, his sanctimonious statements about what the world needs is religion, religion puts fear into people and holds them down from crime, people are getting too much education. His leaning back in his chair, looking at the wall of photos and talking about "his boys" who have died in the chair. His model of the chair in his office in one-third the actual dimensions. Since I am using the County Jail I won't be able to give too realistic a picture of the good warden which irks me. I'd like to really tie into him! I couldn't have imagined a warden as "good" as a character as Sain.

Fri. April 2nd: This weekend or next I have to kill Nick. It is not a pleasant thing to look forward to after three years of living with him, knowing him better than I've ever known anyone and—liking him. Have pages of notes for these last two chapters. They must be good. They must be powerful. They must have punch—deep impact. In them I have to synchronize everything I've said in the book.

Tues. April 6th: Heard from my draft board today. They have allowed me Conscientious Objector's status and have ordered me to a C.O. camp in Maryland. I am supposed to be there on the 20th. Told them at work. I have a new job there now. Am a laboratory technician, Dr. Phenister, one of the finest men I've ever met, being my boss now. Work with Carl Laester another technician who is training me. Wish I had more time to write in this diary and explain what I'm doing on the job. The job is a government job and Dr. Phenister said that no doubt the University could appeal my draft status and get me 2A classification (vital defense work). Our project at work (Phenister, Carl and I being the staff) has to do with experiments—shock—we use animals; rabbits.

Fri. April 9th: Dr. Phenister sent Dr. Schaffer out to my draft board to represent the University.

Fri. April 16th: I got the 2A classification until September at which time the University will again appeal my case. Am working hard on the novel. About a chapter and a half to go.

Thur. April 29th: Started on the last chapter.

Sat. May 1st: Working hard on last chapter. It goes slowly. I have to put all I've got into it.

Fri. May 14th: Still on the last chapter. It's about two-thirds done.

Thur. May 20th: The chapter is down to the last seven minutes of Nick's life.

Mon. May 24th: Finished up the scenic section of the last chapter, writing it at the Marquis. Later Art and I had two glasses of beer. Then home. Yesterday was a dead loss—did no writing; had company all day.

Thur. May 27th: Three minutes of Nick's life left. Should finish over the weekend.

Tues. June 1st: Nick died at 8 o'clock tonight. So, the book is finished and now, with typing, I can send it out. I'm not as happy about ending as I felt I would be. I hadn't realized how long three and a half years are nor how dear Nick had grown to me. I feel as if one of my arms had been cut off. Three and a half years of my life—ten years of Nick's life. Killing him hurt a lot—I ended with tears in my eyes.

    Started tonight on the next book—that is the first couple of pages—"Of Night, Perchance of Death."

    Then, thinking about Nick, went out for a few beers. Met Morry. Had a few more—and a couple shots of whiskey. Got drunk.

INDEX

[*The Diaries of Willard Motley* have been published as a work of their author's imagination, not as a valid historical document. For the privacy of parties concerned, some surnames and other pieces of identifying information have been deleted. As a service to the reader, many of Motley's early friends have been indexed by their first names, since this is how they are identified in the text. One must remember that the judgments expressed in these diaries were Motley's own, which he often admitted were conjecture or outright fantasy. No correspondences to actual persons and events should be drawn, since doing so would be neither Willard Motley's nor the editor's intent.—JK]